Workbook
FOR
DUMMIES®

By Nuala O'Sullivan and Geraldine Woods

WILEY

A John Wiley and Sons, Ltd, Publication

English Grammar Workbook For Dummies®

Published by
John Wiley & Sons, Ltd
The Atrium
Southern Gate
Chichester
West Sussex
PO19 8SQ
England

Email (for orders and customer service enquires): cs-books@wiley.co.uk

Visit our Home Page on www.wiley.com

Copyright © 2010 John Wiley & Sons, Ltd, Chichester, West Sussex, England

Published by John Wiley & Sons, Ltd, Chichester, West Sussex

For general information on our other products and services, please contact our Customer Care Department within the US at 877-762-2974, outside the US at 317-572-3993, or fax 317-572-4002.

For technical support, please visit www.wiley.com/techsupport.

Wiley also publishes its books in a variety of electronic formats. Some content that appears in print may not be available in electronic books.

British Library Cataloguing in Publication Data: A catalogue record for this book is available from the British Library

ISBN: 978-0-470-68830-4

Printed and bound in Great Britain by TJ International Ltd

10 9 8 7 6 5 4 3 2 1

WILEY

About the Authors

Nuala O'Sullivan graduated from Edinburgh University and later received her Certificate and Diploma in English Language Teaching to Adults. She taught English as a foreign language for more than 10 years in Britain, Singapore, Indonesia and Thailand. She trained teachers in the University of Cambridge Certificate in Teaching English Language to Adults (CELTA) in Thailand and the USA. In 2005, Nuala devised and created *The Flatmates* for the BBC. This award-winning, online soap opera was designed specifically for English language learners. She wrote and produced weekly episodes of the soap for four years. She is also the author of *Teaching English in South-East Asia*.

Geraldine Woods began her education when teachers still supplied ink wells to their students. She credits her 35-year career as an English teacher to a set of ultra-strict nuns armed with thick grammar books. She lives in New York City, where with great difficulty she refrains from correcting signs containing messages such as 'Bagel's for sale.' She is the author of more than 40 books, including *English Grammar For Dummies*.

Dedication

From Nuala: For Natalie, with all my love. And in memory of Dima Kostenko (1966–2009), a gentle man and much-missed BBC Learning English colleague.

From Geraldine: For the students who labour (and occasionally smile) in the grammar portion of my English classes.

Authors' Acknowledgments

From Nuala: I'd like to thank the students, teachers, trainers and radio and online producers I've had the privilege and pleasure of working with over the years.

Thanks to all at Wiley who helped bring this book to life, especially Rachael Chilvers, Nicole Hermitage and Andy Finch.

From Geraldine: I owe thanks to my colleagues at the Horace Mann School, who are always willing to discuss the finer points of grammar. I appreciate the work of Kristin DeMint, Sarah Faulkner and Neil Johnson. I also appreciate the efforts of Lisa Queen, my agent, and of Roxanne Cerda and Kathy Cox.

Publisher's Acknowledgments

We're proud of this book; please send us your comments through our Dummies online registration form located at www.dummies.com/register/.

Some of the people who helped bring this book to market include the following:

Acquisitions, Editorial and Media Development

Project Editor: Rachael Chilvers

Content Editor: Jo Theedom

Commissioning Editor: Nicole Hermitage

Production Manager: Daniel Mersey

Copyeditor: Andy Finch

Cover Photos: © Corbis Premium RF / Alamy

Cartoons: Ed McLachlan

Composition Services

Project Coordinator: Lynsey Stanford

Layout and Graphics: Claudia Bell, Carl Byers, Christin Swinford, Christine Williams

Indexer: Claudia Bourbeau

Contents at a Glance

Table of Contents

Introduction

....

Good grammar pays. No, we're not making a sentimental statement about the importance of a job well done or the satisfaction of learning for its own sake, although we believe in both these values. We're talking about cold, hard cash. Don't believe us? Fine. Try this little test: the next time you go to the cinema, tear yourself away from the story for a moment and concentrate on the dialogue. The chances are that the characters who have fancy jobs or piles of cash sound different from those who don't.

We're not making a value judgement here; we're just describing reality. Proper or standard English, written or spoken, tends to be associated with the upper social or economic classes. Toning up your grammar muscles doesn't guarantee your entry into the Bill Gates income bracket, but poor grammar may make fighting your way in that much harder.

Another payoff of good grammar is doing better at school, college or university. Teachers always look more favourably on nicely written, grammatically correct sentences.

The good news is that you don't have to spend a lifetime improving your English. Ten minutes here, ten minutes there, and before you know it, your grammar muscles are toned to fighting strength. This book is the equivalent of a gym membership for your writing and speaking skills. Like any good gym, it doesn't waste your time with lectures on the physiology of flat abs. Instead, it sends you right to the mat and sets you up with the exercises that actually do the job.

About This Book

English Grammar Workbook For Dummies doesn't concentrate on what English teachers (yes, we admit it, we're teachers!) call *descriptive grammar* – the kind where you circle all the nouns and draw little triangles around the prepositions. A closely guarded English-teacher secret is that you don't need to know any of that terminology (well, hardly any) to master grammar. Instead, this book concentrates on *functional grammar* – what goes where in real-life speech and writing.

Each chapter begins with a quick explanation of the rules (don't smoke, don't stick your chewing gum under the table, make sure that your sentences are complete – that kind of thing). We start off telling you what's right and wrong in standard English usage. Next, we give you an example and then hit you with ten or so quick questions. Just so you know that we're not wasting your time, in every chapter we give you a sample from real-life English (albeit in a slightly weird situation, which we offer merely for your delectation and amusement), so you can see how proper grammar aids communication.

After filling in the blanks, you can check your answers at the end of the chapter. In *English Grammar Workbook For Dummies*, we also tell you why a particular choice is correct, not for the sake of discovering a set of rules but to help you make the right decision next time – when you're deciding between *their* and *they're* or *went* and *had gone*, for example. As teachers for more decades than we care to count, we believe that if you truly understand the logic of grammar – and most rules do rest upon a logical base – you become a better, more precise communicator.

If you have English as your second language, we want to offer you a special welcome. You've probably picked up quite a bit of vocabulary and grammar already, but this book lets you practise the little things – the best word choice for a particular sentence, the proper way to create a plural and so on. This book moves you beyond mere comprehension towards mastery.

Conventions Used in This Book

To make your practice as easy as possible, we use certain conventions throughout this book so that from chapter to chapter or section to section you're not wondering what in the world is going on. Here are a few conventions to note:

- As in all *For Dummies* titles, we use an informal, chatty style throughout this book. Please bear in mind, however, that such an approach may not be the right tone in more formal writing, such as when submitting a report to your boss or an essay to your teacher. As we mention a few times in the text, we're exploring *standard* English, which is why we make occasional references to 'your boss', 'your teacher' and so on to steer you towards correct writing in formal situations.

- At the end of each chapter is an 'Answers' section, which covers all the exercises in that chapter. You can find the answers by thumbing through the book until you come to the pages with the grey border.

- The last exercise in each chapter is comprehensive and takes you to the next level, so that you can check your understanding of the material in that chapter and sharpen your editing skills. We provide a figure containing a piece of writing filled with errors. You can find the corrections to these errors, along with an amended figure, in the 'Answers' section. The numbers in the corrected figure correspond with the numbered explanations in the text. Also, we supply an Appendix devoted entirely to giving you comprehensive practice of all the topics covered in this workbook.

We promise to keep the grammar jargon to a minimum in this workbook, but we have to include a couple of terms from Grammarland. If you struggle with a definition, run away as fast as you can and try the sample question instead. If you can get the point without remembering the grammatical term, you win a gold star. Likewise, feel free to skip the explanation of any question that you get right, unless of course you want to gloat. In that case read the explanation while crowing, 'Well of course! I knew that.'

Foolish Assumptions

We assume that you fall into one or more of these categories:

- You know some English but want to improve your skills.
- You aspire to a better job.
- You feel a bit insecure about your language skills and want to communicate with more confidence.
- You're discovering how to speak and write English fluently.

In addition, we make two more general assumptions about you. First, you have a busy life with very little time to waste on unnecessary frills. With this important fact in mind, we try to keep the explanations in this book clear, simple and short, so you can dive right in and practise. We leave the fancy grammar terms – *gerunds, indicative mood* and the like – by the wayside, where in our humble opinion they belong. We don't want to clutter up your brain; we just want to give you what you need to know to speak and write standard English. For further explanation on terms, pick up a copy of the companion book, *English Grammar For Dummies* (also published by Wiley).

Second, we assume that you hate the boring, schoolbook style. You prefer not to yawn as you read. No problem! Everyone glazes over when faced with sentences such as, 'The administrative council approved the new water-purification project outlined in by-law 78-451 by a margin of three votes to two.' For our questions we create some strange little creatures living in peculiar little worlds. You may think that they're there just to make you smile, but no. Our cunning plan is to slip in some grammar practice while you're distracted by the silly tales.

How This Book Is Organised

Life gets harder as you go along, doesn't it? So, too, does this book. Parts I and II concentrate on the basics – popping the right verbs into each sentence, forming singulars and plurals, creating complete sentences and so on. Part III moves up a notch to the pickier stuff, not exactly to world ranking but definitely the county-championship level. In Parts III and IV, you get to try your hand at the most annoying problems presented by pronouns (those pesky little words such as *I, me, theirs, whomever* among others), advanced verb problems and comparisons. Part V is completely practical, polishing up your writing style and explaining some common word traps into which you may fall. Now for more detail.

Part I: Laying the Foundations: Grammar Basics

In this part we take you through the building blocks – *verbs* (words that express action or state of being) and *subjects* (who or what you're talking about) – with a quick side trip into basic *pronouns* (*I, he, her* and so on). We show you how to create complete sentences. In this part you practise choosing the correct verb tense in straightforward sentences and find out all you need to know about singular and plural forms.

Part II: Mastering Mechanics

This part's devoted to two little things that can make or break your writing: punctuation and capital letters. If you're unsure whether to head *North* or *north* or if you want to know where a comma belongs, this part's for you.

Part III: The Pickier Points of Correct Verb and Pronoun Use

This part tackles all the fun stuff associated with pronouns, including the reason why everyone must bring their *lunch* is still a controversial statement, as far as grammar-geeks are concerned. Part III also solves your time problems, helping you to decipher the shades of difference in verb tense *(wrote? had written?)* and voice (not alto or soprano, but active or passive).

Part IV: All You Need to Know about Descriptions and Comparisons

Part IV puts you through your paces in selecting the best descriptive words (such as *good* or *well*?). We also weed out illogical or vague comparisons.

Part V: Writing with Style

Part V allows you to stop cracking your knuckles and twiddling your pen, and start to compete with the world-class writers. You face the toughest grammatical situations, plus exercises that address fluidity and variety. We also throw in some misunderstood words (*imply* and *infer*, to name just two) and give you practice in using them properly.

Part VI: The Part of Tens

Here you find ten ways in which people trying to be hyper-correct end up being super-wrong. You can also find out about ten errors that can ruin your chances of promotion or lower the mark you get for an essay. In the Appendix we give you a Final Challenge – four documents designed to test your grammar skills to their limit.

Icons Used in This Book

Icons are the cute little drawings that attract your gaze and alert you to key points or pitfalls. In *English Grammar Workbook For Dummies*, we use four icons.

Have you ever been a tourist lost in a foreign city, desperate for a local to show you the ropes? The Tip icon is the equivalent of a friendly guide whispering in your ear, 'Psst! Want the inside story to make your life easier?'

If you're on a hunt for treasure, the map you're following needs to warn you, 'Here be pirates!' The Warning icon tells you where the booby traps are so you can turn round and run like mad from them.

Theory doesn't go very far when you're working on grammar. You have to see the language in action, so to speak. The Practice icon alerts you to an example and a set of exercises so you can practise what you've just finished reading about.

Under the Remember icon, we highlight important points for you to bear in mind.

Where to Go from Here

To the fridge for a snack. Just kidding. Now that you know what's where, turn to the section that best meets your needs. If you're not sure what's going to benefit you most, take a moment to think about what bothers you. What parts of writing or speaking make you pause for a lengthy head scratch? Do you have trouble picking the right verb tense? Is finding the right word a cinch but deciding whether to use a comma or not a nightmare? Do you go out of your way to avoid sentences containing *who* because you never know when to opt for *whom*?

After a little grammatical reconnaissance, select the sections of this book that meet your needs. Use the 'How This Book Is Organised' section earlier in this introduction, the comprehensive table of contents and the index to find more detail about what's where. Turn to the exercises that address your issues and use the rest to line the budgie's cage if you want! Of course, if you decide to read every single word, we're going to be secretly chuffed. But if you pick and choose from the different sections of *English Grammar Workbook For Dummies*, we're still going to be chuffed anyway. Talk about a win-win situation!

If you aren't sure whether a particular topic is a problem, no problem! Cast your eyes over the explanation and sample question. Try a couple of sentences and check your answers. If you glide through easily enough and you understand the answers, move on. If you stub your toe, go back and do a few more questions until the grammar rule becomes clear (and your foot stops hurting).

When you understand each concept separately you may still have trouble putting all the elements together correctly. That's when the comprehensive exercise at the end of each chapter comes into its own. This is a short piece of text that's littered with mistakes for you to find and correct. Now you get to be teacher – red pen at the ready!

One more thing: don't try to do everything at the same time. Do short, sharp, ten-minute bursts of grammar activity. In this way, more is going to stick with you, and you have the added bonus of more time to get on with the rest of your life.

Part I
Laying the Foundations: Grammar Basics

'I'd like you to seriously consider
my offer of marriage.'

In this part . . .

If you've ever built a house with bricks or even a tower with playing cards, you know that the whole thing is likely to fall down unless it's sitting on top of a solid foundation. This part gives you the stuff you need to lay the best foundation for your writing. Chapter 1 takes you through verbs, explaining how to select the best verb for present, past and future situations. In the same chapter, you find the most popular irregular verbs and everything you need to know about the ever-helpful helping verbs. Chapter 2 moves inside the house, to the kitchen, and sorts your verbs into singular and plural piles and helps you match each verb to the correct subject. Then you're ready to pair pronouns and nouns (Chapter 3) and to distinguish complete from incomplete or too-long sentences (Chapter 4). Ready? We promise we won't let the grammar roof fall on your head!

Chapter 1

Placing the Proper Verb in the Proper Place

*V*erbs can be as short as two letters and as long as several words; they communicate action or a state of being. Plus, without even looking at a watch, a verb can tell you the time. Unfortunately, that handy little time-keeping function can be confusing.

In this chapter, we look at basic time questions. No, not 'You're late again because. . . ?', but 'Which verb do I need to show what's completed, not yet begun or going on right now?' We look at the basic tenses (past, present and future) and the perfect tenses, which are anything but perfect. We also work on irregular and auxiliary verbs.

Choosing Past, Present or Future

Verbs indicate time using a quality known as *tense*. Before you reach for a tranquilliser, here's a rundown of the three basic tenses: present, past and future. Each tense has two forms: *plain* or *simple* (called by its basic time designation) and *progressive* (the *-ing* form of a verb). The progressive places a little more emphasis on process or action that spans a time period, and the present progressive may reach into the future. In many sentences, plain and progressive verbs may be used interchangeably. Here's a taste of each type:

✔ **The past tense tells you what happened at a specific time in the past or describes a pattern of behaviour in the past.** In the sentence 'Diane painted a skull on her bike', *painted* is a past tense verb describing a single past action. In 'During the Biker Festival, Diane was drinking more than usual', *was drinking* is a verb in the past progressive tense describing an action that recurred over a period of time – the duration of the festival.

✔ **The present tense tells you what's going on right now or, more generally speaking, what action is recurring.** The present tense also touches the future. In the sentence 'Diane rides to work', *rides* is a present tense verb and riding to work is something that Diane does regularly – she has done it for some time and you expect her to go on doing it in the future. In 'Diane is polishing her bike', the verb *is polishing* is in the present progressive tense and polishing her bike is what Diane is doing right now. But in 'Diane is riding her bike to Cornwall on Friday night', the present progressive verb *is riding* indicates that this action is something that Diane is going to do in the future. This double use of the present progressive as a present or future time indicator is just one of the interesting features of English!

> ✔ **The future tense moves into fortune-telling.** The verb in 'Diane will give Grace a ride on her new bike' is *will give*, which is in the future tense. In 'Diane will be showing off her new bike for months', *will be showing off* is in the future progressive tense.

Okay, time to try out a sample problem. The infinitive (the grandma of each verb family) follows every sentence. Stay in that family when you fill in the blank, choosing the correct tense. When you're finished with this example, try the practice problems that follow.

Q. Clothes have always been important to David. He remembers quite clearly the day in 1976 he _____ his first pair of platform boots. (*to wear*)

A. **wore**. The clue here is *in 1976*, which tells you that you're talking about past events.

1. Fashion is important to David, and so he always _____ the latest and most popular style. (*to select*)

2. Last year's tight, slim lines _____ David, who, I must admit, doesn't have a tiny waist. (*to challenge*)

3. When David _____ new clothes, his fashion consultant is busy on the sidelines, recommending stripes and understated plaids to minimise the bulge factor. (*to buy*)

4. David hopes that the next fashion fad _____ a more mature, oval figure like his own. (*to flatter*)

5. Right now, Diane _____ an article for the fashion press stating that so-tight-it-may-as-well-be-painted-on leather is best. (*to write*)

6. She once _____ a purple suede trouser suit, which clashed with her orange hair. (*to own*)

7. When she _____ her hair black, her mother was relieved. (*to dye*)

8. Two days after Diane's shopping spree, Grace _____ her new jacket. (*to borrow*)

9. Diane knows, however, that as soon as she raises enough cash, Grace _____ in a jacket of her own. (*to invest*)

10. David, as always, _____ on having the last word when he gave Grace and Diane the Fashion Train Wreck of the Year Award. (*to insist*)

11. After she received the award, Diane _____ it on a shelf next to her Best Dressed, Considering medal. (*to place*)

12. Until yesterday, whenever I saw the medal, I always _____ what 'considering' meant. (*to wonder*)

13. Just 24 hours ago Grace finally _____ to me what it meant. (*to explain*)

14. She _____ me, 'We earned the medal for considering many fashion options.' (*to tell*)

15. David _____ Diane tomorrow. I wonder if he will have any more awards to give her then. (*to visit*)

Shining a Light on Perfect Tenses

The perfect tenses add *has*, *have* or *had* to a verb. Each perfect tense – present perfect, past perfect and future perfect – also has a progressive form, which includes an *–ing* verb. The difference between the plain perfect tense and the progressive perfect is subtle. The progressive perfect is a bit more immediate than the plain, simple form and refers to something that's ongoing – putting the emphasis on the action – or to something that continues over a period of time. In many sentences the plain and progressive forms are interchangeable. Here's when to use the perfect tenses:

✔ **The present perfect links the past and the present and is used for an action or state of being that began in the past and is still going on.** In the sentence 'Despite numerous reports of sightings around the world, Matt has lived round the corner from his mum for the last ten years', the verb *has lived* is in the present perfect tense. In 'Matt's mum has been trying to get him to spread his wings for the last decade', *has been trying* is in the present perfect progressive tense.

✔ **The past perfect places one event in the past before another event in the past.** In 'Matt had dumped his dirty washing in his mother's kitchen long before she decided to change the locks', the verb is *had dumped*, which is in the past perfect tense. In the sentence 'Matt's mother had been threatening a laundry strike for years, but his sudden interest in playing football pushed her to breaking point', the verb *had been threatening* is in the past perfect progressive tense: it stresses that the threat of strike action happened again and again.

✔ **The future perfect implies a deadline in the future.** In the sentence 'By the end of the year, Matt will have played in 23 football matches', the verb *will have played* is in the future perfect tense. The verb in 'By then he will have been playing football seriously for six months' is *will have been playing*, which is in the future perfect progressive tense.

Practice, especially with these verbs, makes perfect, and so dip your toe in the water with the following example and then jump right in and try the other questions. The verb you're working on appears as an infinitive (the basic, no-tense form) at the end of the sentence. Change it into the correct perfect tense and fill in the blank.

---

0. Matt put on his scarf, hat and ice-skates, and then realised that he _____ his gloves in the car (*to leave*).

A. **had left**. With two events in the past, *had* signals the earlier event. The putting on of the scarf, hat and skates took place before the leaving of the gloves, and so *had left* is the form you want.

---

16. Matt _____ on the pond for two hours when he heard the first crack. (*to skate*)

17. Diane _____ Matt for years about his skating on the pond, but he just wouldn't listen. (*to warn*)

18. Just last week Matt pointed out that Diane's motorbike _____ her more often than his skates _____ him. (*to harm, to harm*)

19. David, who is a delicate, sensitive soul, took Matt to the hospital. When this event is over, David _____ for a total of 132 hours for his friend. (*to wait*)

20. While David _____ for Matt, he called Diane but she said she wouldn't come to the hospital. (*to wait*)

21. Grace _____ to speak to Matt ever since he declared that a little thin ice shouldn't scare anyone. (*to refuse*)

22. By 3 o'clock Matt's mother had arrived and _____ the doctor how Matt was before she saw him. (*to ask*)

23. Sonia was also in Casualty, because she _____ her ankle. (*to sprain*)

24. Sonia has worn killer stiletto heels for years, but she _____ recently that she can look good without them. (*to realise*)

25. While she waited, Sonia calculated that she _____ fashionable but painful shoes for over seven years. (*to wear*)

26. Sonia swears that she _____ wearing heals completely by the time she's 30. (*to stop*)

27. Dick was also in hospital because he _____ his leg when he tried to push his brother Joe down the stairs. (*to injure*)

28. Dick _____ to kill Joe for the last three months. (*to try*)

29. By the middle of next month, Diane _____ for two years on the bike that she's restoring. (*to work*)

30. David would like to help her. He _____ with Diane for months but she still hasn't noticed him. She has time only for her precious bike. (*to be in love*)

Navigating the Irregular Forms

Irregular verbs seem designed to test your mettle, because they stray from the usual *-ed* form in the past tense. The irregularity continues in a form called the past participle. You don't need to know the terms: you just need to know what words replace the usual *-ed* verb configuration (for example, *sang* and *sung* rather than *singed*).

It's hard to memorise every possible irregular verb. If you're unsure about a particular verb, look it up in the dictionary: the definition includes the irregular form.

We provide a set of irregular problems to tax your brain below. Fill in the blanks with the correct irregular form, working from the infinitive indicated in brackets. Here's an example to get you started:

0. Nina seldom arrived on time, but she was always quiet as she _____ into whatever house she was cleaning. (*to go*)

A.   **went.** No *-ed* for this past tense! *Went* is the irregular past form of *to go*.

31. If you discover a piece of pottery on the floor, look for Nina, who has _____ a lot of vases because of her tendency to dust far too enthusiastically. (*to break*)

32. Nina _____ with dismay on her first day as a cleaner when she broke a priceless Ming vase. (*to weep*)

33. David, no mean duster himself, has _____ four manuals of 'domestic maintenance'. (*to write*)

34. His latest one, 'A Clean Sweep', _____ to the top of the bestseller list a few months ago. (*to rise*)

35. Nearly all the copies had been _____ by fanatical cleaners, apparently. (*to buy*)

36. The fire brigade was amused the first time David's dusting _____ off the fire alarm. (*to set*)

37. However, the 19th time the alarm _____ off, the fire fighters didn't think it was so funny. (*to go*)

38. The Chief Fire Officer told David, 'Best seller or not, it's time to stop setting off the alarm.' David finally admitted that cleaning had _____ over his life. (*to take*)

39. 'I hear you've _____ a branch of Cleaners Anonymous,' _____ David to Nina, 'and I suppose I'll have to go along to it.' (*to find, to sigh*)

40. To cheer him up, Nina showed David a scarf she had _____ from yarn she had _____ herself. (*to weave, to spin*)

41. David then discovered a new hobby and became completely obsessed by it. Last week he _____ to be allowed into the local children's knitting circle to be with knitters whose skills were at a level similar to his own. (*to fight*)

42. Although he won his battle, David was still frustrated by the number of stitches he dropped, and so he _____ the bullet and asked Matt's mum for help. (*to bite*)

43. 'You just need more practice,' she _____, as she _____ her coffee. (*to say, to drink*)

44. If he _____ her advice, she thought he would soon be very skilled. (*to take*)

45. David _____, 'Thanks for all your help but I think it's time to go back to my first love – cleaning. It seems so much simpler.' (*to reply*)

Mastering the Two Most Common Irregulars: Be and Have

Two irregular verbs, *to be* and *to have*, appear more frequently than movie stars on the red carpet with a new film to promote. Both these verbs change according to time and according to the nouns or pronouns with which they're paired. Because they're used a lot in English, you need to be sure that you master all their forms, as shown in Table 1-1.

Table 1-1	Verb Forms for the Irregular Verbs *To Be* and *To Have*		
Pronoun(s)	Verb Form for To Be	Pronoun(s)	Verb Form for To Have
I	am	I	have
you/we/they	are	you/we/they	have
he/she/it	is	he/she/it	has
I/he/she/it	was	I/he/she/it	had
you/we/they	were	you/we/they	had

Note that the past participle of *to be* is *been*. The past particle is used in the perfect tenses (for example, 'She has been a doctor for years' or 'They will have been married for 20 years next week').

Fill in the blanks in the following conversation with the correct form of *to be* or *to have*. In some cases, you may find the process easier if you think of the contracted form first (for example, *he's*) but then write the full form (for example, *he is*) in the blank, as in this example:

Q. I _____ delighted to announce that the winner of this year's Potato Salad Competition _____ Mrs Edna Williams, who came second last year and the year before.

A. ('m) am, is.

46. 'Her birthday _____ next week, and I don't know what present to get her,' said Tim.

47. 'Don't look at me – I never _____ any good ideas!' protested June.

48. 'I _____ a good idea last week, but I can't remember what it _was_,' murmured Betty.

49. 'Chocolate _____ my last resort for years whenever I can't think of anything better,' suggested June.

50. 'Oh, chocolates _____ boring,' said Tim, 'and she _____ on a diet.'

51. 'I think the flowers we bought her last year _____ nice,' said Betty.

52. 'Well, Grace and I _____ firmly in favour of more imaginative presents,' said Gill, who _____ irritated by their lack of imagination in the past.

53. Then Kristin _____ a brilliant idea.

54. 'If she wants to keep on winning the Potato Salad Competition, now _____ the time to plant her next crop of potatoes.'

55. 'Why don't we all go over to her place on Saturday and help her with her new crop. I _____ sure she _____ pleased if we do that,' said Tim.

Getting By with a Little Help from Some Other Verbs

In addition to *has*, *have*, *had* and the *to be* verbs (*am*, *is*, *are*, *was*, *were* and so on) you can attach a few other (modal auxiliary) verbs to a main verb and in doing so change the meaning of the sentence slightly. Modal auxiliary verbs that you need to consider include the following:

✔ *Should* and *must* add a sense of duty. Note the sense of obligation in these two sentences: 'David should put the ice cream away before he eats the whole thing' and 'David must reduce his cholesterol, according to his doctor.'

✔ *Can* and *could* imply ability. By the way, *could* is the past tense of *can*. Choose the tense that matches the tense of the main verb or the time period expressed in the sentence. (For example, 'If Hanna can help, she will' and 'Courtney could paint beautifully when she was a child but now she says she can't paint at all.')

✔ *May* and *might* add possibility to the sentence. Both are used where the possibility exists as far as you know, with *might* often suggesting a lower probability. The sentence 'I may go to the picnic if I can find the insect spray' suggests that you do want to go to the picnic, whereas 'I might go to the picnic' suggests that you don't. To say 'I may have caught the early train on Tuesday' is acceptable if you can't remember whether you did or not but the possibility exists that you did, but *might* is correct (and *may* is not) in the sentence 'I might have taken you to the picnic if you'd put your toys away as I asked you' because we both know that you threw a tantrum and weren't taken to the picnic.

✔ *Would* usually expresses willingness or a habit. *Would* may express willingness (as in 'He would be happy to help with the garden'). Also, *would* sometimes communicates repeated past actions (for example, 'Every Saturday he would mow the lawn').

Note that all these modal auxiliary verbs (*should*, *must*, *can*, *could*, *may*, *might*, *will* and *would*) can also be used in sentences that express a theory or hypothesis. These types of sentences have a condition clause and a clause that shows the result of that clause, for example 'If you do that again', (condition clause) 'I'll kill you' (result of the condition clause).

Lots of combinations are available for expressing your theories or hypotheses, but the underlying pattern is as follows: if clause, result clause (or vice versa: you can have the result clause at the beginning). In the result clause, a modal auxiliary verb is often used, such as *would*, *might*, *can* and so on.

Have a look at Table 1-2 to see just a few of the modal auxililary verbs in action in the result clause.

Table 1-2	Examples of If and Result Clauses
If Clause	*Result Clause*
If it's sunny tomorrow,	we *might* go to the park.
If we can get up on time,	we really *should* tidy the garden.
If you wash the dishes,	I'*ll* dry them.
If I were a blackbird,	I'*d* whistle and sing.
If you go to Leeds,	you *can* see the castle.
If he were famous,	he *might* sign autographs, he *might* not.
If she could help you,	she *would*.

Now take a crack at the following example and exercises. Add an auxiliary verb to the main verb. The information in brackets after the fill-in-the-blank sentence explains what meaning the sentence needs to have.

0. Malcolm said that he_____ consider standing for Parliament, but he hasn't made up his mind yet. (possibility)

A. **may** or **might**. *May* indicates that Malcolm hasn't ruled out standing, but *might* suggests that he's not keen on the idea.

56. He thinks that the campaigning _____be exciting, but the prospect of travelling up and down the country fills him with dread. (condition)

57. If he could win the election without stepping on a train, he _____ have no difficulty deciding whether to stand or not. (condition)

58. You see, Malcolm has a fear of buffet-car sandwiches. When he was a boy he _____ hop on and off any kind of transport and eat whatever was on offer. But those days are long gone now. (ability)

59. He's not quite sure when the phobia started. It _____ have been on the overnight sleeper from Manchester to Edinburgh. (possibility)

60. But then again, it _____ have been on the 7:45 from Bristol to Cardiff. (possibility)

61. Whatever the trip, he _____ clearly remember crossing a British border faced with a breakfast of wilted lettuce and soggy crusts. (ability)

62. Ever since then, rail journeys have been problematic for him. He _____ fly of course, but it's too expensive. (ability)

63. The members of his campaign team say that he _____ forget the train. 'Why not travel by rickshaw instead?' they suggest. (duty)

64. 'But who _____ pull me?' he asks them. (willingness)

65. As soon as his PA says, 'You know I _____ if I could but my back's been playing up, and so I _____,' the others start getting their excuses ready. (willingness, ability)

Extra Practice with Verbs

The time has come to sharpen all the tools in your verb kit. Read the memo in Figure 1-1 and correct all the verbs that have strayed from the proper path: you should find ten.

Figure 1-1:
A sample memo with some confused verbs.

To: All Employees

From: Cathy

Subject: Paper Clips

It had come to my attention that some employees will be bending paper clips nearly every day. A few office juniors even bended an entire box. Each employee would remember our dear founder's words: 'I'm the boss, do as I say.' My current mantra is: 'Paperclips have been expensive, don't waste them.' In my ten years as your boss, I always gave you a fair deal. I will have given you a fair deal in the future too, but only if you showed some responsibility. Therefore, I will begin inspecting all desks in this office this morning. By close of play, I will have been checking every single one. If your desk contains a bent paper clip, you would find yourself out of a job.

Answers to Problems on Verbs and Verb Tenses

1 **selects**. Did you notice the time clues? The first part of the sentence contains the word *is*, a present-tense verb, and the second part includes the word *always*. Clearly you're in the present with a recurring action.

2 **challenged**. Another time clue: *last year's* places you in the past.

3 **is buying** or **buys**. The second verb in the sentence (*is*) takes you right into the shop with David, watching the unfolding action. The present progressive tense gives a feeling of immediacy, and so *is buying* makes sense. The plain present tense (*buys*) works nicely, too.

4 **will flatter**. The key here is *next*, which puts the sentence in the future.

5 **is writing**. The time clue *right now* indicates the present and the writing is an activity that continues for some time, and so the present progressive form *is writing* works well here.

6 **owned**. Diane's bad taste splurge happened *once*, which means it took place in the past.

7 **dyed**. The second part of the sentence includes the verb form *relieved*, which places you in the past.

8 **borrowed** or **was borrowing**. The clue to the past is *two days after*. The second answer gives more of an 'again and again' feel, but either is correct.

9 **will invest**. The time words here, *as soon as*, tell you that the action hasn't happened yet.

10 **insisted**. If David *gave*, you're in the past tense.

11 **placed**. The first verb in the sentence (*received*) is in the past tense, and so you know that the action of placing the award on the shelf is also in the past tense.

12 **wondered**. The time clue here is *Until yesterday*, which tells you that this action happened in the past and needs to be in the past tense.

13 **explained**. The *24 hours ago* is a dead giveaway – go for the past tense.

14 **told**. The saga of Grace and Diane's award is in the past, and so you need a past tense verb *told*.

15 **is visiting** or **will visit**. The time clue is *tomorrow*, which places the action in the future, and so the future tense *will visit* is correct, but so is the present progressive tense *is visiting*, used in its future sense.

16 **had been skating** or **had skated**. You have two actions in the past – the skating and the hearing. The two hours of skating came before the hearing, which means that you need the past perfect tense. The plain or the progressive form works here, and so give yourself a gold star for either answer.

17 **had been warning** or **had warned**. The second half of the sentence indicates the past (*wouldn't listen*). The warning came before the listening, and so you need the past perfect for the verb *warn* to show that it came first.

18 **had harmed** and **had harmed**. The harm (in both cases) preceded the pointing out, and both occurred in the past, and so you need to use the past perfect. The sentence is talking about distinct events completed in the past, and so the progressive isn't appropriate.

19 **will have waited**. The deadline in the sentence (*when this is over*) is your clue that the future perfect tense is needed.

20 **was waiting**. The waiting and the calling both happened in the past and so you need past tenses for both of those verbs. The waiting happened over a longer period of time than the calling and so the past progressive (*was waiting*) is correct here.

21 **has refused**. Did you note the present–past link? *Since* is often a sign to use the present perfect. Matt *declared* (past) and Grace is acting now (present), which means that you need the present perfect tense.

22 **had asked**. The asking (and the arriving) happened before the seeing, and so you need the past perfect tense.

23 **had sprained**. The sprain happened before the visit to Casualty, and so you need the past perfect tense.

24 **has realised**. This sentence has a present-tense clue (*now*). The sentence tells you about the past (*for years*) and the present (*recently*), and so the present perfect tense is the one you want.

25 **had been wearing** or **had worn**. The calculating happened after the wearing. Because both are in the past, you need the past perfect tense (progressive or plain) for the earlier action.

26 **will have stopped**. A deadline at some point in the future (*by the time she's 30*) calls for the future perfect tense.

27 **had injured**. The being in hospital started in the past, but the injury took place before that. You use the past perfect tense for the earlier of two past actions.

28 **has been trying**. The time clue *for the last three months* tells you that something has been happening over a period of time (and so you need a progressive tense) and that it started in the past and continues up to now, indicating that the present perfect is correct. Putting them both together, you end up with the present perfect progressive. Give yourself full marks if you answered this one correctly!

29 **will have been working**. A future deadline (*the middle of next month*) requires the future perfect tense. The work on the bike is ongoing, and so the progressive form is ideal.

30 **has been in love**. The sentence tells you that David was and still is in love with Diane. To link the past and present, go for the present perfect tense.

31 **broken**. The verb *to break* has two irregular forms, *broke* (*she broke*) and *broken* (*she has broken*).

32 **wept**. *To weep* has only one irregular form (*she wept, she has wept*).

33 **written**. Two irregular forms apply here (*he wrote, he has written*), and because a *has* appears before the blank, you need *written*.

34 **rose**. Be sure to rise to the occasion and choose *rose* (the other irregular form is *risen*).

35 **bought**. Let this verb remind you of other irregulars, including *caught, taught* and *thought*. In each case, only one past form applies. And no, *thunk* (as in *who'd've thunk?*) doesn't exist but is a made-up word appropriate only in light-hearted moments among friends.

36 **set**. Only one past form for this verb applies, and it's the same as the present and the infinitive!

37 **went**. Take a memo: I *go*, I *went* and I have or had *gone*.

38   **taken**. The plain past tense form is *took*, and the form that combines with *has*, *have* or *had* is *taken*.

39   **found**, **sighed**. The past tense of *find* is *found*. *Sigh* is regular, making the past tense a plain and simple *sighed*.

40   **woven**, **spun**. These two forms are used in the past perfect tense; the simple past form is the same (*spun*) for *to spin*, but is *wove* for *to weave*.

41   **fought**. The past tense of *to fight* is *fought* (just the one form here).

42   **bit**. The past forms of *to bite* are *bit* and *bitten*.

43   **said**, **drank**. The irregular past tense of *to say* is *said* (just one form: *I said*, *I have said*). *To drink* follows the *i–a–u* pattern: *drink*, *drank*, *drunk*. Other verbs that follow this pattern are *ring*, *rang*, *rung* and *sing*, *sang*, *sung*.

44   **took**. Two past forms of *to take* exist: *took* and *taken*. You need the plain, simple form *took* here.

45   **replied**. The verb *reply* in the past tense is *replied*.

46   **'s** or **is**. Here Tim's talking about a set or timetabled event in the future and the best way to convey that is to use the present tense (with a future meaning).

47   **have**. You need a singular, present tense verb to match *I* in this sentence.

48   **had**, **was**. Here you need two past-tense verbs. *Had* agrees with *I* and *was* goes with *it*.

49   **has been**. The sentence requires a link between the past and the present, and so the simple past won't do. You need the present perfect to bridge the two time periods. *Has been* does the job.

50   **are**, **'s** or **is**. You need two present tense verbs here. The verb *to be* becomes *are* to agree with *chocolates* and *is* (*'s*) to agree with *she*.

51   **were**. The sentence is talking about a single event in the past, and so the simple past tense is required and *were* agrees with *flowers*.

52   **are**, **had been**. The first part needs a simple present tense verb to agree with the plural subject (*Grace and I*). The second part is no longer part of the speech. The speech is already in the past tense (*said Gill*), and so the comment on how Gill felt before she said this needs to go in the past perfect tense: *had been* is the answer.

53   **had**. Here you need a simple past tense, in line with the past tense words (*said*, *murmured*, *protested*) throughout the conversation.

54   (**'s**) **is**. You're in the present here, when the time is *now*, and so you need a present verb *is* (*'s*).

55   (**'m**) **am**, **will be**. You need the present tense to begin with (*I'm* or *I am*) followed by the future tense *will be* for the birthday girl's anticipated reaction.

56   **would**. The excitement of the campaign is dependent on the travelling, making *would* the best choice.

57   **would**. Another condition, and so *would* wins the prize.

58   **could**. To talk about an ability, use *can*. To talk about past ability, use *could*.

59   **may** or **might**. To talk about possibility, you can use *may* or *might*.

60 **may** or **might**. Possibility is expressed by *may* or *might*.

61 **can**. You're talking about Malcolm being able to remember in the present, and so *can* is what you need here.

62 **could**. You're talking about ability and so you need *can*, but because an element of condition applies here, *could* is a good choice to show that the possibility is quite remote.

63 **should**. When duty calls, opt for *should*.

64 **would**. Malcolm is testing his team's willingness and so *would* is the best choice here.

65 **would, can't**. His PA is showing willingness and talking about ability. Give yourself top marks if you chose *would* and *can't*.

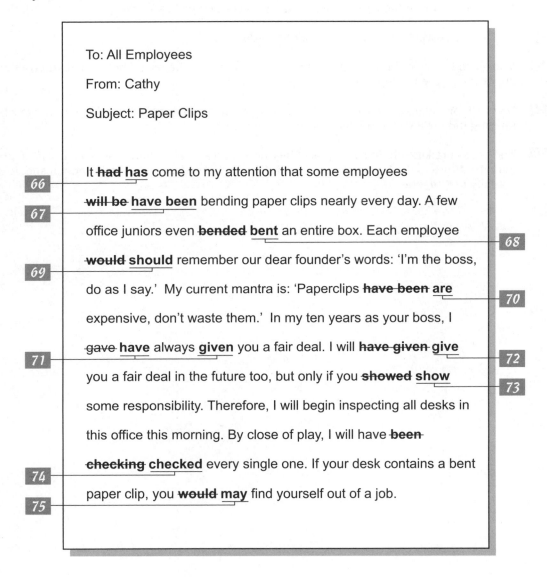

To: All Employees

From: Cathy

Subject: Paper Clips

It ~~had~~ **has** come to my attention that some employees

66

~~will be~~ **have been** bending paper clips nearly every day. A few

67

office juniors even ~~bended~~ **bent** an entire box. Each employee

68

~~would~~ **should** remember our dear founder's words: 'I'm the boss,

69

do as I say.' My current mantra is: 'Paperclips ~~have been~~ **are**

70

expensive, don't waste them.' In my ten years as your boss, I

~~gave~~ **have** always **given** you a fair deal. I will ~~have given~~ **give**

71   72

you a fair deal in the future too, but only if you ~~showed~~ **show**

73

some responsibility. Therefore, I will begin inspecting all desks in

this office this morning. By close of play, I will have ~~been~~

~~checking~~ **checked** every single one. If your desk contains a bent

74

paper clip, you ~~would~~ **may** find yourself out of a job.

75

66 *Had come* is wrong because it places one action in the past before another action in the past – not the meaning expressed by this sentence. Instead, this sentence needs a verb to link past and present, and *has come* fills the bill.

67 *Will be* places the action in the future, but the memo again seeks to establish that the bending went on in the past and continues in the present, and so the present perfect tense (*have been bending*) does the job.

68 *Bent* is an irregular past form. *Bended* is never correct.

69 Because you're talking about duty, *should* works nicely here.

70 The present tense is better because the boss is concerned about the current cost of paper clips.

71 The boss is bragging about fairness in the past, which continues in the present, and so the present perfect (*have given*) is perfect here. Note that the *always* is placed between the verbs of the present perfect (*have always given*), and this rule would be the case if you'd used any other adverb of frequency – such as *usually, never, sometimes* – here.

72 *Will give* is correct; *will have given* implies a deadline.

73 *Showed* is incorrect because the boss isn't talking about the past. She's talking theoretically about the future result (*will give*) of a present action (*you show*).

74 No need for the progressive (*-ing*) here, because the boss wants to tell the underlings when the investigation will end, not when it will be going on.

75 The boss is talking about a real possibility here, and so *will* or *may* works well. *Will* is more definite. *May* lets the boss threaten but still leaves herself enough wiggle room if she doesn't actually fire anyone.

Chapter 2

Matchmaker, Make Me a Match: Pairing Subjects and Verbs Correctly

In This Chapter

▶ Forming plural nouns

▶ Pairing subject and verb forms in common sentences

▶ Dealing with difficult subjects

*I*n the world of grammar, the difference between singular (the one, the only, the solitary) and plural (anywhere from two to a crowd) is a big deal. In this respect, grammar follows real life. When the obstetrician reports on the ultrasound or your date lists ex-spouses, the difference between one and more than one is a matter of considerable interest.

This chapter shows you how to tell the difference between singular and plural nouns, pronouns and verbs, and gets you started on pairing them up correctly in some common sentence patterns. We also help you to tackle difficult subjects such as *everyone*, *somebody*, *either* and *neither*.

Coping When One Just Isn't Enough: Plural Nouns

When we were at school, the only spell-check was the teacher. Rules were drummed into us and we were in trouble if we forgot them. Here's a recap on the rules, minus the punishments:

✔ **Regular plurals pick up an *s*** (*one snob/two snobs, one pound/two pounds*).

✔ **Nouns ending in *s, sh, ch* and *x* tack on *es* to form the plural** (*class/classes, splash/splashes, catch/catches, hex/hexes*) **unless the noun has an irregular plural** (more about irregular plurals in a moment).

✔ **Nouns ending in *ay, ey, oy* and *uy* – in other words, a vowel before *y* – simply add an *s*** (*monkey/monkeys, boy/boys*).

✔ **Nouns ending in a consonant before *y* change the *y* to *i* and add *es*** (*butterfly/butterflies, mystery/mysteries*).

✔ **Irregular nouns do some very weird things!** Sometimes the noun doesn't change at all, making the plural and singular forms exactly the same (*sheep/sheep, deer/deer*); and sometimes the noun does change (*leaf/leaves, child/children*). When you're unsure about an irregular plural, look the word up in a dictionary. The definition lists the plural form for each noun.

When making the plural of a proper name – say, Smith – just add *s*. Don't change any letters even if the name ends with a consonant *y* combo (*Smithy*, perhaps). Just add *s* for the *Smiths* and the *Smithys*.

Are you up for some multiplication? At the end of each sentence is the singular form of a noun (or in some cases two or three nouns) in brackets. Write the plurals in the blanks, as in this example:

Q. Jennifer's temperature was high, and her mother was threatening to take her to one of the local health _____. (*clinic*)

A. **clinics**. Don't you just love those regular plurals? Just add s.

1. Jennifer didn't want to go to the clinic but felt that she was too ill to do her homework, which required her to write two ____*essays*____. (*essay*)

2. Jennifer has never understood the ____*joys*____ of homework. (*joy*)

3. She would rather be outside, exploring the local _____, although she has a tendency to fall into nearby _____. (*hedgerow, ditch*)

4. She has encountered a lot of wildlife on her walks, including ____*deer*____, _____ and _____. (*deer, fox, goose*)

5. She likes nothing better than kicking up _____ while she's out walking in the ____*woods*____. (*leaf, wood*)

6. If Jennifer had her way, ____*teachers*____ and _____ would be banned from giving out any written homework at all. (*teacher, coach*)

7. Instead, all _____ would be observational. (*task*)

8. Dull maths _____ would become more interesting, she thinks, if they were based on the _____ of her _____. (*problem, life, pet*)

9. For instance, her teacher could ask her to do some _____ about her three pet _____. (*calculation, mouse*)

10. Jennifer thinks that this is a good sample question: 'If your three _____ eat eight ____*boxes*____ of cheese a day, how many micey _____ do you have to buy every fortnight?' (*pet, box, treat*)

Bringing Together Subjects and Verbs

To make a good match, as every computer-dating service knows, you have to pair like with like. In Grammarworld, you have to link singular subjects with singular verbs and plural subjects with plural verbs. The good news is that most of the time English verbs have only one form for both singular and plural. *I smirk* and *the boys smirk* are both correct, even though *I* is singular and *boys* is plural. You have to worry only in the following few special circumstances:

✔ **Talking about someone in the present tense requires a different verb form for *he*, *she* and *it* and for *I*, *you*, *we* and *they*.** For *he*, *she* and *it*, verbs end in *s* but for I, you, we and they, you don't need an *s* on the end ('he spits' versus 'they spit'). This rule may seem a little strange, because *he*, *she* and *it* are singular and yet their matching verbs end in *s*. Usually you expect an *s* at the end to signal a plural not a singular ('one elephant' versus 'a herd of elephants').

✔ **The rule above also applies to the verbs *does/do* and *has/have* (on their own or when they are helping another verb).** *Therefore, he, she* and *it* require an *s* ending, whereas *I, you, we* and *they* don't: for example, 'Does John paint his toenails blue?', 'They *have* three kittens', 'We *do* enjoy opera' and 'She *has* been living in Madrid'.

✔ **The verb *to be* changes form according to the noun or pronoun paired with it.** The verb forms and matching pronouns are: *I am, he/she/it is, we/they/you are, I was, he/she/it was* and *we/they/you were*.

✔ **Two subjects joined by *and* usually make a plural and take a plural verb.** As you discovered very young, one plus one equals two, which is a plural. (In 'Kristin and David plan to take a holiday every two years', *Kristin and David* forms a plural subject, and *plan* is a plural verb.) But then you grew up and realised that sometimes when you add one and one you still have one (such as, 'Gin and tonic is my favourite drink'). You have two items but you use a singular verb. This arrangement is true for certain other combinations, such as *bubble and squeak* and *fish and chips*.

✔ **Two or more subjects joined by *or* are just plain troublesome.** The logic here is that you're talking about just one subject (take your pick), and not them all, and so you don't add them up. But here's a simple rule that makes life easier: the verb takes a shortcut and agrees with the subject to which it's nearest, no matter whether you have a mixture of singular and plural subjects. (In 'David or Susan is cooking dinner on Friday', *David* being a singular subject is completely irrelevant because the verb – *is cooking* – is nearer to *Susan*. The verb would still agree with *Susan* if the sentence started 'David, Billy or Susan. . .' or 'The twins or Susan. . .'.)

✔ **Ignore interrupters when matching subjects to verbs.** Interrupters include phrases such as *except for, as well as* and *which takes the biscuit*. Some interrupters (*as well as, in addition to*) appear to create a plural, but grammatically they aren't part of the subject and, like all interrupters, have no effect on the singular/plural issue. (In 'Kristin, as well as all her friends, is marching in protest today', the subject, *Kristin*, is singular and matched with the singular verb *is*.)

✔ *Here* **and *there* can't be subjects:** it's in their contract. In a *here* or *there* sentence, look for the subject after the verb. (In the sentence 'Here are five red beans', *beans* is a plural subject and *are* is a plural verb.)

✔ **The subject usually precedes the verb but may appear elsewhere.** (In 'Across the palace hall race the royal cats and dogs', *the royal cats and dogs* forms a plural subject, which is matched with *race*, a plural verb.)

Test yourself with the following questions, starting with an example. In the blanks, write the correct form of the verb in the brackets.

0. John's chiropodist _____ interested in the toenail-colour issue. (*remain/remains*)

A. **remains**. The subject is singular, and so the verb must also be singular. The letter s is used with the *he*, *she* or *it* form. (Here, *chiropodist* = 'he' or she').

11. Hinting delicately that blue _____ not a natural colour for nails, Nadine _____ her pearly pink varnished toenails at John. (*is/are, wriggle/wriggles*)

12. John, who _____ that he dyes his hair, says that he _____ from a rare toe condition. (*admit/admits, suffer/suffers*)

13. We _____ not buying his toenail story. (*am/is/are*)

14. You probably _____ John because you _____ everyone the benefit of the doubt. (*believe/believes, give/gives*)

15. _____ you think that John always _____ the truth? (*Does/Do, tell/tells*)

16. _____ his story ever fallen on disbelieving ears? (*Has/Have*)

17. No one ever _____ when John _____ avoiding reality. (*know/knows, am/is/are*)

18. He _____ created some very convincing tales over the years. (*has/have*)

19. Why _____ everyone believe him? (*does/do*)

20. It turns out that he really is telling the truth. He _____ a potentially life-threatening condition. (*has/have*)

21. Apparently there _____ only six other people in the country with the same rare condition, but now there are seven. (*was/were*)

22. Although it's contagious, only genetically predisposed individuals _____ likely to catch it. (*is/am/are*)

23. He _____ now receiving the appropriate treatment. (*is/are*)

24. I heard that a movie director and a literary agent _____ interested in the story of John and his toenails. (*was/were*)

25. John's offers, in addition to a serious marriage proposal, _____ a ghostwritten autobiography and a reality TV show. (*includes/include*)

26. The producer of the series _____ guaranteed a hit. (*has/have*)

27. John, as well as his girlfriend, driven by a desire for fame and fast cars, _____ bound to be interested in the deal. (*is/are*)

28. Neither John's girlfriend nor the starlet who proposed marriage _____ aware that John wants to live with his mother for the rest of his life. (*is/are*)

29. _____ there any hope that either of them can make him change his mind? (*Is/Am/Are*)

30. I don't know. All I do know is that his girlfriend, the starlet and his mother all _____ in hope. (*live/lives*)

Taming the Terrible Twos: Difficult Subjects to Match with Verbs

Like a child at that awkward age, some subjects delight in being difficult. Despite being difficult, however, words such as *most*, *all*, *either* and *each* turn quickly, with a bit of attention, from tiny tearaways into well-behaved angels. Here are the rules:

- ✔ **Pronouns ending in *-one*, *-thing* and *-body* (*everyone*, *something* and *anybody*, for example) are singular, even though they sometimes sound plural.** (In 'Everyone is here', the singular subject *everyone* must be matched with the singular verb *is*.)

- ✔ ***All*, *some*, *most*, *none* and *any* can be singular or plural depending on what you're talking about. Some nouns can be counted, whereas others can be measured.** Subjects that can be counted (*alien*, *UFOs*, *spacecrafts*) can be singular or plural and subjects that can be measured (*space*, *love*, *happiness*) can only be singular. (In 'All ears that stick out are going to be super-glued to the scalp', the subject *all* is plural because it refers to *ears*. You can count *ears*, and so you use a plural verb *are*.) A subject that's measured but not counted is singular. (In 'All the excitement was too much for Tilley', *all* refers to *excitement*, which is a noun that can only be measured but not counted, and so the verb to use is the singular *was*.)

- ✔ ***Either* and *neither* alone, without *or* or *nor*, are singular.** (So in 'Neither of my uncles has agreed to take me to the cinema this afternoon', the singular subject *neither* matches the singular verb *has*.)

- ✔ **In *either . . . or . . .* and *neither . . . nor . . .* sentences, match the verb to the closest subject.** (In 'Either Josh or his partners are going to jail', the verb is *are going* because it's closer to the plural *partners* than to the singular *Josh*. If the sentence were reversed, the verb would be singular: 'Either his partners or Josh *is* going to jail.')

- ✔ ***Each* and *every* are always singular, no matter what they precede.** ('Each of the computers that Elizabeth bought was on sale.' 'Every computer and printer in the office has been stolen.' In these sentences the addition of *each* and *every* creates a singular subject that must be paired with a singular verb.)

Ready to relax? We don't think so. Try these problems. Underline the correct verb from each pair.

Q. Neither the theatre fire warden nor the health and safety officers (*was/were*) aware of the fireworks Mortimer wants to use on stage in his musical.

A. **were**. The subject *health and safety officers* is closer to the verb than *fire warden*. Because *health and safety officers* is plural, the verb must also be plural.

31. All the dancers in Mortimer's musical (*is/are*) required to get tattoos.

32. Either of the principal singers (*has/have*) enough talent to carry the musical.

33. Every seat in the stalls and the circle (*is/are*) sold already.

34. Why (*does/do*) no one understand that the musical is extremely boring?

35. Most of the songs (*has/have*) been written already, but the out-of-town tryouts suggest that more work is needed.

36. Everyone (*has/have*) invested a substantial amount, but no one (*is/are*) expecting a profit, despite the strong ticket sales.

37. Neither Mortimer nor the members of the cast (*is/are*) willing to speculate on the critical reception.

38. Any of the reviews (*has/have*) the ability to make or break the production.

39. (*Has/Have*) either the director or the musicians agreed on a contract?

40. Everyone (*agrees/agree*) that they should cut the fifth song.

41. The director is much more interested in tattoos than most of the members of the audience (*is/are*).

42. I don't understand his tattoo fixation because neither of his parents (*has/have*) any tattoos.

43. I've heard that every one of the leading lady's 20 tattoos (*is/are*) fake.

44. Some of Lola's tattoos (*is/are*) to be covered in the early scenes when Lola's character is an innocent schoolgirl.

45. However, each of the tattoos (*has/have*) special meaning to the director, and he is reluctant to conceal anything.

46. 'Artistic integrity,' he says, 'is important. All the fame in the world (*is/are*) not as valuable as honesty.'

47. Lola puts up a good argument for using her fake tattoos, but all her accountants (*believes/believe*) that she will give in and get real tattoos. She needs the part. She has bills to pay.

48. (*Has/Have*) anyone mentioned the Olivier Awards to Lola?

49. Either Lola or her producers (*is/are*) sure to win at least one award – if nobody else (*enters/enter*) the contest.

50. Every Olivier and Oscar on Lola's shelf (*is/are*) a testament to her talent.

51. Neither of her Olivier awards, however, (*has/have*) been polished for a long time.

52. Perhaps someone (*has/have*) neglected to hire a cleaning professional to spruce up Lola's house.

53. Both of Lola's brothers (*is/are*) in the field of furniture maintenance.

54. (*Was/Were*) either of her brothers called in to consult about trophy cleaning?

55. If so, perhaps either Lola's brothers or even Lola herself (*is/are*) on the verge of a cleaner future.

56. Most of us (*believe/believes*) that Lola would never dream of dusting her own statuettes.

57. However, all the Oscars that the director has won (*sparkles/sparkle*) blindingly.

58. None of the award-night excitement (*is/are*) very appealing to Mortimer, who can never bring himself to attend these ceremonies.

59. His wife and his brother (*attends/attend*) when they get the chance, but Mortimer makes a point of being sick on the big night.

60. Each of the award ceremonies, however, (*is/are*) a sacred obligation as far as Lola is concerned.

Brain Strain: Extra Practice with Hitching Subjects and Verbs

Time to sharpen up your error-spotting skills. Tucked into the letter in Figure 2-1, written by a master criminal, are ten errors in subject-verb agreement and ten incorrect plural forms, making a total of 20 mistakes. Cross out each incorrect verb and replace it with a new, improved version.

Dear Adelie,

Oh, my little fluffy sweetheart, how I long to be with you on this cold, cold day! Neither of the iron bars of my cell have kept me from dreaming about sweeping you away on our long-planned trip to Antarctica. Through the vast blue skys, speeding swiftly as wild turkies, go my heart.

Either the wardens or my honey, who is the sweetest of all honies, have taken over every thought in my brain. I never think about the sharkes in the sea any more. Every single one of my waking moments are devoted to you, cuddliest of all the cuddly teddy bear, or Frank, the burliest of all the big burly prison guards.

But, Pookie Snookie, all the other prisoners (except for my cellmate, of course) and I has waited impatiently for your visit. Two months has passed, and everyone (though not the cellmate, naturally) are impatient. I know you was busy. Your last letter said that all the taxs are paid, your new downhill racing skies are waxed (I know you love to ski!), and still you is not here. I wonder why.

Here is two tickets for the police officers you befriended. From what you said in your last letter, they seem like very friendly mans. That's nice you've got some new pals. That means they can come with you on the train, the next time you visit. (I know you hate to travel alone.) Speaking of alone (alone, a loan. Get it?), please bring the loots from our last job. I need escape money. Also bring two gold watchs, which are very handy for bribes.

Your Cutie Patootie,

Charlie

Figure 2-1: Criminal letter with subject and verb errors.

Answers to Subject and Verb Pairing Problems

1 **essays**. For any word ending in *ay*, just add *s*.

2 **joys**. For any word ending in *oy*, add an *s*.

3 **hedgerows, ditches**. *Hedgerow* has a regular plural: just add *s*. For *ditch*, add *es* because it ends in *ch*.

4 **deer, foxes, geese**. *Deer* and *geese* are irregular plurals. *Fox* ends in *x*, and so just add *es* to form the plural.

5 **leaves, woods**. *Leaf* has an irregular plural. *Woods* is a regular plural.

6 **teachers, coaches**. *Teacher* has a straightforward regular plural, and so just add *s*. *Coach* ends in *ch* and so needs *es* when you make it plural.

7 **tasks**. The plural of *task* is *tasks*.

8 **problems, lives, pets**. Regular plurals are fun: just add *s*. That rule works for *problems* and *pets* but *life* has an irregular plural.

9 **calculations, mice**. *Calculation* is regular but *mouse* is irregular.

10 **pets, boxes, treats**. *Pet* and *treat* are regular, and so you just need to add an *s*. Words ending in *x* (such as *box*) require *es* in the plural form.

11 **is, wriggles**. You need two singular forms here: *blue is* and *Nadine wriggles*.

12 **admits, suffers**. The verbs *admits* and *suffers* are singular, as they should be, because the subject-verb pairs are *who admits* and *he suffers,* and they both refer to the singular *John*.

13 **are**. The plural verb *are* matches the plural subject *we*.

14 **believe, give**. The pronoun *you* (whether singular or plural) goes with *believe* and *give*.

15 **Do, tells**. *Do* is plural, matching the plural subject *you,* and *tells* is singular to agree with *John*. In the first pair, the subject is tucked between the two parts of the verb (*do think*) because the sentence is a question.

16 **Has**. You need a singular form here to pair with the singular subject *his story*.

17 **knows, is**. Both answers are singular and match the singular subjects *no one* and *John*.

18 **has**. Because *he* is singular, the verb *has* must also be singular.

19 **does**. The pronoun *everyone* is singular, and so it matches the singular form *does*.

20 **has**. The singular verb *has* matches the singular subject *he*.

21 **were**. The subject is *six other people*. (*There* is never a subject.) *People* is plural and takes the plural verb *were*.

22 **are**. Match the plural subject, *individuals*, with a plural verb, *are*.

23 **is**. The subject is *he*, meaning that you need the singular verb *is*.

24 **were**. Add one movie director to one agent and what do you get? A plural subject that takes the plural verb *were*.

25 **include**. Ignore the interrupter (*in addition to a serious marriage proposal*) and just concentrate on the real subject (*offers*), which matches the plural verb *include*. Everything else is just there to distract you.

26 **has**. Pay no attention to *series,* which is a red herring. The real subject is *producer,* which needs the singular verb *has*.

27 **is**. Ignore the girlfriend – anyone or anything introduced with the words *as well as* is irrelevant. The subject is *John*, which needs the singular verb *is*.

28 **is**. The little word *nor* tells you to take the subjects one at a time, thus requiring the singular verb *is*.

29 **Is**. The subject is *hope*, which takes the singular verb *is*.

30 **live**. The word *and* gives you a clue that all the women count here. Three women = one plural verb, and *live* is the solution to this plural problem.

31 **are**. You can count *dancers*, and *dancers* is a plural noun, indicating that *are* is correct.

32 **has**. Without a partner, *either* is always singular and requires a singular verb, such as *has*.

33 **is**. The word *every* is singular because it treats each theatre seat individually. Therefore, it requires the singular verb *is*.

34 **does**. The subject is *no one,* which is singular, and so it must be paired with *does,* a singular verb.

35 **have**. The pronoun *most* can be singular only if it's used with a measurable quantity, but it can be singular or plural if it's used with a countable quantity. You can count *songs,* and *songs* is plural, and so the plural *have* is needed.

36 **has, is**. The pronouns ending in *-one* are always singular, even though they seem to convey a plural idea at times. Therefore, they need to be matched with singular verbs.

37 **are**. The closest subject is *members*, and so the plural verb wins the prize (the only prize likely to be associated with this very dull musical).

38 **have**. The pronoun *any* may be singular or plural, depending on the quantity to which it refers. *Reviews* may be counted (and you can be sure that the investors are going to count them extremely carefully), and *reviews* is a plural noun; therefore, *any* takes the plural verb *have* in this sentence.

39 **Has**. The sentence has two subjects, *director* and *musicians,* and the correct verb form can be decided on by distance. The verb has two parts, *has* and *agreed*. But *agreed* is the same for both singular and plural subjects. The subject *director* is closer to the part of the verb that changes (the *has* or the *have*), and so the singular *has* is correct.

40 **agrees**. The singular verb *agrees* matches the singular subject *everyone*.

41 **are**. The pronoun *most* can be singular or plural. In this sentence, *members* can be counted (and the counting isn't going to take long when the reviews are in). *Members* is also a plural noun, and so you require the plural verb *are*.

42 **has**. The pronoun neither *is* always singular and so needs to be paired with the singular verb *has*.

43 **is**. Did we catch you out here? The expression *20 tattoos* is plural, but the subject is actually *every one*, which is singular.

44 **are**. You can count tattoos, and *tattoos* is a plural noun, and so the pronoun *some* is plural here and needs to match the plural verb *are*.

45 **has**. The word *each* makes any subject singular; *has* is correct because it's a singular verb.

46 **is**. You can measure, but not count, *fame*, and so you need the singular verb *is* here with the singular pronoun *all*.

47 **believe**. Accountants are countable and plural, and so *all* is plural in this sentence and needs the plural verb *believe*.

48 **Has**. The pronoun *anyone*, like all the pronouns ending in *-one*, is singular, and so is the verb *has*.

49 **are, enters**. In an *either . . . or . . .* sentence, go with the closer subject, which in this case is *producers*. Because *producers* is plural, it's paired with *are*, a plural verb. The singular verb *enters* matches the singular pronoun *nobody*. All pronouns ending with *-body* are singular.

50 **is**. The word *every* makes the subject singular, which means that the correct matching singular verb is *is*.

51 **has**. The pronoun *neither* is singular, and so the singular verb *has* is needed here.

52 **has**. Pronouns ending in *-one* are always singular, and so you need to use a singular verb. Here the subject is *someone*, indicating that *has* wins.

53 **are**. The pronoun *both* is plural because it always means *two*, and so the verb must be *are*.

54 **Was**. Using *were* with *either* is a common mistake. However, *either* (without *or*) is always singular. You don't even need to bother thinking about what it's *either of* (here, *brothers*), you just need to know that you're after a singular verb and *was* fits the bill perfectly.

55 **is**. In this sentence, the *or* is what matters, not the *either*. When you realise that, all you have to do is match the verb to the closest subject. The singular *Lola* is closer to the verb than *brothers*, and so you need a singular verb.

56 **believe**. The pronoun *most* shifts from singular to plural and back, depending on the item attached to it. If *most* is associated with something that you can count (such as *us*), it's plural. Tacked onto something that you can measure but not count (*fame*, perhaps), *most* becomes singular. Here *most* is plural and requires the plural verb *believe*.

57 **sparkle**. *All* is a pronoun that can be singular or plural, like *most* in the preceding sentence. Here it's associated with *Oscars*, a countable, plural item. Therefore, you want the plural verb *sparkle*.

58 **is**. This sentence has another changeable pronoun; this time it's *none*. Similar to the previous two answers, *none* is one of those words that can only be singular if it's attached to something that you can measure but not count, such as *excitement*. Go for the singular verb *is* here.

59 **attend**. This situation is a straightforward 1 + 1 = 2 equation: his *wife and brother* gives you a plural subject requiring a plural verb, *attend*.

60 **is**. *Each* is always singular, no matter what. The logic is that *each* requires you to think of the subject as a series of singular units. Pair *each* with the singular verb *is*.

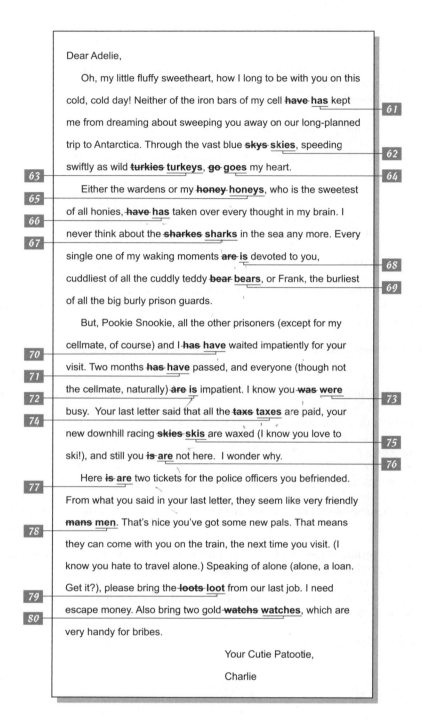

Dear Adelie,

Oh, my little fluffy sweetheart, how I long to be with you on this cold, cold day! Neither of the iron bars of my cell ~~have~~ has kept **[61]** me from dreaming about sweeping you away on our long-planned trip to Antarctica. Through the vast blue ~~skys~~ skies, speeding **[62]** swiftly as wild ~~turkies~~ turkeys, ~~go~~ goes my heart. **[63]** **[64]**

Either the wardens or my ~~honey~~ honeys, who is the sweetest **[65]** of all honies, ~~have~~ has taken over every thought in my brain. I **[66]** never think about the ~~sharkes~~ sharks in the sea any more. Every **[67]** single one of my waking moments ~~are~~ is devoted to you, **[68]** cuddliest of all the cuddly teddy ~~bear~~ bears, or Frank, the burliest **[69]** of all the big burly prison guards.

But, Pookie Snookie, all the other prisoners (except for my cellmate, of course) and I ~~has~~ have waited impatiently for your **[70]** visit. Two months ~~has~~ have passed, and everyone (though not **[71]** the cellmate, naturally) ~~are~~ is impatient. I know you ~~was~~ were **[72]** busy. Your last letter said that all the ~~taxs~~ taxes are paid, your **[73]** new downhill racing ~~skies~~ skis are waxed (I know you love to **[74]** ski!), and still you ~~is~~ are not here. I wonder why. **[75]** **[76]**

Here ~~is~~ are two tickets for the police officers you befriended. **[77]** From what you said in your last letter, they seem like very friendly ~~mans~~ men. That's nice you've got some new pals. That means **[78]** they can come with you on the train, the next time you visit. (I know you hate to travel alone.) Speaking of alone (alone, a loan. Get it?), please bring the ~~loots~~ loot from our last job. I need **[79]** escape money. Also bring two gold ~~watchs~~ watches, which are **[80]** very handy for bribes.

Your Cutie Patootie,

Charlie

[61] The subject of this sentence is *neither,* which when it appears alone is always singular; therefore, you require the singular verb *has.*

[62] To form the plural of a word ending in a consonant before *y,* change the *y* to *i* and add *es.*

[63] To form the plural of a word ending in a vowel before *y,* just add *s.*

[64] The singular subject of the verb *to go* is *heart,* which in this sentence is located after the verb, an unusual but possible spot. Singular subjects take singular verbs, and *goes* is singular.

65 *Honey* has a vowel before the *y*, and so just add *s* to form the plural.

66 The sentence has two subjects connected with *either/or*. The closer subject is *my honey*, which is singular and takes a singular verb. The interrupter *sweetest of all* has no bearing on the subject/verb match.

67 *Shark* has a regular plural - just add *s*, not *es*.

68 *Every* creates a singular subject, and so you need the singular verb *is*.

69 *Bear*, unlike *fish* and *deer*, forms a regular plural; just add *s*.

70 The *except for my cellmate* may distract you, but the true subject is *all the other prisoners and I*, a plural that pairs with *have*.

71 *Two months* is plural, and so use the plural verb *have*.

Time may sometimes be singular ('Five minutes is a long time') when you're referring to the total amount as one block of time. In question 71, however, Charlie is counting the months separately, and so the plural *have* is better.

72 *Everyone*, as well as all the pronouns with the word *one* tucked inside, is singular and takes the singular verb *is*.

73 The pronoun *you* can refer to one person or to a group, but it always takes a plural verb.

74 To form the plural of a noun ending in *x*, add *es*.

75 The noun *ski* is regular, and so to form the plural, just add *s*.

76 *You* always takes a plural verb, in this case it's *are*.

77 *Here* can't be a subject, and so look after the verb. Voila! *Tickets*, a plural, takes the plural verb *are*.

78 Many things separate men and women, but both form their plurals in the same way – by changing the *a* to *e*. Hence, *men*, not *mans*.

79 *Loot* is whatever you get from a crime (not counting a criminal record), whether it's one diamond or a thousand pounds. *Loots* doesn't exist.

80 To form the plural of a noun ending in *ch*, add *es*.

Chapter 3

Who Is She, and What Is It? The Lowdown on Pronouns

*P*ronouns aren't for amateurs in the world of formal grammar. These tricky little words (most are quite short) take the place of nouns and frequently come in handy. Who can make a sentence without using *I, me, ours, them, us, that* and similar words? Unfortunately, pronouns can trip you up in a hundred ways.

Never fear: in this chapter we show you how to distinguish singular from plural pronouns (and when to use each type) and how to use possessive pronouns (the kind that don't let you go out on a Saturday night). We also help you avoid vague pronouns and guide you through the maze of *its/it's, their/there/they're, whose/who's* and *your/you're*.

Separating Singular and Plural Pronouns

Pronouns bump nouns from your sentences and make the words flow more smoothly. When choosing pronouns, you must follow two basic rules:

✔ Replace a singular noun with a singular pronoun.

✔ Replace a plural noun with a plural pronoun.

Pronouns have another characteristic – gender. Fortunately, the rules governing pronoun gender are nowhere near as complicated as the ones about who pays for what on a first date. Masculine pronouns (*he, him, himself*) take the place of masculine nouns, and feminine pronouns (*she, her, herself*) fill in for feminine nouns. Some pronouns are noncombatants in the gender wars (*it, itself, who, which* and *that*, for example) and function in a neutral way.

Other rules also govern pronoun behaviour, but we leave those for another time and place – specifically Chapters 2, 10 and 11, and for those who want to perfect the most obsessive points of pronoun usage, Chapter 21.

Just for the record, here are the most common singular and plural pronouns:

✔ **Singular:** *I, me, you, he, she, it, my, your, his, her, its, myself, yourself, himself, herself, itself, either, neither, everyone, anyone, someone, no one, everything, anything, something, nothing, everybody, anybody, somebody, nobody, each* and *every*.

┃ ✔ **Plural:** *we, us, you, they, them, our, ours, your, yours, their, theirs, ourselves, yourselves, themselves, both* and *few*.

The *-self* pronouns – *myself, himself* and so on – have very limited usage. They can add emphasis (*I myself will blow up the mud balloon*) or circle back to the person doing the action in the sentence (*She will clean herself later*). If you're tempted to use a *-self* pronoun without the circling back action (*Rachel and myself hate mud balloons*, for example), resist the temptation because that usage is wrong.

Okay, are you ready to get to work? Without peeking at the answers (and we're watching), decide which pronoun needs to replace the underlined noun. Consider the singular/plural and gender issues. Write your choice in the blank provided.

Q. I hope that Charlie Burke and Dr Eileen Burke will attend tonight's symphony, even though Charlie is tone deaf and <u>Dr Eileen Burke</u> tends to sing along during the quieter moments. _____

A. **she.** Dr Eileen has been known to overdo the doughnuts now and again, but Eileen is still just one person. *She* is a singular, feminine pronoun.

1. Eileen wore a purple and red tartan hat last year, and <u>the hat</u> made quite an impression on the fashion press. _____

2. 'Who is your designer, Eileen?' <u>the photographers</u> screamed. _____

3. Charlie's hairpiece, on the other hand, attracted almost no attention. No one mentioned <u>Charlie's hairpiece</u>. _____

4. At the end of the evening Eileen muttered, 'Charlie, you should have ordered a taxi for <u>Charlie and Eileen</u>. _____

5. Unlike his mother, Charlie likes to travel in style; <u>Charlie's mum</u> usually takes public transport. _____

6. Charlie and Eileen told <u>Charlie and Eileen</u> that they would never set foot on a bus again after what happened to Eileen. _____

7. Charlie's mum says Charlie and Eileen are snobs. Charlie's mum says she likes buses. Charlie's mum says that if you're in trouble, you can always ask the bus driver and <u>the bus driver</u> will help. _____

8. Eileen says she once tried the bus but fainted when the driver said to her, 'Miss, <u>Eileen</u> will need a ticket.' _____

9. Until Eileen hit the floor, <u>the buses</u> had never before been touched by mink. _____

10. 'Give <u>Eileen</u> a ticket, please,' gasped Eileen when she came to. _____

11. After Eileen's bus experience, <u>Eileen</u> opted for taxis. _____

12. The last time Eileen hailed a taxi, the taxi driver, Henry Todd, was as gracious to his passenger as <u>Henry Todd</u> was to all passengers. _____

13. Because Eileen was a little slow, the driver of the taxi parked <u>the taxi</u> at the side of the road for five minutes. _____

14. As Eileen got into the taxi, Eileen said, 'Thank you, Driver, for waiting for <u>Eileen</u>.
_____

15. 'I am happy to wait for <u>Eileen</u>,' replied the driver. 'I have 12 more years until retirement.'
_____

Taking Possession of the Right Pronoun

You probably know that possession is nine-tenths of the law. But are you aware that possessive pronouns (*my, mine, your, his, her, hers, its, our, ours, their, theirs* and *whose*) are governed by the law, too? Here are a few easy rules for possessives:

- ✔ Use a possessive pronoun to show ownership.

- ✔ Match singular pronouns with singular owners.

- ✔ Match plural pronouns with plural owners.

- ✔ Take note of masculine (for males), feminine (for female) and neutral pronouns.

- ✔ Never insert an apostrophe into a possessive pronoun. (If a pronoun has an apostrophe, it's a contraction (like that one!). See the next section 'Discovering that it's All in the Details: Possessives versus Contractions' for more information.)

Okay, here's a mini-test. Choose the correct possessive pronoun from the options in brackets and plop it into the blank.

Q. The little boy grabbed a grubby handkerchief and wiped _____ nose. (*his/her/its/he's*)

A. **his**. Because you're talking about a little boy, you need a masculine pronoun. Did we catch you with the last option? *He's = he is.*

16. Jessica spent the morning polishing _____ new motorbike, which she bought for a rock-bottom price. (*her/hers/she's/her's*)

17. She found two scratches, and so she took the bike back to the shop to get _____ mudguard repaired. (*it/its/her*)

18. When the sales assistants didn't satisfy her demand for a new mudguard, Jessica threatened to scratch something of _____. (*their/theirs/their's*)

19. Jessica talks a lot, but she's never taken revenge by damaging a single possession of _____. (*my/mine/mines/mine's*)

20. However, Neil and Rachel claim that Jessica once threw paint on something of _____. (*his/hers/her's/their/their's/theirs*)

21. Also, I heard a rumour that Neil had to bury _____ favourite wig, the one he styled himself, after Jessica got hold of it. (*his/her/he's*)

22. When Rachel's dog dug up the wig, Rachel had to use paint remover to clean _____ paw. (*it/its/their*)

23. Just to be safe, Neil will never let Jessica borrow another wig of _____ unless she takes out an insurance policy. (*his/his'/he's*)

24. Tomorrow, Neil is going to Matthews Hair Emporium to buy a spare wig. The shop is having a half-price sale, and _____ wigs are Neil's favourites. (*its/their*)

25. Whenever Neil yells at Jessica, she screams, 'Don't criticise _____ actions!' (*my/mine*)

26. Neil usually replies, in a voice that is just as loud, 'I wouldn't dream of criticising any action of _____.' (*your/your's/yours/yours'*)

27. When Neil speaks to _____ hairdresser, he will ask her what she thinks of the wigs in Matthews Hair Emporium. (*his/his'/he's*)

28. 'Neil will never get his hands on any hairpiece of _____,' declared Rachel and Jessica. (*our/ours/our'/ours'/our's*)

29. I think that Rachel took _____ hairpiece, and I told Neil so. (*his/his'/he's*)

30. Neil explained that he's itching to get his hands on a wig of _____ someday. (*my/mine*)

31. 'Over _____ dead body,' I replied. (*my/mine*)

32. 'I can't work on _____ dead body,' answered Neil in a puzzled voice. (*your/yours/you're*)

33. As she dipped _____ fingers in paint remover, Jessica added, 'You can't work on a live one either.' (*her/hers/her's*)

34. Jessica and Neil seriously need to work on _____ people skills. (*his/her/their*)

35. I'll buy Jessica, Neil and myself a wig and then style _____ new hairpieces. (*our/ours/our's*)

Discovering that it's All in the Details: Possessives versus Contractions

Think of this section as a map of a desert island with 'scary monster's favourite cave', 'poisoned water source' and 'cannibal headquarters' clearly labelled. In other words, this section points out some dangers in the pronoun world and shows you how to steer clear of them. Specifically, we look at the wonderful world of *its/it's*, *their/there/they're* and *whose/who's*. Briefly, here's how to tell them apart:

- ✔ **Its/it's:** The first word shows possession (the bird grasped a seed in *its* beak) and the second is a contraction meaning *it is* (*it's* a lovely day today).

- ✔ **Their/there/they're:** The first word shows possession (the birds grasped seeds in *their* beaks). The second is a location (don't go *there*) and the third is a contraction meaning *they are* (*they're* hungry birds).

- ✔ **Whose/who's:** The first word shows possession (the bird *whose* beak is longest) and the second is a contraction meaning *who is* (*Who's* cleaning out the birdcage?).

Take a look at the following questions. Choose the correct word from the options in brackets by underlining your selection.

Q. Miss Mitchell told the children to button (*their/there/they're*) lips and be as quiet as mice.

A. **their**. The sentence expresses possession, and so you need to use the first option. The second *there* refers to location, and the third means *they are*. If you put *they are* into the sentence, you're not making any sense.

36. George and Josh need watches because (*their/there/they're*) always late.

37. George found a watch that keeps atomic time, but (*its/it's*) too expensive.

38. Josh, playing with the atomic watch, broke (*its/it's*) strap.

39. I notice that (*your/you're*) strap is broken too.

40. '(*Whose/Who's*) watch is this?' Josh asked innocently.

41. '(*Your/You're*) sure that (*its/it's*) not Jessica's?' asked George.

42. 'Put it over (*their/there/they're*) and pretend you never touched it,' said George.

43. 'I can't lie,' whispered Josh. '(*Their/There/They're*) security cameras caught me.'

44. (*Its/It's*) impossible for Josh to lie anyway because he's so honest.

45. '(*Your/You're*) honour demands only the truth,' sighed George.

46. (*Whose/Who's*) going to pay for the watch, you may wonder. Do you think Josh will?

47. (*Your/You're*) wrong; Josh isn't willing to pay the full cost.

48. (*Their/There/They're*) funds are limited, and so each will probably pay half the cost of a new watch strap.

49. George, (*whose/who's*) ideas of right and wrong are somewhat fuzzy, asked Rachel whether she would contribute to (*their/there/they're*) 'charity campaign for underprivileged watches'.

50. Rachel replied, '(*Your/You're*) joking!'

51. '(*Whose/Who's*) going to help my watch?' she asked.

52. 'I don't think (*its/it's*) battery has ever been changed,' continued Rachel.

53. (*Its/It's*) slowing down, according to Rachel, because the battery is beginning to die.

54. George told Rachel, '(*Your/You're*) battery is crucial and should be changed or recharged regularly.'

55. 'Who thinks about batteries?' commented Jessica. '(*Their/There/They're*) easy to overlook.'

Avoiding Double Meanings

Unless you're a politician trying to hide the fact that you've just increased taxes on everything but bubble gum, you're probably interested in communicating clearly. Double meanings, the darling of all sorts of elected officials, have no place in your speaking and writing, right? If you want your audience to interpret your meaning correctly, you need to use pronouns that are accurate and specific. One basic rule says it all:

> If any confusion arises about the meaning of a pronoun, get rid of it and use a noun instead.

In practice, this rule means that you shouldn't say things like 'My aunt and her mother-in-law were happy about her success in the Scrabble tournament', because you aren't making clear who had success: the aunt, the mother-in-law or some other woman.

Try the following exercises on pronoun use, rewriting if a pronoun can have more than one meaning. (When you rewrite, choose one of the possibilities or, if you love to work, provide two new unmistakably clear sentences.) If everything is hunky-dory, write 'correct' in the blank.

Q. Stacy and Alice photographed her tattoos.

A. **Stacy and Alice photographed Alice's tattoos.** Or, **Stacy and Alice photographed Stacy's tattoos.** The problem with the original is the *her*. Does *her* mean Stacy's or Alice's? In the original sentence it could be either possibility. To make the meaning clear, rewrite the sentence without the pronoun.

56. Matt and his sister are campaigning for an Oscar nomination, but only she is expected to get one.

_____

_____

57. Matt sent a donation to Mr Hobson in hope of furthering his cause.

_____

_____

58. If Matt wins an Oscar, he will place the statue on his desk, next to his Emmy, Tony, Obie and Best-of-the-Bunch awards. It's his favourite honour.

_____

_____

59. Matt's sister has already won one Oscar for her portrayal of a kind but slightly cracked artist who can't seem to stay in one place without extensive support.

_____

_____

60. Rachel, who served as a model for Matt's sister, thought her interpretation of the role was the best.

_____

_____

61. In the film, the artist creates giant sculptures out of discarded hubcaps, although these are seldom appreciated by museum curators.

_____

_____

62. When filming was finished, Rachel was allowed to keep the leftover chair cushions and hubcaps, which she liked.

_____

_____

63. Rachel loves what she calls 'found art objects', which she places around her flat.

_____

_____

64. Matt's sister kept one for a souvenir.

_____

_____

65. Rachel, Matt, and Matt's sister went out for a cup of coffee, but he refused to drink his because the cafe didn't have any fresh cream.

_____

_____

66. Rachel said to Matt's sister that Matt could drink her iced tea if he was thirsty.

_____

_____

67. Matt called his brother and asked him to bring the cream from his fridge.

_____

_____

68. 'Are you crazy?' asked Rachel as she gave Matt's sister her straw.

_____

_____

69. Matt's sister took a straw and a packet of sugar, stirred her coffee and then placed it on the table.

_____

_____

Brain Strain: Extra Practice with Basic Pronouns

Time to sharpen up your (that's *your*, not *you're*) editing skills. Look for ten mistakes involving pronouns in the letter in Figure 3-1, written by a disgruntled merchant. After you find an error, correct it. Take note of singular/plural, gender, clarity and confusion.

---

31 May 2010

Dear Mr Baker,

Its come to my attention that the watch you looked at yesterday in our Princess Street branch is broken. The strap is disconnected from the watch, which is quite valuable. Their is no record of payment beyond a very small amount. The sales assistant, Mr Sievers, told me that you paid her exactly 1% of the watch's price. When you and you're brother left the store, Mr Sievers was still asking for additional funds. He's blood pressure still has not returned to normal levels.

Frankly I do not care whose to blame for the broken watchstrap or Mr Sievers's medical problem. I simply want it fixed. The watch and it's strap are not your property. The store needs their merchandise in good condition.

Yours sincerely,

E. Neil Johnson

Sales Supervisor

Figure 3-1:
Error-filled sample letter.

Answers to Pronoun Problems

1 **it**. The hat is singular, and so is *it*.

2 **they**. More than one photographer means that you need the plural pronoun *they*.

3 **it**. The hairpiece is singular and has no gender, making *it* the best choice.

4 **us**. Two nouns are underlined, and so you're in plural territory. Because Eileen is talking about herself and Charlie, *us* fits here.

5 **she**. Charlie's mum is singular and feminine, and so *she* is your best bet.

6 **themselves**. Two people make a plural, and so *themselves*, a plural pronoun, is right.

7 **he or she**. You don't know whether the bus driver is male or female, though you do know that you're talking about one and only one person. The best answer is *he or she*, covering all the bases.

8 **you**. Because the bus driver is talking to Eileen, *you* is the best choice. *You*, by the way, functions as both a singular and a plural.

9 **they**. Buses is a plural noun, and so *they* works best.

10 **me**. Because Eileen is talking about herself, *me* is your answer.

11 **she**. The singular, feminine Eileen calls for a singular, feminine pronoun, in this case, *she*.

12 **he**. The singular, masculine Henry Todd calls for a singular, masculine pronoun, *he*.

13 **it**. The singular taxi isn't masculine or feminine, and so *it* fills the bill.

14 **me**. Eileen is talking about herself (not a surprise, because she never talks about anyone else!), and so *me* is appropriate.

15 **you**. The driver is talking to Eileen, using the pronoun *you*.

16 **her**. You need a feminine singular pronoun (no apostrophe); therefore, the answer is *her*.

17 **its**. Did you fall for *her*? The sentence does refer to a female, but the female doesn't have a mudguard; the bike does, and so you need the possessive pronoun *its*.

18 **theirs**. One of the options – *their's* – doesn't exist in standard English. The first possibility, *their*, should come before the thing that's possessed (*their books*, for example). The middle option – *theirs* – is just right.

19 **mine**. The last two options – *mines* and *mine's* – don't exist in standard English. *My* needs a possession (for example, *my blanket*), whereas the second option, *mine*, can stand alone.

20 **theirs**. You need a word to express plural possession, because you're talking about Neil and Rachel. Of the three plural possibilities (the last three options), the first should go before the possession (*their* motorcycle, for example) and the second has an apostrophe, a giant no-no in possessive-pronoun world. Only the last option works.

21 *his*. The hairpiece belongs to Neil, and so *her*, a feminine pronoun, is out. The last option is a contraction of *he is*.

22 *its*. The first option isn't possessive, and so you can rule it out easily. The third possibility is plural, but the pronoun refers to a dog, a singular noun. Therefore, the second option, a singular possessive, is correct.

23 **his**. No possessive pronoun ever contains an apostrophe, and so the first option is the only correct possibility. *He's*, by the way, means *he is*.

24 **its**. In everyday speech, people often refer to shops and businesses as 'they', with the possessive form 'their'. However, a shop or a business is properly referred to with a singular pronoun. The logic is easy to figure out: one shop = singular. Therefore, Matthews Hair Emporium is singular, and the possessive pronoun that refers to it is *its*.

25 **my**. The pronoun *mine* stands alone and doesn't precede what is owned. *My*, on the other hand, is a pronoun that can't stand being alone. A true party animal, it must go before what is being owned (in this sentence, *actions*).

26 **yours**. In contrast to question 25, this sentence needs a pronoun that stands alone. *Your* must be placed in front of whatever is being possessed – not a possibility in this sentence. All the options with apostrophes are out because possessive pronouns don't have apostrophes. The only thing left is *yours*, which is correct.

27 **his**. The contraction *he's* means *he is*, which doesn't make sense here. The second option is wrong because possessive pronouns don't have apostrophes.

28 **ours**. Okay, first get rid of all the apostrophe options, because apostrophes and possessive pronouns don't mix. You're left with two possibilities – *our* and *ours*. The second is correct because *our* needs to go before the thing that's possessed, and *ours* can stand alone.

29 **his**. The possessive pronoun *his*, like all possessive pronouns, has no apostrophe. The last choice, *he's*, is short for *he is* and isn't possessive at all.

30 **mine**. The pronoun *mine* works alone (it secretly wants to be a private detective, operating solo). In this sentence *mine* has a slot for itself after the preposition *of*. Perfect!

31 **my**. The form that attaches to the front of a noun is *my*. In this sentence, *my* precedes and is linked to *dead body*.

32 **your**. The second option isn't right because *yours* stands alone, but in this sentence a *dead body* is attached to the *yours*. The last option, *you're*, is short for *you are*. Therefore, by a process of elimination, the right answer must be *your*.

33 **her**. Right away you can get rid of the last possibility, *her's*, because possessive pronouns are allergic to apostrophes. The pronoun *hers* works alone, but here the blank precedes the item possessed, *fingers*. *Her* is the possessive you want.

34 **their**. Because you're talking about both Jessica and Neil, go for *their*, the plural.

35 **our**. In this sentence the possessive pronoun has to include *me*, and so *our* is the winner. *Ours* isn't appropriate because you need a pronoun to precede what's being possessed (*hairpieces*). As always, apostrophes and possessive pronouns don't mix.

36 **they're**. The sentence tells you that *they are* always late, and the short form of *they are* is *they're*.

37 **it's**. The meaning needed here is *it is* too expensive. No possessive is required.

38 **its**. The strap belongs to the watch, and so possession is indicated. The possessive pronoun *its* does the job.

39 **your**. The contraction *you're* is short for *you are*, clearly not correct in this context.

40 **Whose**. The sentence doesn't say, '*Who is* watch is this?', and so go for the possessive *whose*.

41 **You're, it's**. Here you have two pronouns, neither possessive. The sentence really means '*You are* sure that *it is* not Jessica's?'

42 **there**. The meaning of the sentence calls for a location, and so *there* is the word you want.

43 **Their**. The security cameras belong to them, and so *their* is needed to show possession.

44 **It's**. The sentence, in its full form, would begin with '*It is* impossible' and *it's* = *it is*.

45 **Your**. A possessive is called for here, not a contraction (*You're* = *You are*).

46 **Who's**. In its full form, the sentence would begin with *Who is*, and *who's* = *who is*.

47 **You're**. Here you require the contraction *you're* = *you are*.

48 **Their**. The funds belong to them, and so *their* is needed to show possession.

49 **whose, their**. Both answers require a possessive, showing that the *fuzzy ideas* belong to George and that the *campaign* belongs to both George and his more honest brother Josh.

50 **You're**. The *joking* isn't a possession. The sentence calls for the contraction of *you are* = *you're*.

51 **Who's**. You need the shortened version of *Who is* in this sentence, and so go for the contraction *who's*.

52 **its**. The battery belongs to the watch, meaning that the possessive pronoun *its* is correct. The contraction *it's* (for *it is*) doesn't belong here at all.

53 **It's**. In this sentence you need the contraction of *it is*.

54 **Your**. Here the possessive pronoun is required, to show that the battery belongs to *you*.

55 **They're**. The contraction *They are* makes sense in this sentence, not the possessive *their* or the location word *there*.

56 **correct**. Matt is male and his sister is female, and so *she* can refer only to one person, Matt's sister. No double meanings are involved and so no corrections need to be made.

57 **Matt sent a donation to Mr Hobson in hope of furthering Matt's cause. Or, Matt sent a donation to Mr Hobson in hope of furthering Mr Hobson's cause.** The problem with the original is the confusion that *his* causes. Does *his* mean *Matt's* or *Mr Hobson's*? The way the original reads means that either answer is possible.

58 **If Matt wins an Oscar, he will place the statue on his desk, next to his Emmy, Tony, Obie and Best-of-the-Bunch awards. The Oscar is his favourite honour.** Okay, maybe the Tony is his favourite honour, or maybe the Obie. The original sentence is unclear because *it* could refer to any one of the awards.

59 **correct**. The two pronouns in this sentence, *her* and *who*, can refer only to Matt's sister. Everything is clear, and no changes are necessary.

60 **Rachel, who served as a model for Matt's sister, thought her own interpretation was the best.** Or, **Rachel, who served as a model for Matt's sister, thought the sister's interpretation was the best.** Either answer is okay, illustrating the problem with the original. You can't tell what *her* means – *Rachel's* or *Matt's sister's*.

61 **In the film, the artist creates giant sculptures out of discarded hubcaps, although the hubcaps are seldom appreciated by museum curators.** Or, **In the film the artist creates giant sculptures out of discarded hubcaps, although these sculptures are seldom appreciated by museum curators.** The problem with the original sentence is the pronoun *these*. (Did you know that *that*, *this, these,* and *those* can function as pronouns?) You have two groups of objects in the sentence: *the sculptures* and *the hubcaps*. Therefore, *these* could refer to either group. To eliminate the uncertainty, replace *these* with a more specific statement.

62 **Rachel was pleased to be allowed to keep the leftover chair cushions and hubcaps.** Or, **Rachel liked the leftover chair cushions, which she was allowed to keep. She also held onto the hubcaps.** Or, **Rachel liked the leftover hubcaps, which she was allowed to keep. She also kept the chair cushions.** If you've read all three suggested answers (and more variations are possible), you understand the problem with the original sentence. What does *which* mean? *Cushions? Hubcaps? Keeping leftovers?* That last possibility, by the way, can't be expressed by a pronoun, at least not according to the strict grammar police. Reword your sentence so that your reader knows what *which* means.

63 **correct**. Surprised? All the pronouns are clear, in the context of this story about Rachel. The *she* refers to *Rachel* and the *which* refers to *objects*.

64 **Matt's sister kept one hubcap for a souvenir.** Or, **Matt's sister kept one sculpture for a souvenir.** Or, **Matt's sister kept one Rachel for a souvenir.** (Just kidding with that last one; only one Rachel exists!) In the original sentence, *one* is too vague, and so you need to add a specific souvenir to clarify.

65 **correct**. The sentence refers to two females (Rachel and Matt's sister) and one male. Because only one male is in the sentence, the masculine pronouns *he* and *his* are clear.

66 **Rachel said to Matt's sister, 'Matt can drink my iced tea if he is thirsty.'** Or, **Rachel said to Matt's sister, 'Matt can drink your iced tea if he is thirsty.'** In the original sentence, you can't tell whether *her* refers to *Rachel* or to *Matt's sister*.

67 **Matt called his brother and asked him to bring the cream from Matt's fridge.** If you want to make Matt a cheapskate, reword the sentence so that Matt is asking for his brother's cream, perhaps using a direct quotation, such as: ***Matt called his brother and asked, 'Bring me some cream from your fridge.'***

68 **'Are you crazy?' asked Rachel, giving her own straw to Matt's sister.** Or, **'Are you crazy?' asked Rachel as she picked up Matt's sister's straw and gave it to her.** The original sentence doesn't make clear who owns the straw.

69 **Matt's sister took a straw and a packet of sugar, stirred her coffee and then placed the coffee on the table.** The original sentence contains a pronoun (*it*) with several possible meanings (*the straw*, *the sugar packet* or *the coffee*).

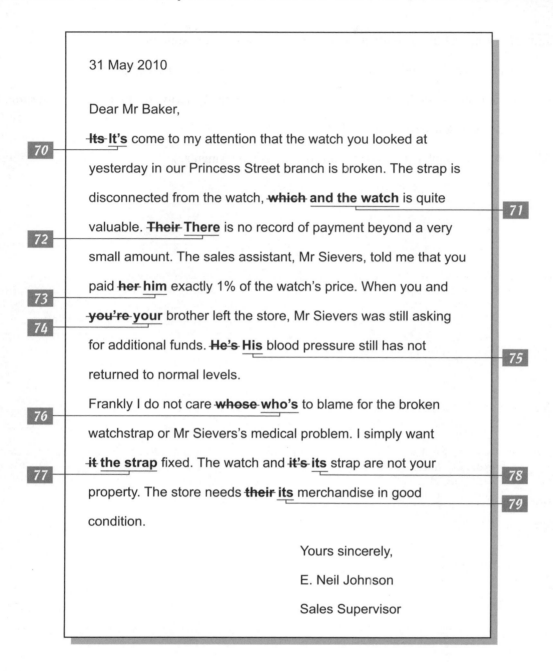

31 May 2010

Dear Mr Baker,

70 ~~Its~~ **It's** come to my attention that the watch you looked at yesterday in our Princess Street branch is broken. The strap is disconnected from the watch, ~~which~~ **and the watch** is quite **71** valuable. ~~Their~~ **There** is no record of payment beyond a very **72** small amount. The sales assistant, Mr Sievers, told me that you paid ~~her~~ **him** exactly 1% of the watch's price. When you and **73** ~~you're~~ **your** brother left the store, Mr Sievers was still asking **74** for additional funds. ~~He's~~ **His** blood pressure still has not **75** returned to normal levels.

Frankly I do not care ~~whose~~ **who's** to blame for the broken **76** watchstrap or Mr Sievers's medical problem. I simply want ~~it~~ **the strap** fixed. The watch and ~~it's~~ **its** strap are not your **77** **78** property. The store needs ~~their~~ **its** merchandise in good **79** condition.

Yours sincerely,

E. Neil Johnson

Sales Supervisor

70 In this sentence, *it's* is short for *it has*.

71 What's valuable – *the watch* or *the strap*? Best to clarify by inserting the specific information.

72 *Their* is possessive which is not needed here. Go for *There is* instead.

73 Mr Sievers is male and needs a masculine pronoun (*him*).

74 *You're* = *you are*, but the sentence needs the possessive pronoun *your*.

75   *He's* = *he is*, but the sentence calls for the possessive pronoun *his*.

76   *Who's* = *who is*. The sentence needs to read 'I do not care *who is* to blame. . .'.

77   What needs to be fixed, *the band* or *the blood pressure*? Clarify by changing *it* to *the strap*.

78   Here the possessive *its* is needed.

79   A *store* is singular (*one store*), and so you need *its* (singular).

Chapter 4

Finishing What You Start: Writing Complete Sentences

In This Chapter

▶ Recognising what makes a sentence complete

▶ Avoiding fragments and run-ons

▶ Combining sentences correctly

▶ Placing endmarks properly

*H*ave you heard the urban legend about the child who said nothing for the first five years of her life and then suddenly began to speak in perfect, complete sentences? Apparently she grew up to be something important, such as a judge, chief executive of a multinational company or something like that. Who knows whether the story is true, but what isn't in doubt is that most judges, CEOs and most people with good jobs know how to write in complete sentences.

You need to know how to do this too, and in this chapter we give you a complete guide to complete sentences, including how to punctuate and how to combine thoughts using the right grammar.

To write a proper, complete sentence, follow these rules:

✔ **Every sentence needs a subject/verb pair.** More than one pair is okay, but one at least is essential. Just to be clear about the grammatical terms: a verb expresses *an action* or *a state of being;* a subject tells you *who* or *what* is acting or being.

✔ **A complete sentence contains a complete thought.** Don't leave the reader hanging with only half an idea. ('If it rains' = an incomplete thought, but 'If it rains, my paper dress will dissolve' = a complete if slightly weird thought.)

✔ **Two or more ideas in a sentence must be joined correctly.** You can't just bung your ideas together. If you do, you end up with a run-on or 'fused' sentence, which is a grammatical crime. Punctuation marks and what grammar experts call *conjunctions* – joining words – glue ideas together legally.

✔ **Every sentence finishes with an endmark.** Endmarks include full stops, question marks and exclamation marks.

That seems easy enough, right? But sometimes applying the rules gets a little complicated. In the following sections we go through each rule, one at a time, so that you can practise them all.

Seeking Out the Subject/Verb Pair

The subject/verb pair is the heart of the sentence. To check it is complete, first be sure that your sentence contains a verb. At least one word must express action or a state of being. Next, look for a word that expresses who or what is doing that action or is in that state of being; that's the subject. Now for one more, essential step: check to see that the subject and verb match. They must go together and make sense ('Mike has been singing', 'Lindsay suffered' and so on). For practice on properly matching subjects and verbs, flip to Chapter 2.

Some words that look like verbs don't function as verbs, and so you can wrongly identify a verb. Checking for a match between a subject and a verb eliminates these false verbs from consideration, because the pairs sound incomplete with false verbs. A couple of mismatches illustrate this point: 'Lindsay watching' and 'Mike's message having been scrambled'.

Now you try some. In the blank, write the subject (S)/verb (V) pair. If you find no true pair, write 'incomplete'.

Q. Charlie, with a cholesterol count climbing higher and higher, gave in and fried some sausages for Nipper.

_____

A. **Charlie (S)/gave (V), fried (V)**. Did we catch you out with *climbing*? In the preceding sentence, *climbing* isn't a verb. One clue: *cholesterol count climbing* sounds incomplete. Just for comparison, *cholesterol count is climbing* makes a match. See the difference?

1. Rascal, woofing repeatedly and frustrated by her inability to score more than ten points at the dog show. _____

2. Charlie fed a chopped steak to Nipper, his entry in the Dog of the Century contest. _____

3. Rascal, my entry, wolfed down a bowl of liver treats and snoozed for about an hour afterwards. _____

4. Entered in the Toy breed category, Rascal is sure to win the Most Likely to Fall Asleep Standing Up contest. _____

5. Having been tired out by a heavy timetable of eating, chewing and licking my hand. _____

6. Rascal sleeps profoundly. _____

7. Once, having eaten through an entire bag of doggie biscuits and increased the size of her stomach by at least 50 per cent. _____

8. Rascal, biting the vet gently just to make a point about needles and her preference not to have them. _____

9. The vet is not upset by Rascal's reaction. _____

10. Who would be surprised by a runoff between Nipper and Rascal? _____

11. Not surprised by anything, especially with liver treats. _____

12. Nipper, sniffing the new dog toy on the couch. _____

13. Toto, the winner of last century's contest in running, jumping and sleeping.
_____

14. Rascal is guided by a strong handler around the judges' platform and TV booth.
_____

15. Rascal loves her time in the spotlight and all the media attention.
_____

16. Charlie, covered in suntan lotion and catching a few rays at the side of the arena.
_____

17. Nipper and Rascal sniffed the suntan lotion while running around the arena.
_____

18. Swiftly across the arena sped the two dogs. _____

19. Stopping next to Charlie at the arena wall, Nipper and Rascal.
_____

20. They lapped a few gallons of suntan lotion from his skin.
_____

Checking for Complete Thoughts

Some subject/verb pairs form a closed circle: the thought they express is complete. That's the quality you want, because otherwise your reader echoes the outlaw who, with his head in the noose, said 'Don't leave me hanging!'

Some expressions are incomplete when they're statements but complete when they're questions. For example, 'Who won?' makes sense but 'Who won' doesn't.

Try these questions on for size. If you find a complete thought, write 'complete'. If you're left in suspense, write 'incomplete'. Remember, the number of words doesn't indicate completeness, but the thought does.

Q. Whenever the cow jumps over the moon.
_____

A. **incomplete**. Aren't you wondering, 'What happens *whenever the cow jumps over the moon?*' The thought is not complete.

21. The cow, who used to work for NASA until she got fed up with the bureaucracy.
_____

22. On long-term training flights, the milking machine malfunctioned. _____

23. Why didn't the astronauts assume responsibility for milking procedures?
_____

24. For one thing, milking, which wasn't in the manual but should have been, thus avoiding the problem and increasing the comfort level of the cow assigned to the jump. _____

25. The cow protested. _____

26. Because she couldn't change NASA's manual. _____

27. Applying to NASA, her mother, when she was only a calf. _____

28. Not a bad decision, however. _____

29. Still, 20 years of moon-jumping is enough for any cow. _____

30. Unless they come up with a way to combine moon-jumping and milk-producing, the NASA administrators will have to recruit other species. _____

31. Sheep, which were once rejected from moon duty. _____

32. Will NASA send a flock of sheep to the moon someday? _____

33. Not needing milking on a regular basis, though female sheep produce milk. _____

34. This species may be a better fit for life in a spacecraft. _____

35. However much the sheep practise, the training doesn't come as easy to them as it does to cows. _____

Going for Flow: Joining Sentences Correctly

Some sentences are short. Some are long. Joining them is good. Combined sentences make a narrative more interesting. Have we convinced you yet? The choppiness of the preceding sentences makes a good case for gluing sentences together. Just be sure to do so legally, or else you end up with a run-on sentence.

To join sentences correctly, you need one of the following items:

✔ **A conjunction:** Don't worry about the grammatical terminology. But if you must know, a conjunction is a word that lets you bring two sentences together into one while making clear how the two ideas are related. The relationship can be, for example, reason ('They made mud pies at Glastonbury *because* it was raining'), contrast ('Eleanor loves live music *but* can't stand camping') or *addition* ('Rebecca loves live music *and* sleeping in the great outdoors').

Other popular conjunctions include: *or, nor, for, since, when, where, if, although, who, which* and *that* – among others. Conjunctions are sometimes preceded by commas and sometimes not. For more information on comma use, check out Chapter 5.

✔ **A semicolon:** A semicolon (a little dot over a comma) pops up between two complete sentences and glues them together nicely. The two complete thoughts need to be related in some way.

Some words look like conjunctions, but aren't. Don't use *nevertheless, consequently, therefore, however* or *then* to join complete thoughts. If you want to place one of these 'false conjunctions' between two complete thoughts, add a semicolon and place a comma after the 'false conjunction.' We go into more detail about commas in Chapter 5.

Okay, put on your thinking cap and decide whether you have a legally combined, correct sentence or (gasp) an illegal, cobbled-together mess. In the blank after the sentence, write 'correct' or 'incorrect'. If you think the sentence is incorrect, change the mess to a legal, complete one. Notice the teacher trick with the lines? We leave enough space to revise every sentence, including the correct ones, so that you can't judge the legal sentences by the blanks, or the lack of them.

Q. Kathy escaped from jail, five years for illegal sentence-joining was just too much for her.

A. **incorrect. Kathy escaped from jail; five years for illegal sentence-joining was just too much for her.** The comma can't unite two complete thoughts. Change it to a semicolon and you're in business. An alternative correction is **Kathy escaped from jail because five years for illegal sentence-joining was just too much for her.** The *because* connects the two ideas correctly.

36. The Minister for Grammar used to work for the High Court, therefore his word was law.

_____

_____

37. His nickname, 'Grammar Gaffer', which had been given to him by the clerks of the court, was not a source of pride for him.

_____

_____

38. Nevertheless, he didn't criticise those who used the term, as long as they did so politely.

_____

_____

39. He often wore a cloak embroidered with parts of speech, for he was truly devoted to the field of grammar.

_____

_____

40. Kathy's escape wounded him deeply; he ordered the grammar police to arrest her as soon as possible.

_____

_____

41. Kathy hid in a basket of dirty laundry, then she held her breath as the prison linen lorry passed through the gates and headed to the city.

_____

_____

42. Kathy dreams in single words in black and white, although she is able to speak in complete and colourful sentences if she really tries.

_____

_____

43. She's attracted to sentence fragments, which appeal to something in her character.

_____

_____

44. 'Finish what you start,' her mother often exclaimed, 'You don't know when you're going to bump into a grammar minister.'

_____

_____

45. While she is free, Kathy intends to burn grammar textbooks for fuel.

_____

_____

46. Grammar books burn exceptionally well, nevertheless, some people prefer history texts for fuel.

_____

_____

47. History books create a satisfactory snap and crackle while they're burning, the flames are also a nice shade of orange.

_____

_____

48. Because she loves history, Kathy rejected *The Complete History of the Grammatical World,* she burned *Participles and You* instead.

_____

_____

49. *Participles and You,* a bestseller for more than two years, sizzled, therefore it gave off a lot of heat.

_____

_____

50. Kathy found a few sentence fragments in the ash pile, but she disposed of them quickly.

_____

_____

Finishing with Flair: Choosing Endmarks

When you're speaking, the listener knows that you've completed a sentence because the thought is complete and your tone says that the end has arrived. In writing, the tone part is taken care of by a full stop, question mark or exclamation mark. You must have one, and only one, of these marks at the end of a sentence, unless you're writing a comic book, in which characters are allowed to say things such as 'You want my what??!!?' Full stops are for statements, question marks are for (surprise, surprise) questions and exclamation marks scream at the reader. Endmarks become complicated when they tangle with quotation marks. For tips on how endmarks interact with quotation marks, turn to Chapter 8.

So roll up your sleeves now and get to work on this section, which is filled with sentences desperately in need of an endmark. Write the appropriate endmark in the blank provided.

0. Did Lottie really ride to the anti-noise protest on her motorbike _____

A. ? (question mark). You're clearly asking a question, and so the question mark fits here.

51. No, she rode her skateboard to the mathematicians' convention _____

52. You're having a laugh _____

53. No, honestly Lottie is a real fan of triangles _____

54. Does she bring her own triangles or expect to find what she needs at the convention _____

55. I'm not sure, but I think I heard her say that her Maths-club friends always bring triangles that are extraordinary _____

56. Do you think that she really means just plain, old ordinary triangles _____

57. No, I heard her scream that everyone loves triangles because they're the best shape in the world _____

58. Are you going too _____

59. I'd rather pull out my own wisdom teeth without anaesthesia than attend a maths convention _____

60. I heard Lottie squeal that she's really into equilaterals _____

61. Are you sure that Lottie loves equilaterals _____

62. I always thought that she was fond of triangles _____

63. Who in the world wants an 'I love maths' T-shirt _____

64. I can't believe that Lottie actually bought one _____

65. Do you think she'll give me her old 'I love grammar' hat now _____

Complete or Incomplete? That Is the Question

In this section, we bring everything together. If you've worked your way through this entire chapter (and if you have, our compliments), you've practised each sentence skill separately. But to write well, you have to do everything at the same time – create subject/verb pairs, finish a thought, combine thoughts properly and place the appropriate endmark.

Length and completeness aren't related. A very long sentence may be incomplete. Similarly, a very short sentence ('Grammar excites me', for example) may be complete. Don't worry about the length of your sentences. Just make sure that they follow the rules outlined in this chapter so that they're complete.

Take a test drive with the questions in this section. Decide whether the sentence is complete or incomplete and plop a label in the blank. If the sentence is incomplete, repair the damage. We have left plenty of space for your work, whether the sentence is right or wrong. No need for us to give the game away!

Q. Though the spaghetti sticks to the ceiling above the pan on rainy days when just one more problem will send me over the edge.

A. **incomplete**. The statement has no complete thought. Possible correction: take out 'Though' and begin the sentence with 'The.'

66. Bill's holiday concert, happening in early October, honours the centuries-old tradition of his people.

_____

_____

67. The holiday, which is called Hound Dog Day in honour of a wonderful dog breed.

_____

_____

68. Tradition calls for blue suede shoes.

_____

_____

69. Having brushed the shoes carefully with a suede brush, which can be bought in any shoe shop.

_____

_____

70. The citizens lead their dogs to the town square, Heartbreak Hotel is there.

_____

_____

71. 'Look for the ghost of Elvis,' the hotel receptionist tells every guest, 'Elvis has often been seen haunting these halls.'

_____

_____

72. Elvis, ghost or not, apparently does not attend the Hound Dog Day festivities because no one has seen an aging singer in a white jumpsuit there.

_____

_____

73. Why should a ghost attend Bill's festival

_____

_____

74. How can you even ask?

_____

_____

75. The blue suede shoes are a nostalgic touch, consequently, the tourists always wear them.

_____

_____

Brain Strain: Extra Practice with Complete Sentences

Read Flora's letter in Figure 4-1. She's got a bit of a crush on someone in her office. She's written a passionate note to her love object but of the sentences she's written only six are complete and correct. Can you find the five that don't quite finish what they start?

Dear Victor,

Your smile, with its adorable overbite and slightly clattery bottom dentures. I can think of nothing I would rather do than contemplate the manly gap between your two front teeth. Inspired by your eyebrows, I think of stars, constellations, and furry little bears. In the future, when I will have the time to write poetry about those brows. Your nose alone merits a poem, a sonnet should be dedicated to its nostrils. A giraffe would be lucky to have a neck like yours. It contrasts so interestingly with your compact body and pudgy wee legs. Your shoulders slope invitingly, moreover, your hips swivel better than my office chair. Across those noble shoulders slides your hair, as thick as porridge left to set overnight in a drawer. How can I forget your eyes I am yours forever, Victor, unless I get distracted by a better offer.

Your adoring wee Scottish terrier,

Flora

Figure 4-1: Sample letter with incomplete and run-on sentences.

Answers to Complete Sentence Problems

1 **incomplete**. Did you zero in on *woofing?* That's part of a verb (a present participle, if you absolutely have to know), but all by itself it isn't enough to fill the verb category. Likewise, if you try to pair *woofing* with a subject, the only candidate is *Rascal. Rascal is woofing* would be a match, but *Rascal woofing* isn't: no correct subject/verb pair, no sentence.

2 **Charlie (S)/fed (V)**. Start with a verb search. Any action or being verbs? Yes, *fed.* Who or what *fed? Charlie fed.* Bingo! You have a complete subject/verb pair.

3 **Rascal (S)/wolfed (V), snoozed (V)**. Your verb search (always the best first step) yields two: *wolfed* and *snoozed.* Who *wolfed* and *snoozed? Rascal.* There you go – an acceptable subject/ verb pair.

4 **Rascal (S)/is (V)**. Were you tricked by *entered? Entered* may be a verb in some sentences, but in this one it isn't, because it lacks a subject. But *is* does have a subject, *Rascal.*

5 **incomplete**. Something's missing here: a subject and a verb! What you have, in grammarspeak, is a participle, a part of a verb, but not enough to satisfy the subject/verb rule.

6 **Rascal (S)/sleeps (V)**. Start with a verb search, and you immediately come up with *sleeps,* which, by the way, is an action verb, even though sleeping seems like the opposite of action. Who *sleeps? Rascal,* bless her snoring little self.

7 **incomplete**. You have some action – *having eaten* – but no subject.

8 **incomplete**. The sentence has action (*biting*), but when you ask, 'Who's biting?' the answer is 'Rascal' but *Rascal biting* is a grammatical mismatch. Whereas, *Rascal is biting,* matches and is complete.

9 **vet (S)/is (V)**. No action in this one, but *is* expresses being, and so you're covered on the verb front. Who or what *is? The vet is.*

10 **Who (S)/would be (V)**. Are you surprised to see *who* as a subject? In a question, *who* often fills that role.

11 **incomplete**. A quick glance tells you that you have a verb form (*surprised*), but no subject.

12 **incomplete**. Another verb form (*sniffing*) is easy to find here, but when you ask who is doing the sniffing, you come up with a blank. *Nipper sniffing* doesn't work as a subject and verb pair.

13 **incomplete**. In this one you have a subject, *Toto,* but no matching verb. True, the statement talks about *running, jumping* and *sleeping,* but those aren't matches for *Toto.* (If you care, they're nouns functioning as objects of the preposition *in.*)

14 **Rascal (S)/is guided (V)**. Start with a verb search. Can you spot any action or being verbs? Yes, *is guided.* Now ask who or what *is guided. Rascal is guided.* Bingo: you have a good subject/verb match.

15 **Rascal (S)/loves (V)**. A verb hunt gives you *loves,* and asking the universal question (Who *loves?*) yields *Rascal loves.* Yes! You've got a subject/verb pair and a correct, complete sentence.

16 **incomplete**. *Charlie* makes a fine subject, but he's not matched with a verb. The two verb forms in the statement, *covered* and *catching,* describe Charlie. (They're participles, if you're into grammar terms.) Neither makes a good match. *Charlie covered* sounds like a match, but the meaning here is incorrect because Charlie isn't performing the action of covering. Actually, being covered is something that has happened *to* him. *Charlie catching* sounds like a mismatch because it is a mismatch.

17 **Nipper (S), Rascal (S)/sniffed (V)**. First, find the verb. If you sniff around this sentence looking for an action word, you come up with *sniffed*. Who *sniffed*? *Truffle and Rascal sniffed*. You have a good compound (double) subject for a good verb, and so you have a complete sentence.

18 **dogs (S)/sped (V)**. This one may have surprised you because the subject follows the verb – an unusual, but perfectly fine position. If you follow the normal procedure (locating the verb and asking who did the action), you find *sped* and *dogs,* even though *dogs* appears later in the sentence that the verb, *sped*.

19 **incomplete**. This statement contains a verb form, *stopping,* but no subject matches it. Verdict: ten years in the grammar jail for failure to complete the sentence.

20 **They (S)/lapped (V)**. The action here is *lapped,* which unites nicely with *they*. Completeness rules!

21 **incomplete**. The reader is waiting to hear something about the cow. The way the sentence reads now, you have a description of *cow – who used to work for NASA until she got fed up with the bureaucracy* – but no action word to tell the reader what the cow is doing.

22 **complete**. The sentence tells you everything you need to know, and so it's complete.

23 **complete**. The question makes sense as is, making the sentence complete.

24 **incomplete**. The statement gives you an idea – *milking* – and some descriptions but never delivers with a complete thought about milking.

25 **complete**. A short sentence, but you have everything you need to know about the *protesting cow*.

26 **incomplete**. The word *because* implies a cause-and-effect relationship, but the sentence doesn't supply all the needed information.

27 **incomplete**. What did the mama cow do when she was only a calf? The sentence doesn't say, and so it's incomplete.

28 **incomplete**. Not enough information appears in this sentence, which, by the way, also lacks a subject/verb pair.

29 **complete**. All you need to know about moon-jumping (that it's enough for any cow) is in the sentence.

30 **complete**. This sentence contains enough information to reform NASA, should it indeed choose to enter the field of moon-jumping.

31 **incomplete**. The sentence begins to make a statement about *sheep* but then veers off into a description (*which were once rejected from moon duty*). No other thought is ever attached to *sheep,* making the sentence incomplete.

32 **complete**. This question makes sense as is. You may wonder what NASA is going to do, but you don't wonder what's being asked here because the question – and the sentence – is complete.

33 **incomplete**. The first part of the sentence is a description, and the second is a qualifier, explaining a condition (*though female sheep produce milk*). Neither of these two parts is a complete thought, and so the sentence is incomplete.

34 **complete**. You have everything you need to know except why anyone would want to send sheep to the moon. Grammatically, this sentence is a complete thought.

35 **complete**. The statement comparing sheep performance to cow performance is finished, and the cows win. You're not left hanging, wondering what the sentence is trying to say. Verdict: complete.

36 **incorrect**. Here you have two complete thoughts (everything before the comma equals one complete thought; everything after the comma equals another complete thought). A comma isn't strong enough to hold them together. Try a semicolon or insert *and* after the comma.

37 **correct**. No problems here! The extra information about the nickname (*which had been given to him by the clerks of the court*) is a description, not a complete thought, and so it can be tucked into the sentence next to the word it describes (*nickname*). The *which* ties the idea to *nickname*.

38 **correct**. Surprised? The *nevertheless* in this sentence is not used as a joiner, and so it's legal.

39 **correct**. Did you trip up on this one? The word *for* has another, more common grammatical use in such expressions as *for Pete's sake, for you, for the last time* and so on. However, *for* is a perfectly fine joiner of two complete thoughts when it means 'because'.

40 **correct**. The semicolon here joins two complete thoughts correctly.

41 **incorrect**. To connect these two ideas, look for a stronger connection word. *Then* can't do the job. Try *and then* or *but then*. Still another good solution is to replace the comma with a semicolon (*; then*).

42 **correct**. The words *although* and *if* join thoughts to the main idea about the way Kathy dreams.

43 **correct**. The tacked-on description (*which appeal to something in her character*) is legal because the which refers to the preceding word (*fragments*).

44 **incorrect**. Just because you're quoting, don't think you can ignore run-on rules. The quotation itself contains two complete thoughts and thus needs to be expressed in two complete sentences. The easiest fix is to place a full stop after *exclaimed*.

45 **correct**. No grammatical crimes here: Two ideas (*she is free* and *Kathy intends to burn grammar textbooks for fuel*) are linked by *while*.

46 **incorrect**. *Nevertheless* is a long word, but rather weak. It looks strong enough to join two complete thoughts, but in reality it isn't. Pop a semicolon before *nevertheless* and you're legit.

47 **incorrect**. One complete thought (*History books create a satisfactory snap and crackle while they are burning*) is glued to another (*the flames are also a nice shade of orange*) with nothing more than a comma. Oops! Use a semicolon or add a comma after *burning*, followed by the conjunction *and*.

48 **incorrect**. As in the preceding question, one complete thought and another are attached by a comma. We think not! Use a semicolon or place a but after *World*.

49 **incorrect**. *Therefore* isn't a legal joiner. Substitute *so* or place a semicolon before *therefore*.

50 **correct**. The word *but* is short but robust, and so it does the job of joining two complete sentences without straining itself.

51 **.** (full stop). Because this sentence makes a statement, a full stop is the appropriate endmark.

52 ! (exclamation point). An exclamation mark is right here because the speaker is expressing amazement that Lottie likes maths.

53 . (full stop). This sentence is a statement, and so it needs a full stop.

54 ? (question mark). The *does* in this sentence signals a question, and so you need a question mark.

55 . (full stop). The full stop is the endmark for this statement.

56 ? (question mark). Here the question mark signals a request for information.

57 . (full stop). This statement calls for a full stop.

58 ? (question mark). This sentence requests information, meaning that you need to place a question mark at the end.

59 ! (exclamation mark). Okay, a full stop would do fine here, but an exclamation mark adds extra emphasis.

60 . (full stop). This statement needs a full stop at the end.

61 ? (question mark). The sentence requests information, and so a question mark fits the bill.

62 . (full stop). A full stop is fine here, but if you're bursting with emotion, opting for the exclamation point is perfectly okay as well.

63 ? (question mark). If you see this sentence as a true inquiry, you need a question mark; if you interpret it as a scream of disbelief, an exclamation mark works well.

64 ! (exclamation mark). This statement contains a strong blast of surprise, and so an exclamation point is suitable.

65 ? (question mark). If you're asking for information, you need a question mark.

66 **complete**.

67 **incomplete**. The sentence is incomplete because it gives you a subject (*the holiday*) and a string of descriptions (*which is called Hound Dog Day in honour of a wonderful dog breed*) but doesn't pair any verb with *holiday*. Several corrections are possible. Here's one: The holiday, which is called Hound Dog Day in honour of a wonderful dog breed, requires each citizen to attend dog obedience school.

68 **complete**.

69 **incomplete**. This sentence has no subject. No one is doing the *brushing* or the *buying*. Here's one possible correction: Having brushed the shoes carefully with a suede brush, which can be bought in any shoe shop, Bill proudly displayed his feet.

70 **incomplete**. This sentence is a run-on, because a comma can't join two complete thoughts. Change it to a semicolon or reword the sentence. Here's a possible rewording: The citizens lead their dogs to the town square, where Heartbreak Hotel is located.

71 **incomplete**. This sentence is another run-on. The two quoted sections are jammed into one sentence, but each is a complete thought. Change the comma after *guest* to a full stop.

72 **complete**.

Dear Victor,

76 **Your smile, with its adorable overbite and slightly clattery**

76 **bottom dentures.** I can think of nothing I would rather do than

contemplate the manly gap between your two front teeth.

Inspired by your eyebrows, I think of stars, constellations, and

77 furry little bears. **In the future, when I will have the time to**

77 **write poetry about those brows.** **Your nose alone merits a** **78**

poem, a sonnet should be dedicated to its nostrils. A giraffe **78**

would be lucky to have a neck like yours. It contrasts so

interestingly with your compact body and pudgy wee legs.

Your shoulders slope invitingly, moreover, your hips swivel

79

79 **better than my office chair.** Across those noble shoulders

slides your hair, as thick as porridge left to set overnight in a

80 drawer. **How can I forget your eyes** I am yours forever, Victor,

unless I get distracted by a better offer.

Your adoring wee Scottish terrier,

Flora

73 **incomplete.** The sentence is incomplete because it has no endmark. It needs a question mark to complete it.

74 **complete.**

75 **incomplete.** This sentence is a run-on. *Consequently* looks like a fine, strong word, but it's really a bit of a weakling and can't join two complete thoughts, which you have in this sentence. Add a semicolon after *touch,* and lose the comma.

76 **incomplete**: no verb.

77 **incomplete**: *when* implies more information; no complete thought.

78 **run-on.**

79 **run-on.**

80 **incomplete**: no endmark.

Part II
Mastering Mechanics

'It was the way he would have
wanted it – He was a terrible
English grammar teacher.'

In this part . . .

When you see a sign like this: 'Bowl of tomatoe's £1.00', what's your first reaction?· *That's a bargain, I could do with some tomatoes for the pasta tonight* or *Where's my pen? I need to correct that dreadful apostrophe mistake before my sensitive grammar side goes completely ballistic!?*

This section is all about apostrophes (like the one that shouldn't be there in the vegetable seller's sign above) and other aspects of mechanics – punctuation and capitalisation. When you've finished this section you'll be queen or king of the comma (Chapter 5), apostrophe (Chapter 7) and the quotation mark (Chapter 8). Plus, you'll know how to place hyphens and dashes and semicolons, not to mention colons (Chapter 6). Chapter 9 looks at the basics of capitalisation. If all these details fry your brain, feel free to refresh yourself with a ripe tomato or two. Just don't throw them at us!

Chapter 5

Exercising Comma Sense

*T*he well-dressed writing of a hundred years ago boasted far more commas than today's fashionable sentences. The current trend towards what grammar experts term *open style punctuation* calls for commas to be used more sparingly. Although commas may be dwindling in use, these little punctuation marks have their place – in lists, direct address, dates and addresses, introductory expressions, interrupters and in certain types of descriptions. In this chapter you can practise inserting and deleting commas until your writing is both correct and stylish.

Making a List and Checking It Twice

When you're writing a free-standing list, line breaks signal when one item in a list ends and another begins. Commas do the same thing in sentences. For example, suppose that Professor MacGregor wants you to carry out the following tasks:

✔ Go online.

✔ Find the origin of the dish known as colcannon.

✔ Write an essay on the history of colcannon.

When you insert these items into a sentence, some line breaks turn into commas:

> Professor MacGregor wants you to go online, find the origin of the dish known as colcannon and write an essay on the history of colcannon.

Notice that a comma doesn't precede the first item (*going online*) and that *and* separates the last two items (*finding the origin* and *writing the essay*) without a comma in front of the *and*. Using a comma here is optional. Stricter or more traditional style manuals and formal writing may want you to insert a comma before whatever word joins the last two items of the list. In the informal *For Dummies* style, however, we don't use this comma unless it clarifies or helps to avoid confusion.

If any item in a list has a comma within it, semicolons are used to separate the list items. Imagine that you're inserting the following list into a sentence:

> ✔ Ali Advani, the mayor
>
> ✔ Agnes Hutton
>
> ✔ Jeannie Beattie, magic expert

In a sentence using only commas, the reader wouldn't know that Ali Advani is the mayor and may instead think that Ali and the mayor are two separate people. Here's the properly punctuated sentence:

> Because he has only one extra ticket to the magic expo, Daniel is going to invite Ali Advani, the mayor; Agnes Hutton; or Jeannie Beattie, magic expert.

PRACTICE

Time to get to work! Insert the list from each question into a sentence (we supply the beginning of the sentence to start you off) and punctuate it properly.

EXAMPLE

0. List of things to buy at the chemist:

> industrial-strength toenail clippers
>
> green shoe polish
>
> earwax remover

Getting ready to throw the party of the year, Dafydd went to the chemist to buy

_____

A. **Getting ready to throw the party of the year, Dafydd went to the chemist to buy industrial-strength toenail clippers, green shoe polish and earwax remover.** You have three items and one comma; no comma is needed before the first item on the list.

1. Supermarket shopping list:

> pitted dates
>
> chocolate-covered mushrooms
>
> anchovies
>
> pickled radishes

Dafydd planned to serve a tasteful selection of _____

_____

2. Guests:

> Natasha Evans, best over-55s underarm server, Abergavenny tennis club
>
> Brangwen Berry, double-glazing salesperson of the year
>
> Hannah Umbridge, Miss Hillman Imp, 1963
>
> Gladys Ogilbee, supermodel (well, model supermarket checkout employee, Bridgend)

Dafydd's guest list is heavily tilted towards women he fancies, such as _____

_____

3. Activities:

> bobbing for cabbages
>
> pinning the tail on the landlord
>
> playing spider solitaire doubles
>
> After everyone arrives, Dafydd plans an evening of_____
>
> _____

4. Goals:

> get three phone numbers
>
> arrange at least one future date
>
> avoid any of his neighbours complaining about his fabulous Barry Manilow music
>
> Dafydd will consider his party a success if he can_____
>
> _____

5. Results:

> the police arrived, in response to neighbours' complaints of crimes against music at 10:00, 11:00 and 11:30 p.m.
>
> no one gave out any phone numbers
>
> everyone thought his name was Barry
>
> Dafydd didn't meet his goals because _____
>
> _____

You Talkin' to Me? Direct Address

If the name or title of the person to whom you're talking or writing is inserted into the sentence, you're in a direct-address situation. Commas set off direct-address expressions from everything else. In the following examples, *Wilfred* is being addressed:

- ✔ Wilfred, can you pick up some courgettes when you're out shopping?
- ✔ I expect you to remove all the seeds from the courgettes before you fry them, Wilfred.
- ✔ When you chop courgettes, Wilfred, try not to slice them too thinly.

The most common direct-address mistake is to send one comma to do a two-comma job. In the last of the three preceding examples, two commas must set off *Wilfred*.

Can you insert commas to highlight the direct-address name in these sentences?

Q. Listen Champ I think you need to get a new pair of elbow pads.

A. **Listen, Champ, I think you need to get a new pair of elbow pads.** In this example, you're talking to *Champ*, a title that's substituting for the actual name. Direct-address expressions don't have to be proper names, though they frequently are.

6. Ladies and gentlemen I present the Fifth Annual Elbox Championships.

7. I know Clive that you're an undefeated Elbox competitor. Would you tell our audience about the sport?

8. Elboxing is about 5,000 years old Kevin. It originated in ancient Egypt.

9. Really? Man I can't believe you knew that!

10. Yes, the sport grew out of the natural movement of the elbow when someone tried to interfere with a diner's portion by 'elbowing' Kevin.

11. Excuse me a moment. The reigning champion has decided to pay us a visit. Ms McWhirter can you tell us how you feel about the upcoming match?

12. Certainly sir. I'm confident that my new training routine will pay off.

13. Hey, hey lady! Did you see what she did there Kevin?

14. Who do you think you are missus elbowing your way into my interview?

15. Okay, okay, we'll leave it there for now folks. We'll let you get ready for the . . . Oops! She's down. I think we have a new champ already. Let's hear it for Kevin, king of the short, sharp, shove!

Dating and Addressing

No, this section doesn't tell you what to wear when taking a comma to the cinema on a Saturday night. Nor does this section deal with what sort of speech you need to make when you first meet a comma. Instead, we help you to practise placing commas in dates (as in 20 July 2010) and addresses (as in Mablethorpe, Lincolnshire).

The use of commas in dates is different depending on whether you're using UK or American English. In UK English, the number of the month usually comes before the month (as in 20 July 2010), whereas in American English it comes after the month (as in July 20, 2010). As you can see, to avoid the two numbers being beside each other and perhaps looking confusing, a comma is used in American English dates.

Here are the rules for commas in dates:

✔ **For a date that includes (in order) the day, month and year (the UK style),** open-style punctuation favours no commas anywhere – before, after, inside, over or under. You get the idea; no commas. ('On the first Saturday after 14 October 2015 I'll go on a wild shopping spree.') Some very traditional English teachers always place a comma after the month and after the year, unless the year ends the sentence, in which case the full stop follows the year. ('I'll go shoe-shopping on the morning of 17 October, 2015, and meet my friends for lunch in the afternoon.') If you're writing for a particular person (a professor or a boss), you should find out his or her preference and follow it. If you're in charge of your style, choose which style you like and then be consistent throughout your writing.

✔ **For a date that includes (in order) the month, day and year (the American style),** place a comma after the day. If this kind of date is in a sentence that continues beyond the year, place a comma after the year as well. ('I will definitely, 100 per cent, without a doubt, ask for a pay rise by October 14, 2015, unless I decide on the day that midweek isn't a good time to speak to the boss about finances.')

✔ **For a date that includes (in order) only the day and month,** you don't need any commas. ('To keep my bank manager happy, I'll deposit a huge amount of cash in my savings account on 15 October.')

✔ **For a date that includes (in order) the month and year,** no commas are required. ('The last time I had a day off was in December 1996 and that was only because the cold snap forced the boss to close the office for a day.') Traditional punctuation places a comma between the month and the year and after the year within a sentence; however, open-style punctuation favours fewer commas, and that's what we advocate. Many style manuals drop both commas if the sentence continues. Which style you follow is up to you, unless the Authority Figure for whom you're writing has a preference. No matter what you do, be consistent.

As far as addresses are concerned, the following rules apply:

✔ **If you're writing an address in block form (not in a sentence),** put each item onto a separate line if you can. If you don't have enough room and you have to combine items, use a comma to separate them, except for the postcode and whatever comes in front of it (the village, town or city).

✔ **If the address is inserted into a sentence**, separate each item with a comma. If the sentence continues after the address, insert a comma after the last bit of the address. ('I sent the package to Louise O'Hara, 172 Wilton Street, Stoke-on-Trent ST1 2QW, but she told me she didn't get it.').

Punctuation party time! Place commas where you need them in the following sentences. Our answer key is based on the more traditional style of writing dates. Your answers may be slightly different if you favour open-style punctuation and don't think you need to add any commas.

Q. On 12 December 2007 Pearl was sitting at home when a commercial newspaper, *The Chippy Courier*, popped through her letterbox. It had been sent to the wrong address. Pearl lived at 36 Back Wynd Aberdeen AB10 1JB in the centre of the city. The Fryer's Delight, her local fish and chip shop, was across the road at 89 Back Wynd.

A. **On 12 December, 2007, Pearl was sitting at home when a commercial newspaper, *The Chippy Courier*, popped through her letterbox. It had been sent to the wrong address. Pearl lived at 36 Back Wynd, Aberdeen AB10 1JB, in the centre of the city. The Fryer's Delight, her local fish and chip shop, was across the road at 89 Back Wynd.** Commas separate the day from the year and the whole date from the rest of the sentence; in the address, a comma separates the street from the city. No comma is placed between the city and the postcode.

16. An article in The *Chippy Courier* dated 12 November 2009 reported that deep-fried Mars Bars had fewer calories than deep-fried Mars Bar and ice-cream.

17. Pearl was watching her figure and although she never went for the hugely fattening ice-cream option, she was partial to the hot, crispy chocolate snack from The Fryer's Delight at 89 Back Wynd Aberdeen probably the best chippy in north-east Scotland.

18. Pearl was 93 and often considered her own mortality. Her last will and testament was dated 8 April 1990 and specified that she didn't want to be buried or cremated.

19. Her lawyer, Bernie Klangger of 25 Thornhill Drive Bridge of Don AB23 9PE was squeamish about the arrangements but promised to carry them out to the best of his ability when the time came.

20. The time came last week. The Fryer's Delight insisted that Pearl was their most loyal customer and were honoured to be of service. After their 'contribution', a sweet service was held at the Chocolate Makers' headquarters at 16 Springfield Street Craigiebuckler AB15 7XK.

Introducing (and Interrupting) with the Comma

Do you want to start off your sentences with a bang, or at least a small pop? Good. Just don't forget to set off the introductory expression with a comma. Grammatically, *introductory expressions* are a mixed bag of verbals (part verb, part another speech form – described in more detail in Chapter 12), prepositional phrases, adverbial clauses and lots of other things you don't have to know the names of. In short, an introductory expression makes a comment on the rest of the sentence or adds a bit of extra information. It may include a verb form or just mention a place; it may even be as short as *yes*, *no* or *well*; or it may be much longer. Check out the italicised portion of the following sentences for examples of introductory expressions:

> *Driving home from the publisher's office,* Brad Jones thought about the huge amount of money he'd get for his memoirs.

> *To be sure of topping the celebrity memoir list,* Brad planned plenty of big-name kiss and tell moments.

> *While he was waiting at the lights,* he started rehearsing his speech for the autobiography of the year award.

Like introducers, interrupters can also vary in length. A direct-address element (see the 'You Talkin' to Me? Direct Address' section earlier in this chapter) may be considered a type of interrupter and so may some of the introductory expressions in the preceding samples, when you move the introducers to the middle of the sentence. The same principle that applies to direct-address elements applies to interrupters: they comment on or otherwise interrupt the main idea of the sentence and thus commas set them off. In the following sentences, the interrupters are italicised:

> Ms Patel, *even though she was scared of lions,* put on a brave front as she shepherded her pupils past the wild beasts' cages at the zoo.

> There was no guarantee, *of course,* that her brave front would fool all the pupils.

Some short introductory expressions or interrupters don't require commas. For example, in the sentence 'That morning Ms Patel had drunk 12 cups of coffee to get herself ready for the zoo trip', a comma isn't used to set off *that morning*. If the expression doesn't have a verb in it and is tied strongly to the main idea of the sentence, you can sometimes get away without commas. This test may help: say the sentence aloud (or in your head, if you're afraid of attracting the wrong sort of attention). If you hear a natural pause, pop in a comma. If everything runs together nicely, don't pop.

Up for some practice? Insert commas where needed in the following sentences, and resist the temptation to insert them where they're not wanted. You can assume that any commas already included are correct.

Q. Exhausted after a tiring morning at the zoo Ms Patel was in no mood for any nonsense.

A. **Exhausted after a tiring morning at the zoo, Ms Patel was in no mood for any nonsense.** The comma sets off the introductory expression, *Exhausted after a tiring morning at the zoo*. Notice how all that phrase applies to *Ms Patel?* She's the subject of the sentence.

21. Keen to get back to school she decided to do a head count once all the pupils were on the bus.

22. The children on the other hand were in no hurry to get back to Mount Harrington Primary.

23. No an afternoon of difficult sums was nobody's idea of fun.

24. Hoping to make everyone laugh Mark McManus did his usual trick.

25. As Ms Patel took the register Mark answered for each student. He really did think he was the world's best impersonator.

26. Amazingly he pulled it off. Ms Patel was fooled, but not one student cracked a smile at the bully's antics.

27. Convinced she had heard from 17 boys and 11 girls Ms Patel told the bus driver to head back to school.

28. Mark of course knew exactly how many pupils were on the bus.

29. As each student had boarded the bus he'd counted and punched every single one of them.

30. Including Mark there were 27 pupils on the bus.

31. Mark chuckling to himself couldn't believe his cunning plan had gone so smoothly.

32. Well that girl Monica with her practical jokes and funny voices wouldn't be upstaging him anytime soon.

33. With every ounce of courage Monica tried to keep her brave face on. Luckily the zoo-keeper heard a tiny sniffle and decided to investigate.

34. The zookeeper promised to take the courageous girl back to her friends and Ms Patel at school. But first she offered Monica an up-close-and-personal visit with any animal she wanted.

35. Monica delighted to try out her new material delivered her jokes to her most appreciative audience ever – the hyenas. They laughed a lot. Then Monica went back to school with a fabulous tale that would cement her reputation as the bravest, funniest girl in the school.

Setting Off Descriptions

Life would be much simpler for the comma-inserter if nobody ever described anything. No descriptions would mean no comma problems. However, why throw the baby out with the bathwater!

A better plan is to find out more about the basic principles behind punctuating descriptive expressions:

✔ **If the description *follows* the word being described, decide whether the description is extra information or essential, identifying material.** If the description falls into the 'nice to know but I didn't really need it' (extra) category, surround it with commas. If the description is in the 'have to have it' bin, omit the commas. For example, in the sentence 'The dictionary *on the table* is dusty', the description in italics is necessary because it tells *which* dictionary is dusty. However, in the sentence, 'Charlie's dictionary, *which is on the table*, is dusty', commas set off the description in italics because you already know that *Charlie's dictionary* is the one being discussed. The part about the table is extra information.

✔ **For descriptions that precede the word described, place commas only when you have a list of two or more descriptions of the same type and importance.** You can tell when two or more descriptions are equally important; they can be written in a different order without changing the meaning of the sentence. For example, in the sentence, 'The *black, dusty* dictionary has never been opened', the two descriptions – *black* and *dusty* – can be reversed without changing the meaning, and so you need a comma. However, in the sentence, '*Four dusty* dictionaries need some cleaning power now!' the two descriptions aren't the same type – one is a number and one is a condition. You can't say *Dusty four*, and so you don't insert a comma.

✔ **When descriptions containing verb forms introduce a sentence (see the preceding section 'Introducing (and Interrupting) with the Comma'), always use commas to set them off.** For example: 'Sneezing into his handkerchief, Zac looked for a duster.' The description, *Sneezing into his handkerchief*, has a verb form (*Sneezing*) and thus a comma sets it off from the rest of the sentence.

Got the idea? Now try your comma skills on the following sentences. If the italicised words need to be set off, add the commas. If not, leave the sentence alone.

Q. The *purple spotty* top belongs to the slowest jockey in the race *Jerry*.

A. **The *purple, spotty top* belongs to the slowest jockey in the race, Jerry.** The first two descriptions precede the word being described (*top*) and may be interchanged without a problem, and so you need a comma between them. The second description follows the thing described (*the slowest jockey in the race*). Because you can have only one slowest jockey, the name is extra, not essential identifying information, and so a comma sets it off.

36. Jerry's favourite food *which he eats almost constantly* is buttered popcorn. He's quite tubby for a jockey. Jerry's not a very good jockey.

37. His horse *Battle of the Bulge* hates him because he's so heavy.

38. Jerry and Battle have lost every race they've ever ridden in. No matter whether the races are *long short* or in between, they've lost them all.

39. Battle wishes she could run away from all this *dull repetitive* horse racing.

40. One of the regular fantasies *that keep her from going insane* is of being a star in the glamorous world of American rodeos.

41. At the sound of almost any bell (the ping of a microwave oven with a *hot sticky sweet* snack in it, for instance), Battle begins to imagine the scene.

42. Last Saturday she heard a bell and the *deep rumbling* voice of a Texan announcer immediately filled her ears.

43. 'And here's *our one British filly*, the delightfully frisky Ms BB. Oh! Look at her buck! That poor fella is up and off before he's even had a chance to get down and on.'

44. When Battle opened her *brown twinkling* eyes she found that she was dancing at the fourth fence at Aintree.

45. She was surprised (and rather delighted) to see jockey Jerry lying at her *delicate feminine* hooves on his *fat angry* back.

Brain Strain: Extra Practice with Commas

Figure 5-1 shows an employee self-evaluation report with some serious problems, a few of which concern commas. (The rest deal with the truly bad idea of being honest with your boss.) Forget about the content errors and concentrate on commas. See whether you can find five commas that appear where they shouldn't and ten places that need commas but don't have them. Circle the commas you're deleting and insert commas where they're needed.

Annual Self-Evaluation: Kristin DeMint

Well Ms Ehrlich that time of year has arrived again. I, must think about my strengths and weaknesses as an employee, of Toe-Ring International. First and most important let me say that I love working for Toe-Ring. When I applied for the job on 15 September, 2005 I never dreamed how much fun I would have taking two, long lunches a day. Sneaking out the back door, is not my idea of fun. Because no one ever watches what I am doing at Toe-Ring I can leave by the front door without worrying. Also Ms Ehrlich, I confess that I do almost no work at all. Transferred to the plant in Knottingley West Yorkshire I immediately claimed a privilege given only to the most experienced most skilled, employees and started to take an extra week's holiday. I have only one more thing to say. Can I have a raise?

Figure 5-1:
Comma problems in an employee self-evaluation report

Answers to Comma Problems

1. **Dafydd planned to serve a tasteful selection of pitted dates, chocolate-covered mushrooms, anchovies and pickled radishes.** Each item on Dafydd's list, except the last one before the *and*, is separated from the next by a comma. No comma comes before the first item, *pitted dates*.

2. **Dafydd's guest list is heavily tilted towards women he fancies, such as Natasha Evans, best over 55s underarm server, Abergavenny tennis club; Brangwen Berry, double-glazing salesperson of the year; Hannah Umbridge, Miss Hillman Imp, 1963; and Gladys Ogilbee, supermodel (well, model supermarket checkout employee, Bridgend).** Did you remember the semicolons? The commas within each item of Dafydd's dream-date list make distinguishing between one dream date and another impossible with a simple comma. Semicolons do the trick.

3. **After everyone arrives, Dafydd plans an evening of bobbing for cabbages, pinning the tail on the landlord and playing spider solitaire doubles.** Sounds like fun, eh? Don't forget to separate the first two thrilling activities with commas.

4. **Dafydd will consider his party a success if he can get three phone numbers, arrange at least one future date and avoid any of his neighbours complaining about his fabulous Barry Manilow music.** Poor Dafydd's standards of success are fairly low, as is the standard for a correctly punctuated list. All you have to do is pop in a comma.

5. **Dafydd didn't meet his goals because the police arrived, in response to neighbours' complaints of crimes against music at 10:00, 11:00 and 11:30 pm; no one gave out any phone numbers; and everyone thought his name was Barry.** Even with low standards, Dafydd is in trouble. You're in trouble too if you forgot to use a semicolon to distinguish one item from another. Why? The first item on the list has commas in it, and so a plain comma isn't enough to separate the list items.

6. **Ladies and gentlemen, I present the Fifth Annual Elbox Championships.** Even though *Ladies and gentlemen* doesn't name the members of the audience, they're still being addressed, and so a comma sets off the expression from the rest of the sentence.

7. **I know, Clive, that you're an undefeated Elbox competitor. Would you tell our audience about the sport?** Here you see the benefit of the direct-address comma. Without it, the reader thinks *I know Clive* is the beginning of the sentence and then lapses into confusion. Two commas separate *Clive*, and the reader understands that *I know that you're . . .* is the real meaning.

8. **Elboxing is about 5,000 years old, Kevin. It originated in ancient Egypt.** You're talking to *Kevin*, and so his name needs to be set off with a comma.

9. **Really? Man, I can't believe you knew that!** Before you start yelling at us, we know that *Man* is sometimes simply an exclamation of feeling, not a true address. But it can be, and in this sentence, it is. So that's why you need to separate it from the rest of the sentence with a comma.

10. **Yes, the sport grew out of the natural movement of the elbow when someone tried to interfere with a diner's portion by 'elbowing', Kevin.** No one's hitting the middle joint of Kevin's arm. Instead, *Kevin* is being addressed directly, and so you need the comma.

11. **Excuse me a moment. The reigning champion has decided to pay us a visit. Ms McWhirter, can you tell us how you feel about the upcoming match?** Here the person being addressed is *Ms McWhirter*, and so a comma sets off the term.

12 **Certainly, sir. I'm confident that my new training routine will pay off.** The very polite Ms McWhirter talks to *sir* in this sentence, and so a comma sets off that term.

13 **Hey, hey, lady! Did you see what she did there, Kevin?** Both Ms McWhirter (*lady*) and the announcer (*Kevin*) are being addressed, which means that commas are required.

14 **Who do you think you are, missus, elbowing your way into my interview?** The direct address term *missus* (to address the champion) is in the middle of the sentence, and so two commas are needed to separate it from the rest of the sentence.

15 **Okay, okay, we'll leave it there for now, folks. We'll let you get ready for the . . . Oops! She's down. I think we have a new champ already. Let's hear it for Kevin, king of the short, sharp shove!** In this sentence, *folks* are being addressed, and so a comma must set off the term.

16 **An article in *The Chippy Courier dated* 12 November 2009 reported that deep-fried Mars Bars had fewer calories than deep-fried Mars Bar and ice-cream.** Or, **An article in *The Chippy Courier dated* 12 November, 2006, reported that deep-fried Mars Bars had fewer calories than deep-fried Mars Bar and ice-cream.** Surprise! Two answers are possible. The more modern solution calls for no commas. The very traditional, 'I learned English when quill pens were the rage' style calls for commas between the month and year and the year and the rest of the sentence.

17 **Pearl was watching her figure and although she never went for the hugely fattening ice-cream option, she was partial to the hot, crispy chocolate snack from The Fryer's Delight at 89 Back Wynd, Aberdeen, probably the best chippy in north-east Scotland.** A comma sets off both lines of the address from each other. A comma also follows the address because the sentence continues after the address.

18 **Pearl was 93 and often considered her own mortality. Her last will and testament was dated 8 April 1990 and specified that that she didn't want to be buried or cremated.** Or **Pearl was 93 and often considered her own mortality. Her last will and testament was dated 8 April, 1990, and specified that that she didn't want to be buried or cremated.** Again, two answers are possible here. The more modern open-style punctuation calls for no commas. The more traditional style opts for commas between the month and year and the year and the rest of the sentence.

19 **Her lawyer, Bernie Klangger of 25 Thornhill Drive, Bridge of Don AB23 9PE, was squeamish about the arrangements but promised to carry them out to the best of his ability when the time came.** A comma separates the lines of Bernie's address, and the whole thing is followed by another comma. Don't use a comma between the town and the post code.

20 **The time came last week. The Fryer's Delight insisted that Pearl was their most loyal customer and were honoured to be of service. After their 'contribution', a sweet service was held at the Chocolate Makers' headquarters at 16 Springfield Street, Craigiebuckler AB15 7XK.** Another address, another chance for you to add a comma. Again. no comma is placed between the post code and what comes immediately before it (here, *Craigiebuckler*).

21 **Keen to get back to school, she decided to do a head count once all the pupils were on the bus.** The introductory expression here merits a comma because it's fairly long. Length doesn't always determine whether you need a comma, but in general the longer the introduction, the more likely you are to need a comma.

22 **The children, on the other hand, were in no hurry to get back to Mount Harrington Primary.** The expression inside the commas makes a comment on the rest of the sentence, contrasting it with the actions of Ms Patel. As an interrupter, commas must separate it from the rest of the sentence.

23 **No, an afternoon of difficult sums was nobody's idea of fun.** *Yes* and *no*, when they show up at the beginning of a sentence, take commas if they comment on the main idea.

24 **Hoping to make everyone laugh, Mark McManus did his usual trick.** Introductory expressions with verb forms always take commas.

25 **As Ms Patel took the register, Mark answered for each student. He really did think he was the world's best impersonator.** The introductory expression *As Ms Patel took the register* needs a comma after it.

26 **Amazingly he pulled it off. Ms Patel was fooled, but not one student cracked a smile at the bully's antics.** The introductory work *amazingly* is short and clear. No comma is necessary, but you aren't wrong to use one if you prefer a short pause.

27 **Convinced she had heard from 17 boys and 11 girls, Ms Patel told the bus driver to head back to school.** Introductory expressions with verb forms always take commas.

28 **Mark, of course, knew exactly how many pupils were on the bus.** The *of course* interrupts the flow of the sentence and comments on the main idea, and so you need a comma before and after it.

29 **As each student had boarded the bus, he'd counted and punched every single one of them.** The introductory phrase *As each student had boarded the bus* (with its verb *had boarded*) needs a comma.

30 **Including Mark, there were 27 pupils on the bus.** Here you have a choice. The introductory expression is short and closely tied to the flow of the sentence and so you can leave out the comma or put one in if you prefer.

31 **Mark, chuckling to himself, couldn't believe his cunning plan had gone so smoothly.** The expression *chuckling to himself* interrupts the flow of the sentence and calls for commas.

32 **Well, that girl Monica with her practical jokes and funny voices wouldn't be upstaging him anytime soon.** Words such as *well, indeed, clearly* and so forth take commas when they occur at the beginning of the sentence and aren't part of the main idea.

33 **With every ounce of courage, Monica tried to keep her brave face on. Luckily the zookeeper heard a tiny sniffle and decided to investigate.** We admit that this one's a judgement call. You aren't going to get prosecuted for comma failure if you didn't place a comma after *courage*, or be carted off to grammar jail if, like us, you did insert one. This sentence falls into a grey area. With a comma, the introductory expression stands out a little more. You don't need a comma after *Luckily* because it's short, sharp and to the point.

34 **The zookeeper promised to take the courageous girl back to her friends and Ms Patel at school. But first, she offered Monica an up-close-and-personal visit with any animal she wanted.** This question is another opportunity for you to decide whether you want a comma or not. If you use one after *but first*, you set the expression off nicely, but the sentence is also fine without one.

35 **Monica, delighted to try out her new material, delivered her jokes to her most appreciative audience ever – the hyenas. They laughed a lot. Then Monica went back to school with a fabulous tale that would cement her reputation as the bravest, funniest girl in the school.** The interrupter, *delighted to try out her new material*, needs commas to set it off.

36 **Jerry's favourite food,** *which he eats almost constantly,* **is buttered popcorn. He's quite tubby for a jockey. Jerry's not a very good jockey.** After you find out that the food is Jerry's favourite, you have enough identification. The information about how often he eats popcorn is extra, and thus commas need to set it off. Descriptions beginning with *which* are often extra.

37 **His horse,** *Battle of the Bulge,* **hates him because he's so heavy.** The *his* tells you which horse is being discussed, and so the fact that her name is *Battle of the Bulge* is extra, and so commas need to set it off.

38 **Jerry and Battle have lost every race they've ever ridden in. No matter whether the races are** *long, short* **or in between, they've lost them all.** These two descriptions (*long* and *short*) may be reversed without loss of meaning, and so a comma is appropriate.

39 **Battle wishes she could run away from all this** *dull, repetitive* **horse racing.** Because you can interchange *dull* and *repetitive* without changing the sentence's meaning, you need to put a comma between these two adjectives.

40 **One of the regular fantasies** *that keep her from going insane* **is of being a star in the glamorous world of American rodeos.** Which fantasies are you talking about? Without the *going insane* information, you don't know. Identifying information doesn't take commas. **Hint:** descriptions beginning with *that* are nearly always essential identifiers and so commas aren't necessary to set them off.

41 **At the sound of almost any bell (the ping of a microwave oven with a** *hot, sticky, sweet* **snack in it, for instance), Battle begins to imagine the scene.** The order of the three descriptions preceding *snack* can easily be changed, and so commas are needed.

42 **Last Saturday she heard a bell and the** *deep, rumbling* **voice of a Texan announcer immediately filled her ears.** The descriptions *deep* and *rumbling* can be reversed and the meaning would still hold, meaning that a comma between them is needed.

43 **'And here's** *our one British filly,* **the delightfully frisky Ms BB. Oh and look at her buck! That poor fella is up and off before he's even had a chance to get down and on.'** The three descriptions before *filly* aren't of the same type: one (*our*) is possessive and another (*one*) is a number. Commas never set off possessives and numbers.

44 **When Battle opened her** *brown, twinkling* **eyes she found that she was dancing at the fourth fence at Aintree.** These two descriptions may be reversed without loss of meaning, and so a comma is the right choice here.

45 **She was surprised (and rather delighted) to see jockey Jerry lying at her** *delicate, feminine* **hooves on his** *fat, angry* **back.** The two descriptions here have two elements each that are interchangeable, and so commas should set them off.

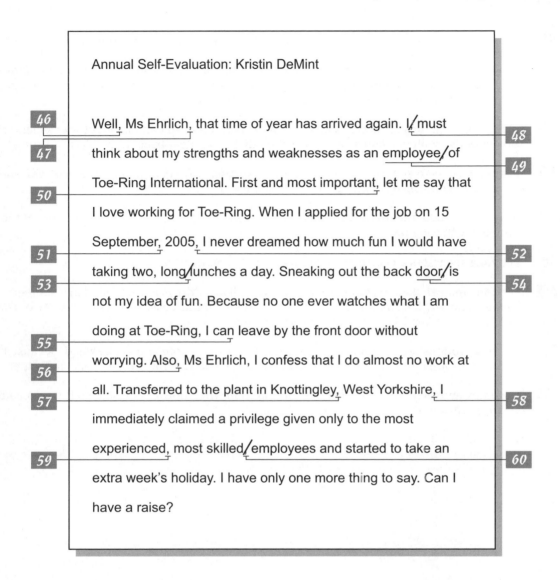

Annual Self-Evaluation: Kristin DeMint

46 Well, Ms Ehrlich, that time of year has arrived again. I must **48**
47 think about my strengths and weaknesses as an employee of **49**
Toe-Ring International. First and most important, let me say that
50 I love working for Toe-Ring. When I applied for the job on 15
September, 2005, I never dreamed how much fun I would have **52**
51 taking two, long lunches a day. Sneaking out the back door is **54**
53 not my idea of fun. Because no one ever watches what I am
doing at Toe-Ring, I can leave by the front door without
55 worrying. Also, Ms Ehrlich, I confess that I do almost no work at
56 all. Transferred to the plant in Knottingley, West Yorkshire, I **58**
57 immediately claimed a privilege given only to the most
experienced, most skilled employees and started to take an **60**
59 extra week's holiday. I have only one more thing to say. Can I
have a raise?

46 Commas surround *Ms Ehrlich* because she's being directly addressed in this sentence.

47 See the preceding answer.

48 The pronoun *I* is part of the main idea of the sentence, not an introductory expression. No comma should separate it from the rest of the sentence.

49 The phrase *Toe-Ring International* is an essential identifier of the type of employee being discussed. No comma should separate it from the word it describes (*employee*).

50 A comma follows the introductory expression, *First and most important.*

51 In this style of date, a comma separates the day from the year. Traditionalists use a comma to separate the month from the year. Open-style punctuation followers says there's no need for commas in this date. It's up to you which style you choose.

52 A comma follows a year when a date of this style is inserted into a sentence.

53 Two descriptions are attached to lunches – *two* and *long*. These descriptions aren't of the same type. *Two* is a number and *long* is a different sort of quantity. Also, a comma never separates numbers from other descriptions. The verdict: delete the comma after *two*.

54 In this sentence the expression *sneaking out the back door* isn't an introductory element; it's the subject of the sentence and so a comma shouldn't separate it from its verb *(is)*.

55 A comma needs to separate the introductory expression *Because no one ever watches what I am doing at Toe-Ring* from the rest of the sentence.

56 *Also* is an introduction to the sentence, and so you need to separate it from the rest of the sentence with a comma.

57 A comma separates a village, town or city from its county.

58 A comma follows *West Yorkshire* for two reasons. If an address is embedded in a sentence, a comma generally follows the last bit of the address – in this case, *West Yorkshire*. Also, *West Yorkshire* is the last bit of an introductory element.

59 Two descriptions are attached to *employees: most experienced* and *most skilled.* Because these descriptions are more or less interchangeable, a comma separates them from each other.

60 No comma ever separates the last description from what it describes, and so the comma before *employees* has to go.

Chapter 6

Made You Look! Punctuation Marks That Demand Attention

. . . .

In This Chapter

▶ Placing hyphens where needed

▶ Using dashes for drama and interruptions

▶ Examining colons and semicolons

. . . .

The punctuation marks we look at in this chapter don't sit in the corner at parties murmuring, 'Oh, don't mind me.' Instead, they scream, 'I'm important! Pay attention, NOW,' wherever they appear. Fortunately, placing these marks in the proper spots is a piece of cake, once you get the hang of a few rules.

Connectors and Dividers: Hyphens

Hyphens (-) are the shortest horizontal marks in the punctuation world. (Dashes are the long ones.) Sometimes, hyphens function as word breakers. When you arrive at the right-hand side of a page in the middle of a word, a hyphen lets you finish the word on the next line. Just break the word at the end of a syllable. Syllables are the separate sounds of a word. *Furniture* and *vegetable* have three syllables each, and *democracy* has four. (A dictionary can help you with this point.) Don't leave only one or two letters all by themselves on one line, and don't attempt to divide any one-syllable words, even a long one such as *through*. If you're working on a computer, though, you can count on your word processing program to take care of the end-of-line hyphens for you.

Hyphens also create compounds (two words linked to create one meaning) and sometimes attach a prefix to a word. Prefixes (*pre-*, *post-*, *ante-*, *un-* and so on) go on the front of other words and change the original word's meaning (*comfortable* and *uncomfortable*, for example). Most prefixes don't need hyphens, but some (such as *self-*, in *self-serving*, for example) tend to appear with hyphens.

As with other punctuation marks, the hyphen is subject to fashion. Many prefixed and hyphenated compounds of 100 years ago have now become single words. (If you were prone to welling up 20 years ago, you may have been called *a cry-baby*, but if you're still blubbering today, you're more of *a crybaby*. And, if you don't mind us saying, you need to get a grip. Stop all that snivelling and pull yourself together!)

To make matters worse, the major style guides and publishing companies sometimes differ on the to-hyphenate-or-not question. The dictionary is a good guide for the everyday writer who's unsure about a particular case. If you can't find a dictionary, follow these guidelines:

✔ **If your reader may become confused without a hyphen, you need one.** You may, for example, be involved in the *re-creation* of a famous work of art or be going to your local park for a spot of *recreation*. Without the hyphen, the reader may have difficulty discerning your meaning.

✔ **If two vowels show up together, chances are that you need a hyphen.** *Anti-inflammatory* and *re-examine,* for example, need hyphens.

✔ **If a prefix latches onto a capitalised word, a hyphen separates the two.** Consider *anti-Conservative* and *post-Renaissance*.

✔ **If you're talking about part of a word (as we did earlier in this section when we listed the prefixes *pre-*, *post-* and others), a hyphen signals that the word isn't complete.** The hyphen functions in this way when you want to link two prefixes to one root word, as in the expression *pre- and postwar anxiety*.

Hyphens also link two words that form one description of the same person or thing. In your driving test, you may make a third-gear mistake (crashing the gears when you're changing down from fourth). Or, if you're having a really bad test, you may make a third gear-mistake (the third of three bad slips in your gear changing). The hyphen brings clarity; though sadly, showing off your hyphenation skills to your driving test examiner is unlikely to improve your chances of passing.

Enough talk – time for some action. Use a caret (^) to tuck a hyphen wherever one is needed in the following sentences. If you find a misplaced hyphen, cross it out. If the description is okay, you don't have to do anything.

Q. When Josh saw a mouse scuttling across his kitchen floor, he went on-line and booked an appointment straight-away with a well known company to deal with his unwelcome visitor.

A. **online**, **straightaway**, **well-known.**
Ten years ago the convention may have been *on-line*, but nowadays it's *online* (unhyphenated). *Straightaway* is also unhyphenated. Both *well* and *known* describe the *company*, and so the descriptions are hyphenated.

1. Josh, who's a second string-violinist, likes to practise in his kitchen because the acoustics are good there.

2. Mags, an agent from the rodent catching company, turned up at Josh's ground-floor flat. She assessed the situation and recommended a new product.

3. 'I'm ex-army myself,' she said, 'and I helped develop this product after seeing a prototype in action behind enemy lines.'

4. Mags ex-plained that The Screecher was an antiinvader noise maker that worked by emitting a high-pitched sound that mice hated.

5. Josh, who was neither anti- not pro-rat, liked the sound of The Screecher.

6. 'You only have to plug it in three-times a day for five-minutes and your little mousey guest will have moved on by next week-end, I guarantee,' Mags promised.

7. Josh switched on the new gadget and, completely oblivious to any sound, got out his violin and started practising Beethoven's-Ninth.

8. A few seconds later, Josh felt a tap on his right-foot. He looked down to see a very chilled out mouse standing there.

9. The mouse said, 'We've lived with that wailing of yours for years and never-once com-plained. I'm so glad we didn't because it seems like today you've finally got the hang of that thing.'

10. The mouse stroked his whiskers and went on, 'I just popped by to say the kids came round today, with the 167 grandchildren, and everyone thinks that new music is extremely-soothing. In fact they like it so much, they've decided to move back in with us. At least till the little ones are ready for nursery-school. See you around, pal.'

Just Dashing Through

The dash is the egotist of punctuation marks, calling for your attention faster than a fire drill in the middle of an exam. And, just as a false fire drill every Tuesday morning can get on your nerves, overused dashes can annoy your readers as well. So use them sparingly, in the following situations only:

✔ **To interrupt the flow of thought with another idea.** 'I will not attend the ball – how could I when my glass slipper is cracked? – no matter how much you beg.' Notice that the material inserted into the sentence between the two dashes doesn't begin with a capital letter, even though in another situation it can stand alone as a complete sentence.

✔ **To summarise or define a list.** 'Lip gloss, insect repellent, stun gun – Megan had everything she needed for her big date.' The dash divides the list from its defini-tion, which is everything Megan thinks she needs on a date.

If you're not feeling dramatic, use a colon to precede a list. A colon does the same job grammatically, with less flash than the dash.

✔ **To show incompleteness.** 'Almost as soon as they sat down Megan said, 'Let me show you my stun gun – hey, hey, come back here. The date isn't over yet!' The dash indicates that Megan's first sentence is incomplete.

✔ **To create drama.** 'May I introduce the best golfer in Antarctica – Sam Spearly.' The dash is the equivalent of a drumroll in this sentence. If you favour a quieter approach, you can also write that sentence using a comma, rather than a dash: 'May I introduce the best golfer in Antarctica, Sam Spearly.' (See Chapter 5 for more information on commas.)

Dashes aren't appropriate in some situations. Keep these points in mind:

✔ Too many dashes can really annoy your reader.

✔ Dashes can't be used to join complete sentences.

✔ You can't send a dash to do a hyphen's job.

Now dash through these questions, inserting dashes where appropriate. By the way, did you notice that we didn't say *where needed*? That's because dashes aren't required anywhere. Other punctuation marks (colons or brackets, for example) may substitute for the dash, though they're usually less dramatic. Note that you may have to knock out another punctuation mark before inserting a dash.

Q. As usual Debbie brought too many snacks, chocolate peanuts, cherry-coated sardines and unsalted popcorn.

A. **As usual Debbie brought too many snacks – chocolate peanuts, cherry-coated sardines and unsalted popcorn.** The dash works better than the comma in this sentence, because the comma after *snacks* blends in with the list.

11. Jim plans to turn up at Debbie's party, I really don't know why, along with his personal trainer.

12. 'I can't believe that he has a trainer because . . .' spluttered Debbie.

13. He needs help with his fitness routine, four push-ups, a walk around the block and a 20-minute nap.

14. His personal trainer is always bragging about how he works with a London Olympic athlete. He usually forgets to mention which London Olympics she competed in, the 1948 ones.

15. The push-ups and walking he makes Jim do aren't exactly demanding exercises. They're so easy, even an old lady, Olympic champ or not, can do them.

Sorting Out Semicolons

A semicolon (;) is the punctuation mark that people use to create winks in electronic messages. You may be a bit surprised to discover that winking isn't its main job. Instead, semicolons link two complete sentences and separate items in a list when at least one of those items contains a comma. (Chapter 5 tells you more about this function of the semicolon.) One important note: don't join two sentences with a semicolon unless the ideas are closely related.

Get to work. Insert or delete semicolons as required in Fran's thoughts on a recent heat wave. If no semicolons need to be added or deleted, write 'correct' in the blank after the sentence.

Q. I swear I'm allergic to hot weather, I plan to crank up the office air con to the max this summer. _____

A. **I swear I'm allergic to hot weather; I plan to crank up the office air con to the max this summer.** The original sentence sends a comma to do a semicolon's job. Not a good idea!

16. The reasons why I hate the summer are sweat; sweat and sweat. _____

17. They say global warming is a myth; I bought a kilo of grapes today. _____

18. Tomorrow I'm planning my summer holidays to the North Pole; Ross, Alaska; and Antarctica. _____

19. I haven't heard the forecast for today; but I'm sure that it will be horribly sunny and mild. _____

20. The printer at work is jammed again; I may buy a winter coat. _____

21. Of course, winter coats are now on sale the fact that winter doesn't arrive for three more months is irrelevant. _____

22. Shops like to sell their goods in advance shoppers prefer to buy clothes that are right for the season. _____

23. Gately's has a sale on boots with fur linings; cashmere scarves; and leather gloves. _____

24. I should shop in Australia for clothes I need here in Manchester; they sell winter clothes in July over there. _____

25. July is quite cool in Melbourne, Victoria, Hobart, Tasmania and Sydney, New South Wales. _____

Placing Colons

You probably know this symbol (:) as the eyes in your smiley emoticon. But a colon also has another job (grammar experts like to think of this use as its day job) and that's to introduce a long quotation or a list.

Don't place a colon after a form of the verb *to be* or a preposition (*from, by, to* and similar words). Also, in the absolute strictest English (and not even we're that picky), a colon may introduce a list or a quotation only when the words before the colon form a complete sentence. If you follow this rule, you can't insert a colon after *for example*, but you can use one after 'take a look at *this example*'. But nowadays most business and technical handbooks allow colons after introductory phrases.

Time to 'colon-ise' (or not) the sentences in this section. Add or remove colons (and, if necessary, subtract other punctuation). If everything's okay, write 'correct' in the blank after the sentence.

Q. The weather, so far this year, can be described with these words, hot, sunny, dry and balmy. _____

A. **The weather, so far this year, can be described with these words: hot, sunny, dry and balmy.** The list of weather descriptions doesn't include *words*. Placing a comma after *words* allows *words* to blend in with the list of descriptions. A colon marks the separation between the introduction and the list.

26. As she watched the thermometer rise, Ellen smiled, frowned and then asked Jack: 'Should I feel guilty for enjoying the warmer weather if the higher temperatures are caused by global warming?' _____

27. Jack suggested that they do some research, and so they jumped in the car and popped down to the bookshop. They bought books by: Marvin Heatfree, Helen Icicle and October Surprise. _____

28. Halfway through the first book, Ellen said: 'Oops'. _____

29. She explained: that, according to Icicle, using the car for such short trips was apparently just the tip of the iceberg, as far as causes of global warming went. _____

30. Jack, who is easily confused, was confused about the iceberg. 'Driving can't be the tip of the iceberg: it says here that global warming has melted all the icebergs already!'

_____

Brain Strain: Extra Practice with Hyphens, Dashes, Colons, and Semicolons

Fran saw the all-inclusive holiday offer in Figure 6-1 online, and reckons that La Bocaville Resort is exactly the package deal she needs. Ignoring the wisdom of her choice, read the excerpt with an eye towards correct (actually, incorrect) punctuation. You need to find ten errors in hyphens, dashes, colons and semicolons. Cross out the offending marks and substitute the correct punctuation. Enjoy your trip!

Figure 6-1:
Sample
brochure
excerpt
from a
less-than-
alluring
resort.

La Bocaville Resort welcomes — you to the best holiday of your life!

When you arrive at the airport, you'll be greeted by: a stretch limo and a

driver, a complimentary box of chocolates and a bottle of mosquito

repellent. No need to hike 10 miles to La Bocaville the limo will take you

to the resort. After you've checked in to our lovingly-restored mansion,

you can choose from loads of fun-filled activities, including — volleyball

played with a water filled balloon and a chat with our secretary treasurer,

who is also our President of Having a Great Time! She's dedicated to

your holiday; and she knows her job depends on your happiness with La

Bocaville. You may also want to visit the BocaBite Restaurant:

conveniently located inside the pool area. Don't forget your

mozzie-spray!

Answers to Punctuation Problems

1 **second-string**. You're not talking about a second 'stringviolinist'. The two words (*second* and *string*) join forces to form one description of *violinist* – one who isn't in the group with the first-string violinists but is instead in with the second-string set.

2 **correct**. The adjective *ground-floor* is hyphenated correctly here.

3 **prototype**. The prefix *proto* doesn't need a hyphen.

4 **explained and anti-invader**. The *ex* in *explained* isn't a prefix so you don't need a hyphen. Two vowels together, created by the attachment of a prefix, call for a hyphen.

5 **correct**. The sentence links two prefixes to one word. The hyphen after the first prefix *anti-* tells the reader to attach it to *rat*.

6 **three times**, **five minutes** and **weekend**. No hyphens are needed here.

7 **Beethoven's Ninth**. *Beethoven* and *Ninth* don't form a compound noun and so no hyphen is needed.

8 **right foot and chilled-out**. Here, the adjective *right* is describing *foot* and so no hyphen is necessary. However, if you were describing a footballer as a '*right-footed* player' you would need one, just as you need one in the adjective *chilled-out*.

9 **never once**. No need for a hyphen here.

10 **extremely soothing and nursery school**. The first word describes the second. How *soothing* is The Screecher? *Extremely soothing*. They aren't linked as one description, and so no hyphen should be inserted. You don't need a hyphen with *nursery school* (or with *primary school* or *high school*).

11 **Jim plans to turn up at Debbie's party – I really don't know why – along with his personal trainer.** The interrupting words *I really don't know why* are set off by dashes. But just so you know, brackets would do the job too.

12 **'I can't believe that he has a trainer because –' sputtered Debbie.** Or, **correct**. The ellipses (three dots) do the job perfectly well, but the dash is more dramatic. The choice is yours.

13 **He needs help with his fitness routine – four push-ups, a walk around the block and a 20-minute nap.** The comma doesn't work after *routine* because otherwise the definition just blends in and creates a list of four things: *routine, push-ups, a walk and a nap*. If you're allergic to dashes, a colon or brackets may substitute here.

14 **His personal trainer is always bragging about how he works with a London Olympic athlete. He usually forgets to mention which London Olympics she competed in – the 1948 ones.** Or, **correct**. The dash makes the revelation of *the 1948 Olympics* more dramatic. But if the comma is your preference, go for it.

15 **The push-ups and walking he makes Jim do aren't exactly demanding exercises. They're so easy, even an old lady – Olympic champ or not – can do them.** A dash sets off the comment *Olympic champ or not* nicely here.

16 **The reasons why I hate the summer are sweat, sweat and sweat.** The items in this list are single words, not phrases containing commas, and so a semicolon isn't needed to separate the items in the list. A comma does the job just fine.

17 **They say global warming is a myth. I bought a kilo of grapes today.** A semicolon can't join two unrelated ideas. These random thoughts shouldn't be linked by a semicolon. Throwing two unrelated ideas together isn't a good idea. The reader requires a logical thread to follow between one sentence and another.

18 **correct.** Surprised? This list contains one item (*Ross, Alaska*) that includes a comma. If the three places were separated only by commas, the reader would not be sure whether *Ross* and *Alaska* were two items or one. The semicolon tells the reader where one item ends and another begins.

19 **I haven't heard the weather forecast for today, but I'm sure that it will be horribly sunny and mild.** The word *but* joins these two sentences, and so you don't need a semicolon as well. Change it to a comma. A comma precedes *and, but, or, nor* and similar words when they connect two complete sentences.

20 **The printer at work is jammed again. I may buy a winter coat.** The semicolon implies a relationship between the things it links. You can argue that the two halves of this sentence show that going shopping is a sensible option if the out-of-order printer is making work in the office impossible, but if the relationship isn't immediately clear to the reader, add some words or make two separate sentences. Better yet, add one or more sentences that join the two ideas in a logical way.

21 **Of course, winter coats are now on sale; the fact that winter doesn't arrive for three more months is irrelevant.** These two complete thoughts both relate to the maddening habit of selling out-of-season merchandise. Both statements are complete thoughts, and so a semicolon joins them correctly.

22 **Shops like to sell their goods in advance; shoppers prefer to buy clothes that are right for the season.** Each of these two statements can stand alone as a complete sentence, and that's why they can't be mashed together without a legal connection. You need a semicolon to link them.

23 **Gately's has a sale on boots with fur linings, cashmere scarves and leather gloves.** Take the semicolons out of this list. You need a semicolon to separate items in a list only if one of the items contains a comma – not the case here.

24 **correct.** In this sentence, two complete thoughts are correctly united by a semicolon.

25 **July is quite cool in Melbourne, Victoria; Hobart, Tasmania; and Sydney, New South Wales.** A comma separates the city and state in each of the items on this list, meaning that a semicolon is needed to separate one item from another.

26 **correct.** This quotation from Ellen is quite long and introduced by a complete sentence, and so introducing it with a colon is fine.

27 **Jack suggested that they do some research, and so they jumped in the car and popped down to the bookshop. They bought books by Marvin Heatfree, Helen Icicle and October Surprise.** Don't place a colon after the preposition *by*; just dive into the list.

28 **Halfway through the first book, Ellen said, 'Oops'.** The colon after *said* isn't a good idea because the quotation is short and run-of-the-mill. The colon is appropriate for long or extremely dramatic quotations only.

29 **She explained that, according to Icicle, using the car for such short trips was apparently just the tip of the iceberg, as far as causes of global warming went.** Drop the colon! It only interrupts the main idea, which shouldn't be interrupted. No punctuation is needed after *explained*.

30 **Jack, who is easily confused, was confused about the iceberg. 'Driving can't be the tip of the iceberg – it says here that global warming has melted all the icebergs already!'** If you want the punctuation equivalent of a drum-roll, go for a dash, not a colon.

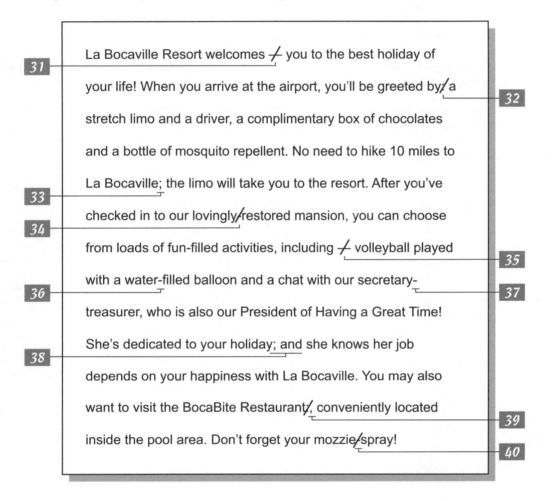

31 No punctuation needed here. Why? The sentence has no interrupting thought to be set off with a dash.

32 No punctuation needed here, because a colon should never follow a preposition (*by*, in this sentence).

33 Two complete sentences can't be placed next to each other without a joining word or appropriate punctuation. Insert a semicolon or make two separate sentences.

34 These two descriptions shouldn't be linked because they don't form a single description of *mansion*. Instead, *restored* describes *mansion* and *lovingly* describes *restored*. In general, words ending in *-ly* aren't linked by hyphens to other descriptions.

35 The dash is out of place here because *including* introduces the list. Leave the dash out.

36 The hyphen is needed to join *water* and *filled* because they create one description of the *balloon* and a very messy volleyball game.

37 The term *secretary-treasurer* is always hyphenated.

38 The two complete sentences are already joined by *and*. The semicolon is overkill, and so leave the *and* out, or drop the semicolon.

39 The colon after *Restaurant* implies that a list or quotation follows, but the next few words don't fit into those categories. A comma goes better here.

40 *Mozzie* describes *spray*. No hyphen is needed.

Chapter 7

One Small Mark, a Whole New Meaning: Apostrophes

In This Chapter

▶ Shortening words and numbers with apostrophes

▶ Showing possession

An apostrophe is a little hook (') that snags many writers at some point. With a little practice, however, you can confidently pop apostrophes into the proper places in your writing.

The most common apostrophe mistake is to place one inappropriately. Don't use an apostrophe in either of the following circumstances:

✔ **To create a plural:** You have *one arrow* and *two arrows,* not *two arrow's.* The no-apostrophe-for-plural rule holds true for names. The golfer Tiger Woods comes from a family whose name is Woods. Other people in his family are the *Woodses*, not the *Woods'.*

✔ **With a possessive pronoun:** Don't use an apostrophe in a possessive pronoun such as *my*, *your*, *his*, *hers*, *its*, *ours*, *theirs*, *whose* and so on.

Traditionally, an apostrophe was used to create a particular (and unusual) type of plural – the plural of symbols and numerals. It was also used to create the plural of a word referred to as a word. (Confused? Keep reading for an example.) In old books you may find a sentence such as *Henry sprinkled 20's and therefore's throughout his story*. Don't panic. Grammar goes through changes and what was once correct is now out-of-date. Just recognise an old-fashioned custom and move on with your life.

Hook into the exercises in this chapter so that apostrophes never catch you out again.

Putting Words on a Diet: Contractions

Apostrophes shorten words by replacing one or more letters. The shortened word, or *contraction* (not to be confused with the thing pregnant women scream through), adds an informal, conversational tone to your writing.

Contractions are rarely used (or acceptable) in formal writing.

We list the most frequently used contractions, paired with their long forms, in Table 7-1.

Table 7-1	Frequently Used Contractions
Long Form	*Contraction*
Are not	Aren't
Cannot	Can't
Could have	Could've
Could not	Couldn't
Do not	Don't
He has	He's
He is	He's
He will	He'll
He would	He'd
I am	I'm
I had	I'd
I will	I'll
I would	I'd
It is	It's
She has	She's
She is	She's
She will	She'll
Should have	Should've
Should not	Shouldn't
They are	They're
They have	They've
They will	They'll
We are	We're
We have	We've
We will	We'll
Were not	Weren't
Will not	Won't
Would have	Would've
Would not	Wouldn't
You are	You're
You have	You've
You will	You'll
You would	You'd

If you want to make a contraction that isn't in Table 7-1, check your dictionary to make sure that it exists and is acceptable. In Scotland, for example, *amn't* is a perfectly acceptable contraction of *am not*. The American English version of that contraction is *ain't* and although in common use, this contraction isn't allowed in standard, formal speech and writing.

An apostrophe shortens a word, and a common mistake is to re-expand a contraction into something it was never meant to be. The contraction *should've*, for example, is short for *should have*, not *should of*. The expressions *should of*, *could of* and *would of* don't exist in standard English.

Contractions aren't just for words. You can also slice numbers out of your writing with apostrophes, especially in informal circumstances. This punctuation mark enables you to graduate in '07, get your first job in '08 and marry in '15.

Feel like flexing your apostrophe muscles? Look at the underlined words in these sentences and change them into contractions. Write your answers in the blanks.

0. Adam said that <u>he would</u> go to the shop to buy nuts. _____

A. **he'd.** This apostrophe is a real bargain because you save four letters.

1. 'Peanuts are not the best choice because a lot of people are allergic to them,' commented Pam. _____

2. '<u>I am</u> sure that <u>you will</u> choose a better appetiser,' she added. _____ _____

3. The shop <u>will not</u> take responsibility for what you buy. _____

4. <u>Do not</u> underestimate the power of a good appetiser. _____

5. Your guests will think that <u>you are</u> cheap if you <u>do not</u> provide at least one bowl of nuts. _____ _____

6. Adam <u>would have</u> bought caviar, but then he <u>would not</u> have had enough money for dessert. _____ _____

7. 'You <u>cannot</u> neglect pudding,' said Adam. _____

8. Adam usually likes to serve a fancy pud, like banoffee pie with ice cream, but <u>he is</u> watching his weight. _____

9. 'If they created a better low-fat ice cream,' he often says, '<u>I would</u> eat a ton of it.' _____

10. 'Yes, and then <u>you would</u> weigh a ton yourself,' snaps Pam. _____

11. <u>She is</u> a bit grumpy when faced with diet food. _____

12. Of course, Adam <u>could have</u> been a little more diplomatic the last time he saw Pam in her new dress and said, 'Oh, is tight the new black?' _____

13. Adam is planning to serve a special dessert wine, Chateau Adam <u>1999</u>, to his guests. _____

14. He's organising a reunion for the class of <u>2006</u>. _____

15. <u>We are</u> planning to attend, but <u>we will</u> bring our own refreshments! _____ _____

16. A few people <u>cannot</u> make it. _____

17. <u>We are</u> preparing a guessing game for the reunion. _____

18. Pam wants to know <u>who is</u> in charge of creating the questions. _____

19. Adam is. <u>He is</u> the best man for the job because he knows the most gossip. _____

20. <u>We will</u> have to check the questions before the party. _____

21. <u>He would</u> like nothing better than to shock everyone with his prying questions. _____

22. At our last reunion, Adam <u>should have</u> been more careful. _____

23. Three people burst out crying because they <u>had not</u> heard the latest bit of gossip about themselves until Adam opened his big mouth. _____

24. Adam applied for a job at one of those celebrity gossip magazines. He <u>did not</u> get it. _____

25. They said his references <u>were not</u> good enough. He <u>should have</u> asked the class of <u>2006</u> to write his references for him! _____ _____

Taking Possession

The *pen of my* aunt that you might of heard about in foreign-language classes becomes *my aunt's pen* in standard English, with the help of an apostrophe. (We're just joking with *might of*; we mean *might have*, of course!) To show possession with apostrophes, keep the following rules in mind:

- ✔ **Singular owner:** Attach an apostrophe and the letter *s* (in that order) to a singular person, place or thing to express possession (*Henry's* tooth, *Rome's* dentists, the *drill's* annoying whine).

- ✔ **Plural owner:** Attach an apostrophe to a regular plural (one that ends in *s*) to express possession (the *cities'* mayors, the *officials'* meetings, the *politicians'* expenses).

- ✔ **Irregular plural owner:** Add an apostrophe and the letter *s* (in that order) to an irregular plural (one that doesn't end in *s*) to express possession (the *women's* children, the *children's* toys).

- ✔ **Joint ownership:** If two or more people own something jointly, add an apostrophe and an *s* (in that order) to the last name (*Jerry and Kaori's* sofa; *George, Danny and Abdul's* flat).

- ✔ **Separate ownership:** If two or more people own things separately, everyone gets an apostrophe and an s (*Joe's* and *Alex's* toys; *Lizzie's*, *Ellen's* and *Isla's* shoes).

- ✔ **Hyphenated owner:** If the word you're working with is hyphenated, just attach the apostrophe and *s* to the end (*mother-in-law's* office). For plurals ending in s, attach the apostrophe only (three *secretary-treasurers'* accounts).

- ✔ **Time and money:** Okay, Father Time and Ms Euro don't own anything. Nevertheless, time and money may be possessive in expressions such as *next week's test, two hours' homework, a day's pay* and so forth. Follow the rules for singular and plural owners, as explained at the beginning of this bulleted list.

Easy stuff, right? Now, here's your chance to apply your knowledge. Turn the underlined word (or words) into the possessive form. Write your answers in the blanks provided.

O. This <u>year</u> back-to-basics cooking competition is right up <u>Jill</u> street.

A. **year's, Jill's**. Two singular owners. The time expression *year* takes an apostrophe and so does *Jill*.

26. <u>Johnny</u> style of baking, on the other hand, is a bit more flamboyant.
_____

27. He invested three <u>months</u> work in finalising his recipe for the competition.
_____

28. Johnny will get a little help from his brothers; <u>Brian and Martin</u> eggs, which they started to sell a few years ago, will be one of his key ingredients.
_____

29. The <u>mens</u> eggs are strictly organic, and come with the association of organic <u>farmers</u> seal of approval. _____

30. <u>Jill</u> budget is pretty small. She can't afford the <u>brothers</u> organic products.
_____

31. However, Jill has a secret ingredient and, even though it costs her a <u>day</u> pay, she thinks it's worth every penny. _____

32. Through offering a friend of a friend the promise of Victoria sponges for life and a small donation to the charity of her choice, Jill found out what the three <u>judges</u> favourite pies are. _____

33. Jill decided to disregard the two minor <u>judges</u> likes and dislikes, and focus all her attention on the main <u>judge</u> preferences. _____

34. It seems the chief <u>examiner</u> fancy is tickled by lemon meringue pies. _____

35. Johnny, meanwhile, is making a six-egg chocolate cake, following his <u>great-grand-mother</u> recipe. He'll use one of his <u>grandmother</u> hand-painted plates to display the cake. _____

36. <u>Johnny</u> success at the competition is not certain because although his chocolate cake is usually very successful, sometimes it doesn't turn out well at all.
_____

37. <u>Jill</u> final preparation for winning involved asking to borrow her <u>mum</u> special silver cake stand. _____

38. Her mum turned down <u>Jill</u> request. _____

39. Ten <u>hours</u> begging did no good at all. _____

40. In the end, Jill thought an old, chipped cake plate may be more in keeping with the <u>competition</u> keep-it-simple theme. _____

41. What <u>Jill</u> informant failed to tell her is that the head <u>judge</u> pet hate is chipped crockery. _____

42. The head judge is in her room now getting the <u>finalists</u> ribbons ready. _____

43. She hopes that after ten <u>years</u> judging, she will finally taste a cake as good as her <u>mother</u>. _____

44. But it's not all about taste. Judge Jean thinks that a <u>cake</u> presentation is equally important. _____

45. <u>Jean</u> toughest choice would be a perfect meringue on a cracked plate versus a so-so chocolate cake on a beautiful platter. _____

46. So will the winning ribbon be pinned on <u>Jill</u> jacket or <u>Johnny</u> jumper? _____

Brain Strain: Extra Practice with Apostrophes

Ciaran's advice for making potato and carrot soup in his kitchen in Figure 7-1 needs some serious editing. Check the apostrophe situation. You need to find 11 places to insert and five places to delete an apostrophe.

Ciaran's Potato and Carrot Soup

A. Peel potatoe's and carrot's and put in pot of boiling water.

B. After 5 minutes boiling, season potatoes'.

C. Put the salt back in the cupboard.

D. Close the cupboard doors gently. You dont want to disturb the peace in the kitchen.

E. Open the cupboard and check whether the salt has moved.

F. If it has, its one of Jennys old tricks.

G. Dont get freaked out. She's been here since 83 and she's in no hurry to go anywhere.

H. Call the Busters number. You know, the one you said youd never call because you don't believe in ghosts'.

I. When you cant find the phone, talk to Jenny calmly but firmly and demand that the phone is put back in it's place at once.

J. While youre waiting for that (and it may be some time), check your potatoes. You wouldnt want them to overcook now, would you?

Figure 7-1:
Recipe
full of
apostrophe
mistakes.

Answers to Apostrophe Problems

1 **aren't**. The contraction drops the letter *o* and substitutes an apostrophe.

2 **I'm, you'll**. In the first contraction, the apostrophe replaces the letter *a*. In the second, it replaces two letters, *w* and *i*.

3 **won't**. This contraction is irregular. Illogical though it may seem, *won't* is the contraction of *will not*.

4 **Don't**. Drop the space between the two words, eliminate the second *o* and insert an apostrophe to create *don't*.

5 **you're, don't**. The first contraction sounds exactly like the possessive pronoun *your*. Don't confuse the two. (For extra help on possessives, take a look at Chapter 3.)

6 **would've, wouldn't**. Take care with the first contraction; many people mistakenly re-expand the contraction *would've* to *would of* (instead of the correct expansion, *would have*). The second contraction, *wouldn't*, substitutes an apostrophe for the letter *o*.

7 **can't**. Did you know that *cannot* is written as one word? The contraction also is one word, with an apostrophe knocking out an *n* and an *o*.

8 **he's**. The same contraction works for *he is* (as in this sentence) and *he has*.

9 **I'd**. You're dropping the letters *woul*.

10 **you'd**. The same contraction works for *you would* (as in this sentence) and *you had*.

11 **She's**. The apostrophe replaces the letter *i*.

12 **could've**. Be careful in re-expanding this contraction. A common mistake is to write *could of*, an expression that's a total no-no.

13 **'99**. A date may be shortened, especially if you're out with Adam. Just be sure that the context of the sentence doesn't lead the reader to imagine a different century (*2099*, perhaps). This one is fairly clear, given that we're nowhere near *2099*, and *1899* is probably not the intended meaning.

14 **'06**. Not much chance of the reader misunderstanding which numbers are missing here (unless he or she is really old)!

15 **we're, we'll**. The apostrophes replace the letters *a* and *wi*.

16 **can't.** The apostrophe replaces the letters *no*.

17 **We're**. The apostrophe replaces the letter *a* in this contraction of *we are*.

18 **who's**. The apostrophe replaces the letter *i* in this one.

19 **He's**. Only one letter is replaced here (*i*), but in this fast-paced world, every letter counts.

20 **We'll**. This contraction is a bargain. Drop two letters (*wi*) and pop in an apostrophe instead.

21 **He'd**. The apostrophe is a real space saver in this contraction; it replaces *woul*.

22 **should've**. If you take out the *ha*, you can insert an apostrophe and create this contraction.

23 **hadn't**. We're not sure why anyone cares about gossip, but we are sure that this contraction has an apostrophe in place of the letter *o*.

24   **didn't**. Drop the *o* and replace it with an apostrophe.

25   **weren't, should've, '06**. You get three contractions for the price of one here. In the first blank, you substitute an apostrophe for the letter *o*. In the second, take out the *av* and put in apostrophe. In the third, the apostrophe replaces the numbers *1* and *9*.

26   **Johnny's**. Johnny owns the style, and so you just need to attach an apostrophe and an *s* to a singular form to create a singular possessive.

27   **three months'**. The value of time and money can be expressed with a possessive form. Because you're talking about *months*, a plural, the apostrophe goes after the *s*.

28   **Brian and Martin's**. The sentence tells you that the men own the eggs together, and so only one apostrophe is needed. It's placed after the last owner's name. The possessive pronoun *his*, like all possessive pronouns, has no apostrophe.

29   **men's, farmers'**. The first form is an irregular plural (not ending in *s*), and so you tack on an apostrophe and an *s*. The second is regular plural possessive, meaning that you just tack an apostrophe onto the *s*.

30   **Jill's, brothers'**. The first form is singular, and so you add an apostrophe and an *s*. The second form is a regular plural, indicating that you just add the apostrophe.

31   **a day's.** This one falls into the time/money category, and because day is singular, you add an apostrophe and an *s*.

32   **judges'**. Here we're talking about more than one judge, and so that's a regular plural. All you have to do is add an apostrophe to the *s*.

33   **judges', judge's**. The first form is a regular plural – more than one judge, and so you add an apostrophe after the *s*. The second one refers to only one judge, and so you put the apostrophe before the *s*.

34   **examiner's**. To create a possessive of a singular noun, just attach an apostrophe and an *s*.

35   **great-grandmother's, grandmother's**. Both these answers are simple, singular possessives, and so an apostrophe and an *s* does the trick, twice.

36   **Johnny's**. This is the *success* that belongs to *Johnny,* and so an apostrophe and the letter *s* is needed.

37   **Jill's, mum's**. An apostrophe and an *s* is needed for the *final preparation*. To show that the *special silver cake tray* belongs to her *mum*, you need to add an apostrophe and the letter *s* to the word *mum*.

38   **Jill's**. An apostrophe and an *s* are all that are needed here.

39   **Ten hours'**. The apostrophe creates an expression meaning *ten hours of begging*. Because *hours* is plural, only an apostrophe is added.

40   **competition's**. A simple, regular singular noun needs only an apostrophe and an *s* to make the word possessive.

41   **Jill's, judge's**. You have to add an apostrophe and an *s* to show that the *informant* belongs to *Jill*. Only one head judge exists and so the apostrophe comes before the *s*.

42   **finalists'**. To create a plural possessive, add an apostrophe after the letter *s*.

43 **years' mother's.** *Years* is plural, and so you need only to add an apostrophe to create an expression that means *ten years of judging*. *Mother*, on the other hand, is singular, and so you add an apostrophe and then the *s*.

44 **cake's.** This regular singular noun needs only an apostrophe before the *s* to become possessive.

45 **Jean's.** Just add an apostrophe and the letter *s* to show that the decision belongs to Jean.

46 **Jill's, Johnny's.** To show that the clothes belong to each of the people, add an apostrophe and the letter *s* to each of their names.

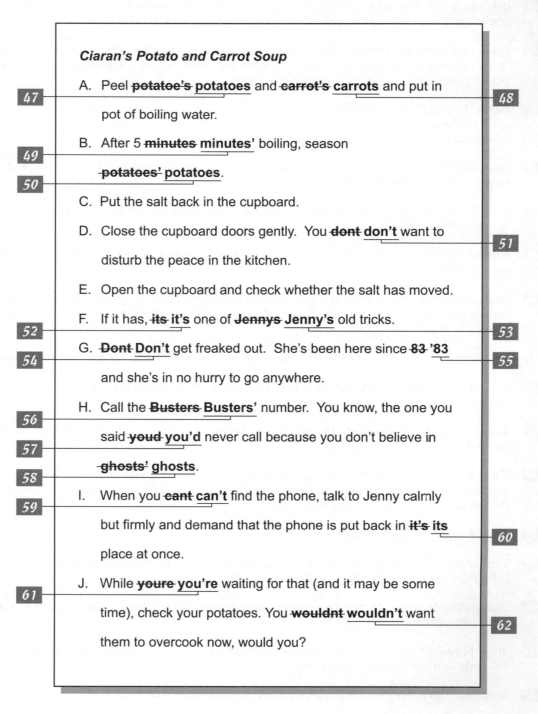

Ciaran's Potato and Carrot Soup

A. Peel ~~potatoe's~~ potatoes and ~~carrot's~~ carrots and put in   **47** ... **48**

   pot of boiling water.

B. After 5 ~~minutes~~ minutes' boiling, season   **49**

   ~~potatoes'~~ potatoes.   **50**

C. Put the salt back in the cupboard.

D. Close the cupboard doors gently. You ~~dont~~ don't want to   **51**

   disturb the peace in the kitchen.

E. Open the cupboard and check whether the salt has moved.

F. If it has, ~~its~~ it's one of ~~Jennys~~ Jenny's old tricks.   **52** ... **53**

G. ~~Dont~~ Don't get freaked out. She's been here since ~~83~~ '83   **54** ... **55**

   and she's in no hurry to go anywhere.

H. Call the ~~Busters~~ Busters' number. You know, the one you   **56**

   said ~~youd~~ you'd never call because you don't believe in   **57**

   ~~ghosts'~~ ghosts.   **58**

I. When you ~~cant~~ can't find the phone, talk to Jenny calmly   **59**

   but firmly and demand that the phone is put back in ~~it's~~ its   **60**

   place at once.

J. While ~~youre~~ you're waiting for that (and it may be some   **61**

   time), check your potatoes. You ~~wouldnt~~ wouldn't want   **62**

   them to overcook now, would you?

47 A simple plural (*potatoes*) doesn't need an apostrophe.

48 This instance is another simple plural (*carrots*), and so there's no need for an apostrophe.

49 The expression *5 minutes* needs an apostrophe after the s.

50 *Potatoes* is just a plain plural, not a possessive, and so it doesn't need an apostrophe.

51 In this contraction, an apostrophe replaces the missing letter *o*.

52 The full form here is *it is*. When you make a contraction, you need an apostrophe to replace the second missing *i*.

53 The tricks belong to Jenny (in a manner of speaking), and so the apostrophe is needed to show possession.

54 In this contraction, the apostrophe replaces the letter *o* again.

55 The missing numbers here are *19* (or, if Jenny is very old, maybe *18* or even *17*).

56 *Busters* is a plural noun (the name of a family or a business, perhaps), and so to show that the number belongs to the Busters, use *s'*.

57 In this contraction, an apostrophe replaces the letters *woul*.

58 This simple plural (*ghosts*) doesn't take an apostrophe.

59 In this contraction, an apostrophe replaces the missing letter *no*.

60 Possessive pronouns (such as *its*, *hers*, *mine*, *yours*) don't have apostrophes.

61 In this contraction, an apostrophe replaces the letter *a*.

62 Here, you use an apostrophe to show that the *o* is missing.

Chapter 8

'Let Me Speak!' Quotation Marks

Quotation marks (' ' – also known as quotes, quote marks or inverted commas) can be confusing because of all the rules connected with them and the fact that many of these rules come from custom and tradition rather than logic. But if you're willing to put in a little effort, you can crack the code of these important punctuation marks.

Quotation marks have several important jobs:

✔ **Directly quoted material:** Quotation marks surround words drawn from another person's speech or writing. In fiction, quotation marks indicate dialogue: *'I wish someone would send me a single rose,' sighed Sandy.* Quotation marks don't belong in a sentence that summarises or reports speech, such as *He said that he had caught a cold.*

✔ **Titles:** Quotation marks are used around the titles of certain types of literary or other works of art: for example, *Emily's first poem, 'Ode on a Grecian Olive', was printed in the school magazine.*

✔ **Distancing:** Quotation marks are sometimes used to indicate slang or to tell the reader that the writer doesn't agree with the words inside the quotation marks: *I don't always appreciate Emily's 'art'.*

In this chapter, you can practise direct quotes and titles, along with a few other delights, including the interaction between quotation marks and other punctuation, and quotes embedded inside other quotes. Let the games begin.

Giving Written Words a Voice: Punctuating Direct Quotations

The basic rule governing quotation marks is simple: place them around words drawn directly from someone else's speech or writing to distinguish their ideas and expression from your own. Or, if you're writing a novel or short story, place quotation marks around dialogue. The tricky part is the interaction between quotation marks and other punctuation, such as commas, full stops and the like:

✔ **If the quotation indicates who speaks (*Alfie screamed, she murmured* and so on), that information needs to be separated from the quotation by a comma:**

   • *Before* **the quotation:** If the speaker information is *before* the quotation, the comma comes before the opening quotation mark: *Sharon sighed, 'I hate hay fever season.'*

- *After* **the quotation:** If the speaker information is *after* the quotation, the comma goes inside the closing quotation mark: *'What a large snout you have,' whispered Richard lovingly.*

- *In the middle of* **the quotation:** If the speaker information appears *in the middle* of a quotation, a comma is placed *between* the first closing quotation mark and the speaker information, and another one is placed after the speaker information: *'Here's the handkerchief,' said Richard, 'that I borrowed last week.'*

Just because you're quoting, don't think you have a licence to create a run-on sentence. (Flip to Chapter 4 for practice with run-ons.) If you have two complete sentences, quoted or not, they need to be written as separate sentences or linked correctly with a semicolon or a joining word such as *and*.

✔ **If the quotation ends the sentence, the full stop goes *inside* the closing quotation mark:** *Richard added, 'I would like to kiss the tip of your mammoth ear.'*

✔ **If the quotation is a question or an exclamation, the question mark or the exclamation mark goes *inside* the closing quotation mark:** *'Why did you slap me?' asked Richard. 'I was complimenting you!'*

Question and exclamation marks serve as sentence-ending punctuation, and so you don't need to add a full stop after the closing quotation mark.

✔ If the quotation is neither question nor exclamation, but the sentence in which the quotation appears is, the question mark or exclamation point goes outside the closing quotation mark: *I can't believe that Richard said he's 'a world class lover'! Do you think Sharon will ever get over his comment about her 'mammoth ear'?*

If the quotation is tucked into the sentence without speaker information, as in the two preceding sample sentences, no comma separates the quotation from the rest of the sentence. Nor does the quotation begin with a capital letter. Quotations with speaker information, on the other hand, always begin with a capital letter, regardless of where the information about the speaker falls. In an interrupted quotation (when the speaker info is in the middle), the first word of the first half of the quotation is capitalised, but the first word of the second half isn't, unless it's a proper name, of course.

✔ **If semicolons and colons are involved, they always go outside the quotation marks:** *Mary claimed that the book was 'way too difficult'; I told her to read it anyway.*

Enough explanation! Are you ready for some practice? Your job is to identify the direct quote and fill in the proper punctuation, in the proper order, in the proper places. You may find extra information in brackets at the end of the sentence.

Q. The annual rounders match is tomorrow said Becky, trying to sound enthusiastic.

A. **'The annual rounders match is tomorrow,' said Becky, trying to sound enthusiastic.** Don't give yourself top marks unless you placed the comma inside the closing quotation marks.

1. Oh goody said Abdul sarcastically.

2. I'll bat if you like offered Gus.

3. Andy interrupted I'll take third base.

4. No one knew how to answer Andy, who in the past has been called overly sensitive.

5. You know you don't have to Becky said.

6. But I suppose someone's got to save the day, as usual, said Andy, walking back into his office.

7. The marketing lot will whip us again Abdul said if we can't get Andy to sit it out this year.

8. But what can we do asked Becky. (Becky is asking a question.)

9. The prospect of losing yet again was beginning to get them down. There will never be an end to our humiliation cried Abdul. (The statement Abdul is making is an exclamation.)

10. The boss can't catch a ball said Gus so we get penalised. It's not fair. (The final statement Gus is making is an exclamation.)

11. The final score line is always blamed on someone else. It's never Andy's fault noted Abdul. (The first sentence isn't a quote from Abdul but the second one is.)

12. It really isn't his fault observed Gus. He couldn't catch a cold if he stood naked in the North Pole for a month.

13. Who's gone to the North Pole for a month asked Andy, sneaking up behind them, pretending to go to the photocopier. (What Andy says is a question.)

14. Don't tell me I'm going to have to bat as well he said.

15. Oh no. I was just saying sometimes the park's like the North Pole so we should warm up before the game said Becky. Isn't that right Gus. (Becky's final sentence is a question.)

16. Just the key details, Becky dear. Bring my kit down to the park like a love, and I'll be there, warmed up and ready to go said Andy.

17. A little later, Becky enquired Do you want a cup of coffee and a bit of a practice for tomorrow's game. (Becky is asking a question.)

18. Sure said the boss. (What the boss says is an exclamation.)

19. Well then, catch shouted Becky, Gus and Abdul together. (The statement is also an exclamation.)

20. Perhaps not surprisingly Andy didn't manage to catch the powdered coffee, the carton of milk or the kettle of hot water. As the three fired employees left the building for the last time, Becky asked Anyone for cricket. (Becky is asking a question.)

Embedding One Quotation inside Another

Speeches inside speeches (or embedded quotes) don't turn up very frequently, but when they do, you have to pay close attention. Here's the deal: the embedded quotation is enclosed in double quotation marks (" ") and the surrounding quotation is placed in the usual single quotation marks (' '). So far, so good. The problem comes when this sort of situation requires other punctuation, and it usually does. Follow these guidelines:

✔ **If the embedded quotation is at the end of the larger quotation,** the two closing quotation marks are next to each other, with the double mark first, followed by the single one. Any commas or full stops you need go between the two sets of closing marks: *'I hate it when he calls me "dear",' said Becky.* Question marks and exclamation marks follow the rule of logic: if the internal quotation is a question or an exclamation, place the *?* or the *!* inside the double closing mark – that is, inside the inner quote. If the internal quotation isn't a question or an exclamation but the larger quotation is, place the *?* or the *!* outside the double closing mark but inside the single closing mark (or, more simply, put the mark in between the two different quotation marks): *Gus screamed, 'I can't believe he thinks he'll "save the day"!'*

✔ **If the embedded quotation is at the beginning or in the middle of the larger quotation,** any commas surrounding it follow the rules described in the preceding section, 'Giving Written Words a Voice: Punctuating Direct Quotations'. In other words, commas that precede the embedded quotation go in front of the opening double quotation mark. Commas that follow the embedded quotation go between the double and single closing quotation mark: *Becky cried, '"A coffee now" is what he demanded!'* and *'When Andy started talking about "saving the day", I wanted to cry,' said Abdul.*

This chapter follows the rules of standard British English. American English reverses the use of single and double quotation marks. If you're in the US or following American writing conventions, you may want to write single quotation marks wherever we use doubles, and doubles wherever we pop in single quotation marks.

Punctuation inside embedded quotations is also slightly different in American English. Any commas, full stops, question marks or exclamation marks go inside both closing quotation marks, unless the embedded quotation itself isn't a question or exclamation, but the whole sentence is. In that case it's similar to UK English and the question mark or the exclamation mark goes between the two sets of final quotation marks.

Can you place the quotation marks and other punctuation in the right places in these sentences? Write the appropriate punctuation marks in the appropriate spots. We provide some information to help you in brackets at the end of the sentence.

Q. I think that I shall never see a summer's romance more lovely and more temperate intoned Richard, who believes that quoting Shakespeare is the best way to impress women. (The embedded quote is *more lovely and more temperate.*)

A. **'I think that I shall never see a summer's romance "more lovely and more temperate",' intoned Richard, who believes that quoting Shakespeare is the best way to impress women.** Notice that the comma after *temperate* goes between the double and single closing quotation marks.

21. Jane Austen would have a lot to say to Richard about his more lovely nonsense commented Clare. It was the day after Sharon and Richard's conversation and Sharon was telling her best friend Clare every last word of it. (The embedded quotation is *more lovely.*)

22. Clare said My favourite quotation concerns a truth universally acknowledged. (The embedded quotation is *a truth universally acknowledged.*)

23. Did Richard really ask about Shakespeare's sonatas asked Sharon's grandma, who still didn't have in her hearing aid even though it was late afternoon. Despite Sharon's best attempts to talk to Clare, Grandma wouldn't stop interrupting. (Grandma is asking a question and the embedded quotation is *Shakespeare's sonatas*.)

24. Sharon replied No, Grandma, he asked about Shakespeare's bonnets. (The embedded quotation is *Shakespeare's bonnets*.)

25. I can't believe he talked about beauteous bonnets snorted Clare. (The embedded quotation is *beauteous bonnets*. Just to make this one harder, make the larger quotation an exclamation.)

26. Clare has no patience for what she terms Richard's posturing explained Sharon to Grandma, who was still looking a bit confused. (The embedded quotation is *Richard's posturing*.)

27. Grandma asked Don't you think that Richard is what you young ones call an educated bloke who means well. (The embedded quotation is *an educated bloke who means well*, and Grandma is asking a question.)

28. No, he keeps telling me he's just an ordinary guy who happens to be a bit of a Romeo said Sharon. (The embedded quotation is *just an ordinary guy who happens to be a bit of a Romeo*.)

29. I can't believe that anyone would call him a bit of a Romeo sneered Clare. (The embedded quotation is *a bit of a Romeo*. The larger quote is an exclamation.)

30. And with his quaint millionaire's mansion, buck teeth and wet-look comb-over said Grandma I can't believe he thinks he's just an ordinary guy. (The embedded quotation is *just an ordinary guy*.)

Punctuating Titles

Punctuating titles is easy and uses these rules:

- ✔ **Titles that are italicised or underlined:** The titles of full-length works – novels, magazines, television series, plays, epic poems, films and the like – are italicised or underlined. Italics are more usual nowadays (underlining was used when most people had only a typewriter).

- ✔ **Titles that are placed in quotation marks:** The titles of shorter works or parts of a whole – a poem, a short story, a single episode of a television show, a song, an article and so on – aren't italicised or underlined; they're placed in quotation marks.

Okay, we admit that pamphlets or newsletters can be a bit problematic. Even though they're short, they fall into the italicised or underlined category because regardless of length, they're still considered full-length works.

These rules apply to titles that are tucked into sentences. Centred titles, all alone at the top of a page, don't get any special treatment: no italics, no underlining and no quotation marks. The centring and placement are enough to call attention to the title, and so nothing else is necessary, unless the centred title refers to some other literary work. In that case the embedded title is punctuated as described in the preceding bulleted list.

When a title in quotation marks is part of a sentence, it sometimes tangles with other punctuation marks. The rules in UK English call for any commas or full stops after the title to be placed outside the quotes. So if the title is the last thing in the sentence, the full stop of the sentence comes after the closing quotation mark. Question and exclamation marks also go outside the quotation marks, unless they're actually part of the title. For example, suppose you write a poem and call it 'Why Is the Sky Blue Again?' The question mark appears inside the closing quotation mark because it's part of the title.

If a title that ends with a question mark is the last thing in a sentence, the question mark ends the sentence. Don't place both a full stop and a question mark at the end of the same sentence.

All set for a practice lap around the track? Decide whether the titles below need to be italicised or put in quotation marks, and add any ending punctuation when necessary. Occasionally, we place some information to help you in brackets at the end of a sentence.

Q. Have you read Sarah's latest poem, Sonnet for the Tax Assessor. (The sentence is a question, but the title isn't.)

A. **Have you read Sarah's latest poem, 'Sonnet for the Tax Assessor'?** The title of a poem takes quotation marks. Question marks don't go inside the quotation marks unless the title itself contains a question.

31. Sarah's hoping that it'll be chosen for the collection entitled Tax Day Blues.

32. The best-seller, Publish Your Poetry Now, inspired Sarah.

33. Some of us, who have been subjected to more than one evening of her poetry reading, wish that she'd read the recent newspaper article, Forget About Writing Poetry.

34. Her sister Julie is a musician. She took pity on Sarah and turned Sarah's poem into a song. She changed the name to Sonata Taxiana.

35. She's including it on her next CD, Songs of April.

36. When Sarah called me, I promised I'd listen to the CD when it came out. I promptly hung up and went back to watching my favourite TV show, Strictly Come Bossy Big Brother and Sister Apprentice.

37. I was in the middle of the episode called Sister Knows Everything in which the main character hacks into her brother's computer and deletes an entire year's worth of his school work.

38. It gave me an idea. Maybe I could log on as Sarah and delete all her dreadful poems. I could write a newspaper article on why I did it called How I Saved the World from Sarah's Truly Awful Verses.

39. When I finally logged onto Sarah's computer the next day, I found the drafts of her latest book – No More Poetry! How to Booby-trap Hackers and Horrible Friends You Can't Trust to Leave your Computer Alone for Two Minutes.

40. I'm writing this blog, provisional title: Keep Out from a chilly, strange kind of waiting room. I was told there's a hell of a wait but that I've not to worry. Apparently I'll be nice and toasty eventually. Forever. Thanks Sarah! (The two word title of the blog is an exclamation.)

Brain Strain: Extra Practice with Quotation Marks

A school report, by one Tommy Brainfree, is reproduced in Figure 8-1. Identify ten places where a set of quotation marks needs to be inserted. Place the quotation marks correctly in relation to other punctuation in the sentence. In addition, make sure that you underline titles (to indicate italics) where appropriate.

What I Did on my Two Week Summer Camping Trip

by Tommy Brainfree

This summer I went to Camp Waterbug, which was the setting for a famous poem by William Long entitled Water, Bugs and Spiders, Yuk! At Camp Waterbug I learned to paddle a canoe without tipping it over more than twice a trip. The camp leader even wrote an article about me in the camp newsletter, Waterbug Bites. The article was called How to Tip a Canoe. The camp leader said, Brainfree is well named. I was not upset because I believed him (eventually) when he explained that the comment was an editing error.

Are you sure? I asked him when I first read it.

You know, he responded quickly, that I have a lot of respect for you. I nodded in agreement, but that night I placed 47 frogs under his sheets, just in case he thought about writing How to Fool a Camper. One of the frogs had a little label on his leg that read JUST KIDDING TOO.

At the last campfire gathering I sang a song from the musical Fiddler on the Roof. The song was called If I Were a Rich Man. I changed the first line to If I Were a Camp Leader. I won't quote the rest of the song because I sang it to my mum when I got home, and then had to sit on the naughty step for the rest of my summer holiday. I am so happy to be back at school. There's a sentence I bet you never thought you'd read, Mrs Jacobs.

Figure 8-1:
School report without quotation marks.

Answers to Quotation Problems

1   **'Oh goody,' said Abdul sarcastically.** The directly quoted words, *Oh goody*, are enclosed in quotation marks. The comma before the speaker information *said Abdul* goes inside the closing quotation mark.

2   **'I'll bat if you like,' offered Gus.** The speaker information comes at the end in this sentence, and so the comma is placed inside the closing quotation mark.

3   **Andy interrupted, 'I'll take third base.'** The speaker information comes first in this sentence, and so you need to place the comma before the opening quotation mark. The full stop that ends the sentence goes inside the closing quotation mark.

4   **No one knew how to answer Andy, who in the past has been called 'overly sensitive'.** The quotation is short, but it still needs some quotation marks. The full stop at the end of the sentence is placed outside the closing quotation mark. Notice that this quote doesn't have any speaker information, and so it isn't preceded by a comma and doesn't start with a capital letter.

5   **'You know you don't have to,' Becky said.** The speaker information (*Becky said*) comes at the end in this sentence, and so the comma is placed inside the closing quotation mark.

6   **'But I suppose someone's got to save the day, as usual,' said Andy, walking back into his office.** Here the speaker information comes after the quote, and so you need a comma after *usual*.

7   **'The marketing lot will whip us again,' Abdul said, 'if we can't get Andy to sit it out this year.'** Here the speaker information comes in the middle. Make sure that the two parts of the quotation are punctuated correctly. In this one, the quoted material makes up one sentence, and so the second half begins with a lowercase letter.

8   **'But what can we do?' asked Becky.** Becky's words are a question, and so the question mark goes inside the closing quotation mark.

9   **The prospect of yet another year of losing was beginning to get them down. 'There will never be an end to our humiliation!' cried Abdul.** Because the second sentence is an exclamation, the exclamation mark takes its rightful place inside the closing quotation mark.

10   **The boss can't catch a ball,' said Gus, 'so we get penalised. It's not fair!'** Gus is exclaiming and so the exclamation mark goes inside the quotation marks. The speaker information is in the middle of the quote and the quote itself makes a complete sentence, and so the second half of the quote begins with a lowercase letter.

If each part of the quotation can stand on its own as a complete sentence, don't run the two together as one sentence (check out Chapter 4 for more details on run-on sentences). Instead, put a full stop after the speaker information and make the second half of the quotation into a separate sentence enclosed in quotation marks. Or, place a full stop after the first half of the quotation and capitalise the first word of the rest of the quotation. Here's an example, adapted from question 10: **'The boss can't catch a ball,' sighed Gus. 'It's not fair that we get penalised.'**

11   **The final score line is always blamed on someone else. 'It's never Andy's fault,' noted Abdul.** The first sentence isn't a quote but the second one is. The speaker information comes at the end of the quote, and so you place a comma inside the closing quotation mark.

12   **'It really isn't his fault,' observed Gus. 'He couldn't catch a cold if he stood naked in the North Pole for a month.** This quote is another where the speaker information is in the middle. Because two complete sentences make up the quotes, you need a capital letter to begin the second one.

13 **'Who's gone to the North Pole for a month?' asked Andy, sneaking up behind them, pretending to go to the photocopier.** The question is part of Andy's quote, and so make sure that you include the question mark in the quotation marks.

14 **'Don't tell me I'm going to have to bat as well,' he said.** If you placed the comma before the closing quotation marks, you're really getting the hang of this now.

15 **'Oh no. I was just saying sometimes the park's like the North Pole so we should warm up before the game,' said Becky. 'Isn't that right Gus?'** The speaker information *said Becky* calls for a comma inside the first closing quotation mark. The second quote is a separate sentence from the first, and so starts with a capital letter. It's also a question, indicating that you need a question mark inside the second set of quotation marks.

16 **'Just the key details, Becky dear,' said Andy. 'Bring my kit down to the park like a love, and I'll be there, warmed up and ready to go.'** The quoted words form two complete sentences. You can't join two complete sentences with a comma, even if the sentences are quotations, the comma is too weak to do the job. The first quotation ends with a comma tucked inside the quotation marks, and the first sentence ends with *Andy*. The second sentence needs to be surrounded by quotation marks, and the last full stop goes inside them.

17 **A little later Becky enquired, 'Do you want a cup of coffee and a bit of a practice for tomorrow's game?'** The speaker information is before the quote, and so you need a comma after *enquired*. The question mark must be included in the quotation marks as well.

18 **'Sure!' replied the boss.** Even though this sentence contains speaker information, you don't need a comma inside the quotation marks. A comma is unnecessary when a full stop, question mark or exclamation mark is in place already.

19 **'Well then, catch!' shouted Becky, Gus and Abdul together.** The exclamation is part of the quote, and so the exclamation mark goes inside the quote.

20 **Perhaps not surprisingly Andy didn't manage to catch the powdered coffee, the carton of milk or the kettle of hot water. As the three fired employees left the building for the last time, Becky asked, 'Anyone for cricket?'** *Becky asked* introduces the quote, and so you need a comma after *asked*. Becky is asking a question, which means that the question mark must be placed inside the quotation marks.

21 **'Jane Austen would have a lot to say to Richard about his "more lovely" nonsense,' commented Clare. It was the day after Sharon and Richard's conversation and Sharon was telling her best friend Clare every last word of it.** When one quote is planted inside another, the embedded words are enclosed by double quotation marks. We're talking about British usage here and in all the answers; in the USA, this practice is usually reversed.

22 **Clare said, 'My favourite quotation concerns "a truth universally acknowledged".'** You may need a magnifying glass to sort out all these squiggles! The embedded quotation gets double quotation marks, and the larger quote gets single quotation marks. When the two occur at the same spot – in this case at the end of the sentence – you pop the full stop between the double and single closing quotation marks.

23 **'Did Richard really ask about "Shakespeare's sonatas"?' asked Sharon's grandma, who still didn't have in her hearing aid even though it was late afternoon. Despite Sharon's best attempts to talk to Clare, Grandma wouldn't stop interrupting.** At first glance this sentence may look far too complicated to punctuate correctly. But if you just take it one step at a time, you can see that the punctuation is quite straightforward. The embedded quotation takes double quotation marks. Because the embedded quotation isn't a question, the question mark follows the closing double quotation marks. The larger quotation, on the other hand, is a question, and so the question mark goes inside the closing single quotation mark. See, told you it was easy!

24 **Sharon replied, 'No, Grandma, he asked about "Shakespeare's bonnets".'** The larger quote takes single quotation marks, and the embedded quotation takes double quotation marks. The full stop goes between the double and single closing quotation marks.

25 **'I can't believe he talked about "beauteous bonnets"!' snorted Clare.** Are you having a good time yet? The embedded quotation isn't an exclamation, and so the exclamation mark stays outside the double quotation marks. The larger quote is an exclamation, indicating that the exclamation mark goes inside the closing single quotation mark (between the two sets of closing quotation marks).

26 **'Clare has no patience for what she terms "Richard's posturing",' explained Sharon to Grandma, who was still looking a bit confused.** When both quotations end at the same spot, any full stops or commas go between both closing quotation marks.

27 **Grandma asked, 'Don't you think that Richard is what you young ones call "an educated guy who means well"?'** This sentence is complicated. The embedded quote isn't a question, and so its closing quotation mark goes before the question mark. The larger quotation is a question, meaning that its closing quotation mark goes after the question mark.

28 **'No, he keeps telling me he's "just an ordinary guy who happens to be a bit of a Romeo",' said Sharon.** Again, both the embedded and the larger quotes end at the same place. The comma goes between both sets of closing quotation marks.

29 **'I can't believe that anyone would call him "a bit of a Romeo"!' sneered Clare.** The larger quotation is an exclamation, and so the exclamation point belongs inside the closing single quotation mark.

30 **'And with his quaint millionaire's mansion, buck teeth and wet-look comb-over', said Grandma, 'I can't believe he thinks he's "just an ordinary guy".'** Both the embedded and the larger quotes end at the same place. The full stop goes between both sets of closing quotation marks.

31 ***Tax Day Blues.*** If the item is a collection, it's treated as a full-length work. Full-length works are italicised (or underlined), and not placed in quotation marks.

32 ***Publish Your Poetry Now,*** The book title is italicised (or underlined).

33 **'Forget About Writing Poetry'.** Use quotation marks for this newspaper article.

34 **'Sonata Taxiana'.** The title of this track needs quotation marks. The full stop goes outside a closing quotation mark, in British English. (In American English the full stop is generally inside.)

35 ***Songs of April.*** A CD is a full-length work, and so the title is italicised (or underlined).

36 ***Strictly Come Bossy Big Brother and Sister Apprentice.*** The title of the whole series is italicised. (You can underline it instead if you want.) The title of an individual episode goes in quotation marks.

37 **'Sister Knows Everything',** The episode title belongs in quotation marks. The series title gets italicised (or underlined). The introductory expression calls for a comma, which needs to be placed outside the quotation marks.

38 **'How I Saved the World from Sarah's Truly Awful Verses'.** This article is in quotation marks.

39 ***No more poetry! How to Booby-trap Hackers and Horrible Friends You Can't Trust to Leave your Computer alone for Two Minutes.*** A book title is italicised (or underlined). The full stop isn't part of the book title and so isn't italicised.

40 **'Keep Out!'** This blog title is in quotation marks. The exclamation mark is part of the title, and so put it inside the quotation marks as well.

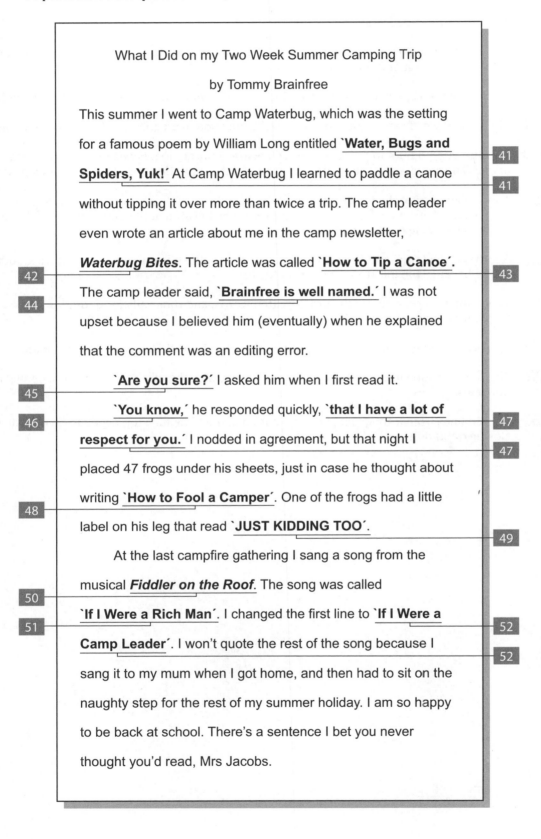

What I Did on my Two Week Summer Camping Trip

by Tommy Brainfree

This summer I went to Camp Waterbug, which was the setting for a famous poem by William Long entitled `**Water, Bugs and Spiders, Yuk!**´ At Camp Waterbug I learned to paddle a canoe without tipping it over more than twice a trip. The camp leader even wrote an article about me in the camp newsletter, *Waterbug Bites*. The article was called `**How to Tip a Canoe**´. The camp leader said, `**Brainfree is well named.**´ I was not upset because I believed him (eventually) when he explained that the comment was an editing error.

`**Are you sure?**´ I asked him when I first read it.

`**You know,**´ he responded quickly, `**that I have a lot of respect for you.**´ I nodded in agreement, but that night I placed 47 frogs under his sheets, just in case he thought about writing `**How to Fool a Camper**´. One of the frogs had a little label on his leg that read `**JUST KIDDING TOO**´.

At the last campfire gathering I sang a song from the musical *Fiddler on the Roof*. The song was called `**If I Were a Rich Man**´. I changed the first line to `**If I Were a Camp Leader**´. I won't quote the rest of the song because I sang it to my mum when I got home, and then had to sit on the naughty step for the rest of my summer holiday. I am so happy to be back at school. There's a sentence I bet you never thought you'd read, Mrs Jacobs.

41 Poem titles belong in quotation marks. The title of a collection of poems, on the other hand, needs to be italicised (or underlined).

42 The newsletter title is italicised (or underlined).

43 An article title belongs in quotation marks. The full stop at the end of the sentence belongs outside the closing quotation mark.

44 Directly quoted speech belongs in quotation marks, with the full stop inside the closing mark.

45 The quoted words are a question, and so the question mark goes inside the quotation marks.

46 The interrupted quotation, with inserted speaker information, needs two sets of quotation marks. The comma at the end of the first part of the quotation goes inside the closing mark.

47 The second part of the interrupted quotation needs two sets of quotation marks (one set beginning before *that,* and one set ending after *you*). The full stop at the end of the sentence goes inside the closing quotation mark.

48 Another article title, another set of quotation marks: the full stop goes outside the quotation marks because the full stop isn't part of the title.

49 This quotation reproduces the exact written words, and thus calls for quotation marks. The full stop goes outside the quotation marks.

50 The title of a play, which is a full-length work, needs to be italicised (or underlined).

51 The title of a song needs to be in quotation marks, with the full stop outside the ending quotation mark.

52 Quoted lines from a song must be in quotation marks. The full stop needs to be outside the closing quotation mark.

Chapter 9

Hitting the Big Time: Capital Letters

. . . .

In This Chapter

▶ Choosing capitals for job and personal titles

▶ Capitalising geographical names

▶ Identifying school and business terms that need capitals

▶ Selecting capital letters for literary and media titles

▶ Placing capital letters in abbreviations

. . . .

*W*hether you love or hate poetry, you have to admit that poets get away with grammatical murder. Specifically, they murder the rules for capital letters whenever they want. A poet can write 'i sent sally to sue' and no one bats an eye. Unfortunately, the rest of us have to conform to capitalisation customs.

Most people know the basics: capital letters are needed for proper names, the personal pronoun *I* and the first letter of a sentence. Trouble can arrive, however, with the finer points of capital letters – in quotations (which we look at in Chapter 8), titles (both people and publications), abbreviations and school or business terms. Never fear . . . in this chapter you get practice in all these areas.

Even for non-poets, the rules for capital letters may vary. The major style setters in the land of grammar (yes, grammar has style, and no, grammarians aren't immune to trends) sometimes disagree about what should be capitalised and what shouldn't. In this workbook we follow the most common capitalisation styles. If you're writing for a specific publication or a particular teacher, you may want to check which rule book (also known as a style manual) you need to follow. A few popular manuals of style are: *New Hart's Rules: The Handbook of Style for Writers and Editors*, *The Times Style and Usage Guide* and *The Economist Style Guide*.

Bowing to Convention and Etiquette: People's Names and Titles

Unless you're a poet or an eccentric musician who wants to buck the trend, you capitalise your name – first, last and initials. Job or personal titles, however, are a different story. The general rules are as follows:

✔ Titles before and attached to a name are capitalised (*Miss Hughes, Professor Wylie, Councillor Chaudhary* and so on). Small, unimportant words in titles (*a, the, of* and the like) are always in lowercase.

✔ Titles written after or without a name are generally not capitalised (for example, *Gil Wylie, professor of psychology* or *Isla Hughes, director of paper distribution*).

✔ Titles that name a post of the highest national or international importance (for example, *Prime Minister, Chancellor of the Exchequer* or *Commander of the Fleet*) may be capitalised even when used alone, although some style manuals go for lowercase regardless of rank.

Now that you get the idea, test yourself. In the following sentences, add capital letters where necessary and change any superfluous capitals into lowercase (just cross out the offending letter and substitute the correct form). Note in this section to correct only personal names and people's titles – you can assume that everything else is correct.

Q. The reverend archie smith, Chief Executive of the Homeless Council, has invited councillor Bickford to next month's fundraiser.

A. **Reverend, Archie, Smith, chief, executive, Councillor.** Personal names are always capitalised, and so *Archie Smith* needs capitals. *Reverend* and *Councillor* precede the names (*Archie Smith* and *Bickford*) and act as part of the person's name, not just a description of their jobs, and so they should be capitalised. The title *chief executive* follows the name and shouldn't be capitalised.

1. Yesterday mayor Victoria Johnson ordered all public servants in her town to conserve sticky tape.

2. Herman harris, chief city engineer, has promised to toe the line on tape spending.

3. However, the City Dogcatcher, Agnes e. Bark, insists on sticking 'Lost Dog – Reward!' signs to every tree.

4. The signs placed by dogcatcher Bark seldom fall far from the tree.

5. The taping done by ms Bark is so extensive that hardly any paper detaches.

6. Few Dogcatchers care as much as agnes about rounding up lost dogs and bringing them back together with their owners.

7. The recent champion of the town dog show, BooBoo, was reunited with his owner last week after being missing for 27 whole minutes.

8. Surely Ms Johnson is wrong when she insists that tape be rationed by Civil Servants.

9. Ms. Johnson, who also serves as director of marketing for a well-known drawing pin company, has an interest in substituting drawing pins for sticky tape.

10. Until the issue is resolved, Agnes, herself the chief executive of Sticking Ltd, will continue to tape to her heart's content.

11. Sticking Ltd has appointed a Vice President to oversee a merger with a drawing pin company.

12. Vice president Corkboard of Pinups Ltd is tired of jokes about his name.

13. When he was appointed Chief Financial Officer, George Corkboard asked the previous holder of the position for advice.

14. Alicia Dough, who is now the President of a large stationery supply chain, had little sympathy for Corkboard.

15. 'With a name like Dough,' she explained, 'everyone thinks you should work as a Bank Manager.'

16. Corkboard next asked reverend Holy how he dealt with his unusual name.

17. However, Holy, who has been a Bishop for 12 years, was puzzled by the question.

18. 'I feel fortunate compared to my brother, who was General Manager of the Dagenham Devils football team,' Bishop Holy remarked.

19. Reginald Holy joined the Devils 20 years ago as a Player Development Director.

20. Holy hopes to be appointed President of the East Essex Football Association someday.

Entering the Worlds of Business and Education

Whether you bring home a salary or a report card, you need to take care to capitalise properly. Surprisingly, the worlds of business and education have a lot in common as regards capitalisation:

- **Where everything happens:** Capitalise the name of the company or school (*Superlative Widgets International* or *University of Rock and Roll*, for example). General words that may refer to a number of businesses or academic institutions (*university, conglomerate* and so on) are written in lowercase.

- **Working units:** Business activities (such as *management, advertising* or *marketing*) and general academic tasks, years and subjects (such as *research, final year* and *history*) aren't capitalised. The name of a specific department (*Research and Development Division* or *Department of Cultural Anthropology*) may be capitalised. Project names (*Zero Task Force*) and course names (*Psychological Interpretations of Belly-Button Rings*) are capitalised. In these capitalised terms, articles and prepositions (*a, the, for* and so on) are generally written in lowercase.

   Course titles and the names of businesses or institutions: Capitalise these items according to the *headline style* rules of titles, which we look at in the later section 'Capitalising Titles of Literary and Media Works'. Briefly, capitalise the first word, all nouns and verbs, and any important words in the title. Short, relational words such as *of, for, by* and *from*, and the articles *a, an* and *the*, aren't capitalised.

- **Products:** General terms for items produced or sold (*widgets, guarantees, consultation fee* and the like) and academic degrees or awards (*master's, chair, fellowship, doctorate* and so on) aren't capitalised. If a specific brand is named, however, roll out the big letters (for example, *Christopher Columbus Award for Round-Trip Travel* or *Universal Widget Groove Simulator*).

Some companies take a tip from poets and change the usual capitalisation customs. Sigh. As a grammar geek you may not be happy, but people (and companies) have the right to ruin their own names. So if you know that a company prefers a particular format (*eBay* or *banjos n strings*, for example), you just have to bow your head and accept it.

Now that you have the basics, try these questions. We thoughtfully include both business and education references so that everyone feels at home. If a word needs a capital letter, cross out the offending letter and insert the capital. If a word has an unnecessary capital letter, cross out the offender and insert a lowercase letter.

0. The eldest daughter of Brendan McLaughlin, founder of belly buttons are we, is a final year student at the university of hogwash, where she is studying navel repair.

A. **Belly Buttons Are We, University of Hogwash.** The name of the company is capitalised, as is the name of the university. The year of study (*final year*) and the subject she's studying (*navel repair*) aren't capitalised.

21. After extensive research, the united nose ring company has concluded that most freshers prefer silver rings.

22. The spokesperson for the Company said silver 'rocks their world'.

23. 'I wore a gold ring to the curriculum critique committee last term,' explained Fred P. Stileless, who is the student rep on all university committees.

24. 'The gold ring definitely turned off some freshers I was interested in romantically,' explained Fred, who hasn't had a date since he was in the sixth form.

25. The spokesperson surveyed competing products, including a silver-gold combination manufactured by in style or else ltd, a division of klepto industrials.

26. The silver that the Jewellers use is imported from four or five major silver-producing countries.

27. The company claims that the silver attracts attention and costs less, although the department of product development has issued a statement denying 'any attractive power' for the metal.

28. Stileless says that he doesn't care about scientific studies because, though he's studying for a degree in chemistry, 'introduction to fashion, a course I took in the first year, opened my eyes to art and beauty'.

29. Stileless expects to receive a bachelor's degree in chemistry and fashion imperatives.

30. He thinks import-export Companies will soon have to switch from gold to silver to satisfy the student market.

Capitalising Titles of Literary and Media Works

If you write an ode to homework or a scientific study on the biological effects of too many final exams, how do you capitalise the title? The answer depends on the style you're following:

✔ **Headline style:** Literary, creative and general-interest works are capitalised in headline style, which specifies capital letters for the first and last word of the title and subtitle, in addition to all nouns, verbs and descriptive words, and any other words that require emphasis. Articles (*a*, *an* and *the*) and prepositions (*among*, *by*, *for* and so on) are usually in lowercase. All the headings in this chapter are in headline style.

✔ **Sentence style:** The titles of scientific works employ sentence style, which calls for capital letters for the first word of the title and subtitle and for proper nouns only. Everything else is lowercase. (The title of a scientific paper in sentence style is as follows: 'Cloning fruit flies: Hazards of fly bites'.)

Ready to get to work? The following titles are written without any capital letters at all. Cross out the offending letters and insert capitals above them where needed. The style to follow (headline or sentence) is specified in brackets at the end of each title. (If you want more information on the punctuation of titles, check out Chapter 8.)

Q. the wonders of homework completed: an ode (headline)

A. **The Wonders of Homework Completed: An Ode.** The first words of the title and subtitle (*The*, *An*) are always capitalised, as are the nouns (*Wonders*, *Homework*) and descriptive words (*Completed*). The preposition (*of*) is left in lowercase.

31. moby duck: a tale of obsessive bird watching (*headline*)

32. an analysis of the *duckensis mobyous*: the consequences of habitat shrinkage on population (*sentence*)

33. call me izzy smell: my life as a duck hunter (*headline*)

34. the duck and i: essays on the relationship between human beings and feathered species (*sentence*)

35. duck and cover: a cookbook (*headline*)

36. the duck stops here: political wisdom from the environmental movement (*sentence*)

37. duck upped: how the duck triumphed over the hunter (*headline*)

38. moby platypus doesn't live here anymore (*headline*)

39. population estimates of the platypus: an inexact science (*sentence*)

40. love a duck: a sentimental memoir (*headline*)

Placing Geographical Capitals

Where am I? I'm in the town (lowercase) of Stromness (capitalised), on the island (lowercase) of Orkney (capitalised), off the northeast coast (lowercase) of the Scottish (capitalised) mainland.

Get the idea? Place names are in lowercase when they're generic, one-term-fits-all (*river, mountain, town, street* and so forth). Place names are capitalised when they're the specific, proper names (*Glasgow, North Wales, Tibet, Amazon River* and so on).

One more point about places: the compass points are in lowercase when they refer to directions (*head south for ten miles*, for example) and capitalised when they refer to areas of a country or region (*the Northeast, the South, the Midlands* and so on).

Place names that have become so much a part of the common vocabulary that they no longer refer to actual locations are still capitalised in UK English but aren't in American English (for example, UK English uses *French fries, Russian roulette, Waterford crystal*).

Now that you're oh-so-savvy about places and capital letters, peer at the underlined words in the following sentences and decide whether a capital letter is appropriate. If so, cross out the small letter and write in the capital one. If not, leave the word alone. (Note that the answers we provide are based on UK English.)

Q. Megan revved up her motorbike and sped <u>south</u>, arriving at the white cliffs, overlooking the <u>english channel</u> just before sunset.

A. **English Channel.** The first underlined word is a direction, not an area, and so lowercase is appropriate for *south*. The second underlined term is a proper, specific name, indicating that capital letters are necessary.

41. She was there to see if Donald von Bon could succeed in becoming the first person to cross the <u>atlantic ocean</u> in a wheelie bin attached to a lilo.

42. Donald, who was born on the <u>isle of wight</u>, had tried to cross <u>oceans</u>, <u>lakes</u> and all kinds of bodies of water in rubbish containers.

43. Megan had read about his latest record attempt in the <u>north american</u> Journal of Junk Junks.

44. The article said that von Bon was a <u>hungarian</u> count, but the minute she clapped eyes on him, Megan knew he was a fake.

45. Megan, who was born on an <u>island</u> just <u>east</u> of the <u>strait of gibraltar</u>, recognised the look of an islander as soon as she spied Donald through her binoculars.

46. 'You are no more from a landlocked principality than I am the Queen of <u>sheba</u>,' she thought, as she saw him beginning to take on water three miles <u>east</u> of the <u>english coast</u>.

47. Even though he was a phony, she couldn't bear to let another islander drown in a sea of stupidity, and so she jumped into the freezing <u>ocean</u> and swam out to rescue him.

48. Two hours later, in a candlelit <u>french</u> bistro, they were tucking into Megan's choice of <u>spanish</u> omelette and a side order of <u>turkish</u> delight.

49. Donald suggested a breath of fresh air, and Megan thought <u>dover's</u> twisty <u>lanes</u> would be perfect for a romantic evening stroll.

50. When they got outside, Donald whipped out his <u>swiss</u> measuring tape and started eyeing up the restaurant's catering dustbins. Clearly, the only thing on his mind was his next rubbish sailing record.

Tackling Abbreviations: AM or p.m.?

Abbreviations save you time, but they also present you with a couple of annoying problems, namely whether or not to use capital letters and whether you need a full stop. The world of time abbreviations can be confusing because you regularly see them written in three different ways: *am*, *AM* or *a.m.* (All these formats are correct, but don't mix them.) So if you're writing for an organisation with a time-formatting chip on its collective shoulder, you're wise to ask in advance for a list of the company's, publication's or university's preferences. In this section we look at a one-size-fits-most abbreviated form style. Here are the general guidelines:

- ✔ Abbreviations formed by removing the end of a word need a full stop on the end: for example, *the Rt. Hon. MP Chris Smith*, *Msgr. O'Neill*.

- ✔ Abbreviations formed by removing the middle of a word but leaving both ends don't need a full stop on the end (these special abbreviations are known as contractions): for example, *Mrs Robinson*, *Dr Singh*, *James Patrick Jr*, *St Joseph*, *Main St* and *Willow Ave.*

- ✔ Acronyms – forms created by the first letter of each word (*NATO*, *UNICEF*, *OPEC* and so on) – take capitals but not full stops.

- ✔ Capitalised long forms normally have capitalised abbreviations (for example, *Saint Patrick's day* and *St Patrick's day*) and lowercase long forms pair with lowercase abbreviations (*kilometre* and *km*).

- ✔ Initials use capitals and full stops (*George W. Bush*, for example).

- ✔ Latin abbreviations aren't usually capitalised but do end with a full stop. Latin abbreviations include *e.g.* (for example), *ibid.* (in the same place) and *etc.* (and so on). The abbreviations for morning and afternoon may be written with capital letters and no full stops (*AM* and *PM*) or without capitals and without full stops (*am* and *pm*) or without capitals but with full stops (*a.m.* and *p.m.*). The choice is yours, but be consistent.

- ✔ In the UK counties are often abbreviated, for example, *Co Armagh* (County Armagh), *Mid Glam* (Mid Glamorgan) and *Yorks* (Yorkshire). The United States Postal Service has devised a list of two-letter state abbreviations, for example, *NY* (New York), *VA* (Virginia) and *KS* (Kansas). However, other systems of abbreviations are more informative for non-Americans, for example, *Fla* for Florida or *Ariz* for Arizona. If you need to abbreviate American states, decide which system you're using and stick to it.

- ✔ When an abbreviation comes at the end of a sentence, the full stop for the abbreviation does double duty as an endmark. Don't place two full stops in a row.

Okay, try your hand at abbreviating. Look at the full word, which we put in lowercase letters even when capital letters are required. Your task is to insert the proper abbreviation or acronym for the following words, taking care to capitalise where necessary and filling in the blanks with your answers.

0. figure _____   *A.* **fig.**

51. illustration _____

52. centimetres _____

53. mister Patel _____

54. united kingdom prime minister_____

55. scottish football association _____

56. reverend Smith _____

57. great britain _____

58. Oxford street _____

59. independent television _____

60. limited _____

Brain Strain: Extra Practice with Capital Letters

Use the information in this chapter to help you find ten capitalisation mistakes in Figure 9-1, which is an excerpt from possibly the worst book report ever written.

Moby, the Life Of a Duck: A Book Report

If you are ever given a book about Ducks, take my advice and burn it. When i had to read *Moby Duck*, the Teacher promised me that it was good. She said that 'Excitement was on every page'. I don't think so! The story is set in Northwest Wales, where a duckling with special powers is born. Moby actually goes to university. We read all about his dull student days, from the very first lecture he goes to in his First Year, through to his tedious gradua-tion ceremony three long, long years later, where he gets his Degree in bird Science. Finally, just as the story gets a tiny bit interesting – Moby becomes a Flight Instructor – the book ends! I can't say I'll be unhappy winging this one back to the library.

Figure 9-1: Book report of a not very interesting novel.

Answers to Capitalisation Problems

1. **Mayor.** Titles and proper names take capitals; common nouns, such as *public servants* and *tape*, don't.

2. **Harris.** Names take capitals, but titles written after the name usually don't.

3. **city dogcatcher, E.** The title in this sentence isn't attached to the name; in fact, it's separated from the name by a comma and should be in lowercase. Initials take capitals and full stops.

4. **Dogcatcher.** Now the title is attached to the name, and so it's capitalised.

5. **Ms.** The title *Ms* is always capitalised.

6. **dogcatchers, Agnes.** The common noun *dogcatchers* doesn't need a capital letter, but the proper name *Agnes* does.

7. **correct.** The name of the champion must be capitalised. About that name – people are allowed to spell their own names (and the names of their pets) as they want. The capital letter inside the name, *BooBoo*, is a style; you may not like it, but the namer's preference needs to be honoured.

8. **civil servants.** Again, the title and name are in caps, but the common job classification isn't.

9. **correct.** This title (*director of marketing*) isn't attached to a name, and so it's in lowercase letters.

10. **correct.** Names have capital letters, but the title doesn't, except when it comes before the name.

11. **vice president.** A title that isn't attached to a name shouldn't be capitalised.

12. **President.** In this sentence the title comes before the name, and so needs to be capitalised.

13. **chief financial officer.** This title isn't attached to a name, and so go for lowercase.

14. **president.** Don't capitalise the title of *president* written without a name unless you're talking about a major world leader such as the President of the United States. (Even then, some style manuals call for lowercase.)

15. **bank manager.** This title isn't connected to a name, and so use lowercase.

16. **Reverend.** The title comes before the name and in a sense becomes part of the name. A capital letter is, therefore, appropriate.

17. **bishop.** In this sentence *bishop* doesn't precede a name; lowercase is the way to go.

18. **general manager.** Lowercase is best for this job title, which isn't connected to a name.

19. **player development director.** Another title that's all by itself; opt for lowercase.

20. **president.** To be president of anything is a big deal, but no need for a big letter here.

21. **United Nose Ring Company.** Although most first year students think they're really important (and, of course, they are), they rate only lowercase letters. The name of the company is specific and so needs to be in uppercase.

22 **company.** A common noun such as *company* isn't capitalised.

23 **Curriculum Critique Committee.** The name of the committee and the person (*Stileless*) should be written in caps, but the other terms (*student rep, university* and the like) aren't cap-worthy.

24 **correct.** Years or levels in school or university aren't capitalised.

25 **In Style or Else Ltd, Klepto Industrials.** The names of companies are capitalised according to the preference of the company itself. Most companies follow headline style, which is explained in the section 'Capitalising Titles of Literary and Media Works' earlier in this chapter.

26 **jewellers.** Don't capitalise common nouns.

27 **Department of Product Development.** The name of a department should be capitalised, but the preposition (of) is lowercase.

28 **Introduction to Fashion.** Course titles get caps, but subject names and school years don't.

29 **Bachelor's.** Use capitals for the type of university degree (Bachelor's, Master's degree) but not for the word 'degree' itself. Degree abbreviations are capitalised (B.A., M.S. and so on). The degree title (like course titles) is written in headline style with capital letters on *Chemistry*, *Fashion* and *Imperatives* but not on *and*.

30 **companies.** This term isn't the name of specific companies, just a common noun, and so you want lowercase.

31 **Moby Duck: A Tale of Obsessive Bird Watching.** In headline style, the first word of the title (*Moby*) and subtitle (*A*) are in capitals. Nouns (*Duck, Tale* and *Watching*) and descriptive words (*Obsessive, Bird*) are in uppercase. The preposition *of* merits only lowercase.

32 **An analysis of the *Duckensis mobyous*: The consequences of habitat shrinkage on population.** In sentence style capitalisation, the first words of the title and subtitle are in caps, but everything else is in lowercase, with the exception of proper names. In this title, following the preferred scientific style, the names of the genus and species are in italics, with only the genus name in caps.

33 **Call Me Izzy Smell: My Life As a Duck Hunter.** Per headline style, the article (*a*) is in lowercase. Did we catch you on *As*? The word is short, but it's not an article or a preposition, and so it rates a capital letter.

34 **The duck and I: Essays on the relationship between human beings and feathered species.** Sentence style titles use capitals for the first word of the title and subtitle. The personal pronoun *I* is always capitalised.

35 **Duck and Cover: A Cookbook.** Headline style calls for capitals for the first word of the title and subtitle and all other nouns. The joining word *and* is in lowercase in headline style, unless it begins a title or subtitle.

36 **The duck stops here: Political wisdom from the environmental movement.** Sentence style gives you two capitals in this title – the first word of the title and subtitle.

37 **Duck Upped: How the Duck Triumphed over the Hunter.** Because this title is in headline style, everything is in caps except articles (*the*) and prepositions (*over*).

38   **Moby Platypus Doesn't Live Here Anymore.** Headline style gives capital letters for all the words here because this title contains no articles or prepositions.

39   **Population estimates of the platypus: An inexact science.** Sentence style calls for capital letters at the beginning of the title and subtitle. The term *platypus* isn't the name of a genus (a scientific category) and so is written in lowercase.

40   **Love a Duck: A Sentimental Memoir.** Headline style mandates lowercase for articles (*a*). However, if articles are the first words of a title and subtitle, they merit capital letters.

41   **Atlantic Ocean.** The proper name (*Atlantic Ocean*) is in capitals.

42   **Isle of Wight, correct, correct.** All proper names are in capitals here, but the common terms (*oceans*, *lakes*) are in lowercase.

43   **North American.** The proper name *North American* is capitalised.

44   **Hungarian.** Countries and nationalities are always capitalised.

45   **Correct, correct, Strait of Gibraltar.** Generic places names (*island*) and compass points directions are in lowercase. The *Strait of Gibraltar* is capitalised but has a lowercase *of*.

46   **Sheba, correct, English, correct.** Countries, or even ancient kingdoms (*Sheba*), are capitalised. Adjectives referring to countries (*English*) are also capitalised. Generic place names (*coast*) and compass point directions (*east*) are in lowercase.

47   **Correct.** The common noun (ocean) is in lowercase.

48   **French, Spanish, Turkish.** All adjectives that describe countries (or products from those countries) use capital letters in UK English.

49   **Dover's, correct.** City names are capitalised; generic geographical terms aren't.

50   **Swiss.** The adjective to describe a measuring tape from Switzerland needs to be capitalised.

51   **illus.**

52   **cms**

53   **Mr Patel**

54   **U.K. P.M. or UK PM**

55   **S.F.A. or SFA**

56   **Rev. Smith**

57   **G.B. or GB**

58   **Oxford St.**

59   **I.T.V. or ITV**

60   **Ltd**

61 *Moby, the Life ~~Of~~ of a Duck:* A Book Report

If you are ever given a book about ~~Ducks~~ ducks, take my advice **62**

and burn it. When ~~i~~ I had to read *Moby Duck*, the ~~Teacher~~ teacher **64**

63 promised me that it was good. She said that **'~~Excitement~~ excite-** **65**

ment was on every page'. I don't think so! The story is set in

66 ~~Northwest Wales~~ northwest Wales, where a duckling with **65**

special powers is born. Moby actually goes to university. We read

all about his dull student days, from the very first lecture he goes

to in his ~~First Year~~ first year, through to his tedious graduation **67**

ceremony three long, long years later, where he gets his ~~Degree~~

68 degree in ~~bird~~ Bird Science. Finally, just as the story gets a tiny **69**

bit interesting – Moby becomes a ~~Flight Instructor~~ flight instruc- **70**

tor – the book ends! I can't say I'll be unhappy winging this one **70**

back to the library.

---

61 In a headline style title, prepositions aren't capitalised.

62 An ordinary term for animals, in this case *ducks*, is in lowercase.

63 The personal pronoun *I* is always capitalised.

64 The name of the teacher isn't given, just the term *teacher*, which should be in lowercase.

65 When a quotation is written without a speaker tag (*she yelled*, *the teacher said*) the first word isn't capitalised. (See Chapter 8 for more on quotations and how to punctuate them.)

66 Compass points aren't capitalised but countries are.

67 University years are in lowercase.

68 The word *degree* is written in lowercase.

69 Course titles and degree subjects are written in headline style.

70 Job titles, when they aren't attached to the beginning of a name, are in lowercase.

Part III

The Pickier Points of Correct Verb and Pronoun Use

'This is a more upmarket product for the brighter child – It contains punctuation.'

In this part . . .

*I*f you're a bit uncertain about the scary-sounding indicative, imperative and subjunctive, this section is just right for you. Most of the issues that grammar students worry about are actually quite simple. Take *who* and *whom,* for example. Deciding which one is appropriate isn't rocket science; it's just a case of knowing about subject and object pronoun cases, which you can practise in Chapter 10. Chapters 11 and 12 help you get to grips with the tricky (okay, picky) points of pronoun and verb usage. If you've ever stumbled over *everyone brought their/his/ her lunch* or *she said she has/had a cold,* these chapters are for you. Finally, Chapter 13 explains how to deal with verb moods (not irritable or ecstatic but indicative, imperative and subjunctive). Ready? Well let's get started!

Chapter 10

The Case of It (And Other Pronouns)

⋯⋯⋯⋯⋯⋯⋯⋯⋯⋯⋯⋯⋯⋯⋯⋯⋯⋯⋯⋯⋯⋯⋯

In This Chapter

▶ Distinguishing between subject and object pronouns

▶ Selecting *who* or *whom*

▶ Placing pronouns in *to be* sentences

▶ Choosing pronouns for prepositional phrases

▶ Using possessive pronouns with *-ing* nouns

⋯⋯⋯⋯⋯⋯⋯⋯⋯⋯⋯⋯⋯⋯⋯⋯⋯⋯⋯⋯⋯⋯⋯

Most children can switch from *He and I are going to do our homework now* (reserved for adult audiences) to *Him and me are playing footie tomorrow* (when talking to friends) faster than the blink of an eye. The second sentence, of course, is nonstandard English, but if you need a way to indicate that you've left behind the world of rules and proprieties, messing up the pronoun case is a great way to do it. *Pronouns* (just to be clear what we're talking about) are the words that stand in for the name of a person, place or thing. Popular pronouns include *I, me* and *my* (fashionable with big-head types); *you* and *yours* (for the less selfish); and *he, she, it, they, them* and a bunch of others (which are good, all-purpose choices).

All pronouns have a case (or family). Subject and object pronouns form two of the three major cases of pronouns. The third case is the possessive. (Possessive pronouns want to know where you are every single minute. Oops, that's your mother, not the possessive case!) In this chapter we deal mainly with subject and object pronouns. You can find the basics of possessive pronouns, along with the lowdown on another quality of pronouns – number – in Chapter 3; for the really advanced (okay, obsessive) pronoun topics, such as double meanings, jump to Chapter 11. Here we discuss only one special possessive situation – when a pronoun goes before a noun that was formed from a verb (called a gerund).

Meeting the Subject at Hand and the Object of My Affection

Subjects and objects have opposite jobs in a sentence. Briefly, the subject is the doer of the action or whatever is in the state of being that's talked about in the sentence. In the first paragraph of this chapter, *he and I* is a better choice than *him and me* because the sentence needs a subject for its verb, *are going*, and *he* and *I* are subject pronouns. In contrast to subjects (which do), objects receive; instead of acting, they are acted upon. If you scold *him and me*, those two pronouns resentfully receive the scolding and so act as objects. Verbs have objects, and so do some other grammatical elements, such as prepositions (which we look at in the later section 'Discovering Whether You're Talking to Me, or I: Pronouns as Objects of Prepositions'.) Here are the contents of the subject- and object-pronoun baskets:

✔ **Subject pronouns** include *I, you, he, she, it, we, they, who* and *whoever.*

✔ **Object pronouns** include *me, you, him, her, it, us, them, whom* and *whomever.*

Some pronouns, such as *you* and *it,* appear on both lists. They do double duty as both subject and object pronouns. Don't worry about them; they're right for all occasions. Other one-case-fits-almost-all pronouns are *either, most, other, which* and *that.*

Another type of pronoun is a reflexive, or *-self,* pronoun (*myself, himself, ourselves* and so on). Use these pronouns only when the action in the sentence doubles back on the subject. (For example, *I told myself that the grammar test would be easy* and *They washed themselves 50 times during the deodorant shortage.*) You may also insert the *-self* pronouns for emphasis, such as *She swore to the judge that she had baked the cake herself.* Don't place a *-self* pronoun in any other type of sentence.

Wrong: If you have a problem, don't hesitate to contact myself.

Correct: If you have a problem, don't hesitate to contact me.

In the following sentences, try your hand at choosing the correct pronoun from the brackets. Take care not to send a subject pronoun to do an object pronoun's job, and vice versa, or wrists will be slapped.

Q. Peyton showed Matt the precious parchment. She asked (he/him) if he'd ever seen anything like it before.

A. **him.** In this sentence, Peyton is the one showing and telling. The pronoun *him* is on the receiving end because Peyton showed the parchment to *him. Him* is an object pronoun.

1. The parchment didn't impress (he/him) much. 'It's just a stupid old piece of paper. Sorry, kiddo,' said Matt patronisingly.

2. He was only two minutes older than Peyton but Matt somehow managed to rub the fact that (he/him) was older and therefore 'wiser' in Peyton's face at every opportunity.

3. Matt asked, in his usual uninterested, older brother kind of way, what (she/her) thought the paper was.

4. 'A treasure map! (I/me) think it's showing the way to a vast fortune,' Peyton said excitedly. But she frowned and sighed, 'If only someone would help (I/me) figure out what the code means.'

5. Matt told his little sister, 'Just between you and me, (I/me) am sure this is just an old tube map or something that's gone through the washing machine once too often.'

6. Peyton said (she/herself) thought the bit that said, 'Here be gold', and the big X in the middle of the page made it more likely to be treasure map than a tube one.

7. Matt suddenly remembered (he/him) had a dentist's appointment and said he had to leave.

8. 'I'll take the rubbish out if you want and pop that old map in the recycle bin on my way too,' (he/him) said helpfully.

9. As soon as he was gone, Peyton turned to (I/me/myself) and said that there was no time to lose.

10. The only decision I needed to make was whether I was with (her/she) or against (her/she).

11. She's my big sister, my best friend in the whole wide world. Why would (she/her) think I was going to let (she/her) down now?

12. I told her she could count on (me/myself) even though (I/me) wasn't quite sure what I was being counted on for.

13. Peyton said that she had to break the code before Matt did so she could find the treasure and, for once in her life, prove that she was smarter than (he/him).

14. 'Then why did you let (he/him) take the parchment?' I asked her, quite reasonably I thought.

15. 'The great thing about being a twin is that you know exactly how your other half thinks,' (she/her) said.

16. As soon as (he/him) saw the parchment, Peyton said she knew precisely what he'd do.

17. 'He can't resist a challenge,' she said. 'That's why I took the precaution of copying the map before I let (him/he) see it.'

18. 'I bet he'll find the best code breakers in town and see if (he/him) and they can figure out where the loot is stashed,' I said.

19. (I/Me) suggested calling Codebusters because (they/them) solved the riddle of the Subway Tapestry last year.

20. Peyton agreed that they seemed to know a thing or two about hieroglyphics but (her/herself/she herself) thought it would be more satisfying if (we/us) figured out the code without any outside help at all.

Choosing Between 'Who' and 'Whom'

The dreaded pronouns *who* and *whom* deserve some, but not all, of the fear associated with them. As with all other subject/object pronoun decisions, you simply have to figure out how the pronoun functions in the sentence. If you need a subject (someone doing the action or someone in the state of being described in the sentence), *who* is your best choice. If you need an object (a receiver of the action), go with *whom*. Why are *who* and *whom* such a pain? Probably because they tend to occur in complicated sentences. But if you untangle the sentence and figure out who is doing what to whom, you're going to be fine.

Bear in mind that fashions in grammar come and go; language changes. Nowhere is this fact more noticeable than in the world of subject and object pronouns, and in the way that people use *who* and *whom* in everyday speech and writing. In informal English, you often hear or read 'Who's that?' 'It's me.' or 'Who did you go to the party with?' In the first example, the subject pronoun (*me*) is used, whereas in formal English the object pronoun (*I*) is more appropriate. In the second example, the informal *who* is fine if you're chatting to your friends, but *With whom did you go to the party?* is better if you're addressing royalty (though why you'd be so impertinent as to ask such a probing question of a queen or king is beyond us). As always, if you want to get ahead, find out whether your teachers, professors or managers are formal or informal types, and then tailor your essays or reports to their tastes.

Please do come aboard the who/whom first class passenger liner and select the appropriate formal pronoun from the following brackets.

0. (Who/Whom) can decode the message? Codebusters! (If you don't count that pesky girl Peyton who's a bit of a know-it-all on the deciphering front.)

A. **Who.** The verb *can decode* needs a subject, someone to do that action. *Who* is for subjects, and *whom* is for objects.

21. Did anyone ever find out (who/whom) phoned in the tip-off that helped Codebusters crack the final part of the Subway Tapestry?

22. Lucy, (who/whom) was the president of Codebusters, never gave any public credit to Peyton for her help back then.

23. Peyton didn't believe Lucy, or (whoever/whomever) else was on the Codebusters' payroll, would ever publicly admit the help Peyton had given the company.

24. Codebusters were willing to crack any code but only if the price was right. And (who/whom) had access to millions?

25. Our dear older brother Matt to (who/whom) our parents had left all their fortune. (Well, they didn't intend to. Matt just hired the world's sleaziest lawyer.)

26. Peyton knew that even though a third of the money really belonged to each of us, Matt would throw it all at (whoever/whomever) was willing to decode the treasure map for him.

27. Matt's competitive side was all-consuming. To (who/whom) would the treasure go? To him, no matter what.

28. Peyton, (who/whom) knew she didn't have much time, got down to the tricky task of trying to make sense of the map, while I made tea and sandwiches.

29. Meanwhile Matt, (who/whom) I didn't trust an inch, was busy schmoozing Lucy at Codebusters.

30. I once heard Matt say that those (who/whom) have an honest face can get away with anything.

31. 'If you are one of those people (who/whom) can fake sincerity,' he said, 'you've got it made.'

32. Peyton and I knew that (whoever/whomever) trusted Matt would be in big trouble.

33. At that moment Lucy, (who/whom) was falling hook, line and sinker for Matt's smooth talk, was in big trouble.

34. 'I'll pay whatever it takes to crack this code. And I'll make this promise to you or (whoever/whomever) is willing to help me do it, too: I'll share the treasure 50-50. I swear,' he said earnestly.

35. Lucy, to (who/whom) the words 'treasure' and '50-50' appealed enormously (because she was as greedy as she was gullible), promised to keep the enigma engines working all hours till a solution was found.

Linking Up with Pronouns in 'To Be' Sentences

Most verbs express action, but mingling with this on-the-go group are forms of the verb 'to be' (_am, is, are, was, were, has been, will be_ and the like). These verbs are like giant equal signs linking two equivalents, and for that reason, they're sometimes called _linking_ verbs. 'Jeremy is the president' is the same as 'Jeremy = president'. If you've studied algebra, or even if you haven't, you know that these statements mean the same even when reversed ('the president is Jeremy'). This knowledge leads to an important pronoun fact: a subject pronoun serves as the subject of a linking verb, and to preserve reversibility, subject pronouns also follow linking verbs, in the same spot where you normally expect an object. Therefore, the answer to 'Who's there?' is 'It is _she_' rather than 'It is _her_', because you can reverse the first ('She is it') and not the second ('Her is it').

When you select pronouns for a sentence with a linking verb, be aware that sometimes the verb changes, and so to sound right a reversible sentence may need a verb adjustment from singular to plural or vice versa. 'It is they' is reversible, at least in theory, because _they_ is a subject pronoun, even though 'they is' doesn't pass a grammar sound check until you change the verb to _are_.

Can you select the appropriate pronoun from the brackets? Give it a whirl in the following example and exercises. Just to make life more interesting, we sprinkle a few action verbs into the mix – for more information on pronouns with action verbs, see the earlier section, 'Meeting the Subject at Hand and the Object of My Affection'.

Q. I think the perfect sibling is (she/her), not Matt.

A. **She.** You want a subject pronoun after the linking verb _is_. Reverse that portion of the sentence to see for yourself: _her is the perfect sibling_? We don't think so. _She is the perfect sibling_. That's more like it.

36. Matt, Peyton and I were called in for questioning by one of Scotland Yard's finest. We promised (her/she) that the parchment would be returned to the rightful owner.

37. The 'rightful owner', according to Peyton, is (she/her), because Peyton herself found the map inside a novel she bought in a second-hand book shop.

38. 'I may not be able to decode a treasure map,' said Peyton innocently, 'but I know a good book when I see one. The lawful purchaser of the novel, and therefore, the map is (I/me).'

39. Matt wasn't so sure; it is (he/him) who will have to go to jail if the police ever figure out that it was (he/him) who had the original map.

40. Suddenly, Inspector O'Brien's phone rang and (she/her) walked over to the other side of the interrogation room.

41. Peyton turned to Matt and whispered, 'I can break us out of here in ten seconds flat. I've got makeup and wigs waiting for us in a van outside. We can be (whoever/whomever) we want to be and ride off into the sunset.'

42. 'What's the catch?' he hissed. 'Simple,' she said, 'you have to let (I/me) be the big sister, forever.'

43. 'Why should (I/me) let you be the boss of me?' he squeaked.

44. 'Because I've got the skeleton key to get us out of here, I know where the treasure's buried. But most of all, because (we/us) both know, it's what mum and dad would have wanted.'

45. And, you know, from that day onwards, the twins and (I/me) lived happily ever after. Sometimes it is true – big sister really does know best.

Discovering Whether You're Talking to Me or I: Pronouns as Objects of Prepositions

Prepositions, not to be confused with propositions (such as *Are you busy tonight?*), are words that express relationships. (Come to think of it, propositions concern relationships too.) Common prepositions include *by, for, from, in, on, of, about, after* and *before*. Prepositions always have objects, and sometimes those objects are pronouns. The objects of prepositions are italicised in the following examples:

> Give that umbrella to *me* or I'll break it over your *head*.

> The embroidery on the *umbrella* was done by *me* alone.

Got the idea? In the first sample sentence, *me* and *head* are objects of the prepositions *to* and *over*. In the second, *umbrella* and *me* are objects of *on* and *by*. Luckily, you don't have to worry about *umbrella* and *head*. They're nouns, and they don't change no matter where they appear in the sentence. But the pronoun does change (sigh), depending upon its job in the sentence. And if its job is to be an object of a preposition, it must be an object pronoun. You can't give an umbrella to *I*, and the embroidery wasn't done by *I* alone. Not in the English grammatical universe, anyway.

Take a stab at the following sentences, selecting the correct pronoun from the pair in brackets. In an attempt to fry your brain, we cleverly (they say modestly) scatter a few subjects in the exercise.

Q. The postie hates delivering mail to (we/us) just because once, years ago, our aunty sent (we/us) some pickled cabbage. How were we supposed to know the postie would get her hand stuck in our letterbox trying to deliver it?

A. **us, us.** The preposition *to* needs an object, and so your first answer has to be *us*. The second needs to be an object pronoun (the subject is *our aunty*), making *us* the one you want.

46. The postie's also no fan of Spike. You can't put much past Spike. That's why (he/him) is a great watchdog.

47. Spike likes to walk behind (we/us) when we get near the house; he growls at (whoever/whomever) comes too close.

48. Mum, who's dead posh sometimes, said to Spike yesterday when we came back from the shops, 'At (who/whom) are you snarling now Spike?

49. 'You know he thinks the postie wants to rob us, so he tries to keep an eye on (she/her),' I told Mum as I tried to piece together another ripped catalogue.

50. 'You have to run around (they/them),' I added helpfully to the postie, speaking of my mum and Spike.

51. Carefully separating the letters addressed to 'Spike' from the letters meant for us, the postie gave the shredded mail to Mum and (I/me).

52. Spike's pawpals generally include a dog biscuit when writing to (he/him).

53. Spike and my mum both enjoy getting mail, but Spike loves letters even more than (she/her).

54. Spike's letters sometimes contain meaty bones from (whoever/whomever) really wants his attention.

55. My mum is as fond of meaty bones as (he/him), but she hardly ever gets any. The postie says that she's constantly surprised by the lack of bones she has to deliver to my mum.

Matching Possessive Pronouns to '-ing' Nouns

We cheated a bit with the title of this section. When we say *-ing* nouns, we mean nouns made from the *-ing* form of verbs (*swimming, smiling, puttering* and similar words). We're not talking about nouns that just happen to contain those three letters, such as *king, wingding* and *pudding,* among others. Nor are we talking about *-ing* verb forms used as verbs or as descriptions of other nouns. For those of you who enjoy grammar terms, the *-ing*-noun-made-from-a-verb-form is called a gerund.

Here's the deal with pronouns and *-ing* nouns. You need to put a possessive form in front of them. Why? Because that form keeps the focus in the right place. Have a look at this sentence:

Chloe hates (me/my) auditioning for the new reality show, *Nut Search.*

Chloe doesn't hate *me*. Instead, Chloe hates the whole reality-show effort. (*My auditioning* threatens her sense of privacy and pretty much guarantees that she isn't going to get chosen to go on the show.) Therefore, the correct choice is *my* because it shifts the reader's attention to *auditioning,* where it belongs (*auditioning* is what Chloe hates).

In the situation described in the preceding paragraph, the possessive form of a noun must also be your choice for the spot in front of an *-ing* noun. In the sample sentence, the correct form is *Chloe hates Rick's auditioning. . .* not *Chloe hates Rick auditioning. . . .* The same reasoning applies; Chloe doesn't hate Rick. She just doesn't want him to try to get on television.

Try your hand at the following example and exercises. Circle the pronouns you love and ignore the ones you hate. To keep you alert, we insert a few sentences that don't call for possessive pronouns. Keep your eyes open!

Q. Although I'm not a movie critic, I think that (he/him/his) writing a film script is a bad idea.

A. **his.** The bad idea here is the *writing,* not *he* or *him*. The possessive pronoun shifts the attention to the task, which is the point of the sentence.

56. Mr Bernard Lawrence of the *Times* needed help with (he/him/his) scripting work and had to hire additional writers.

57. Mr Lawrence said that he loved everything the employment agency did the week before except (they/them/their) sending him too many pronoun-challenged writers.

58. My friend Lori went for an interview on a Tuesday. He saw (she/her/hers) reading *The Pronoun Diet,* a new grammar text by Jinty McKechnie.

59. 'I love (she/her/hers) insisting on only one pronoun per paragraph, don't you?' she asked. She didn't get the job.

60. When I turned up on the Wednesday, I told Mr Lawrence that I took (I/me/my) pronoun usage very seriously.

61. By the Friday afternoon I thought I knew him well enough to talk to him about (he/him/his) filmmaking theme.

62. He was none too happy when I told (he/him/his) swash-buckling pirate adventures were completely out-of-date. Generation Y would be totally uninterested in a film that looked like a boring old Errol Flynn film.

63. Poor deluded Mr Lawrence! I had to admire (he/him/his) sticking to his guns. He insisted his tale of high-seas plundering was bound to be the summer's blockbuster.

64. I said no more and thought it'd be fun to see (he/him/his) eating his words in June, July and August.

65. How was I to know that (he/him/his) is best mates with Johnny Depp, Orlando Bloom and Keira Knightley?

Brain Strain: Extra Practice with Pronoun Case

The advert for a garage sale in Figure 10-1 contains quite a few pronoun problems. Of the 20 that are underlined, ten are correct, and ten aren't. Can you find the ten pronoun-case errors and correct them?

Garage Sale for You

Last weekend, <u>my</u> brother cleared out the garage. His hard work has given you – <u>our</u> neighbours – and <u>I</u> a great opportunity (for a very limited time) to bond over a few bargains. The merchandise, which, just between <u>you</u> and <u>I</u> is mostly rubbish, will go on sale tomorrow, for one day only.

<u>Him</u> taking the initiative to earn a few quid will put money in everyone's pocket as well! The gently used DVDs — a few surprises here for <u>whomever</u> looks really carefully at the subtitles — are priced to sell! <u>I</u> recommend *For <u>Who</u> the Dog Barks*. Why not buy it for your friends and watch it with <u>them</u> and <u>their</u> pets? Other great items include a used fridge, given to Mum by <u>me</u> and my brother Doug, and recently repaired by <u>our</u> dad and <u>I</u>. It only leaks a tiny bit now.

Come early to 38 Greenfield Road and make sure that your pockets are stuffed with dosh, for it is <u>me</u> <u>who</u> will have to cart away unsold merchandise to the dump. I promise a free balloon to <u>whomever</u> buys the most, and <u>he</u> or <u>her</u> may blow it up and then I'll pop it right on the spot! As I always say, 'Let <u>I</u> have my way and then everyone's happy.'

Figure 10-1:
A pronoun-challenged advert for a garage sale.

Answers to Pronoun Case Problems

1 **him.** The pronoun *he* is an actor, but *impress* takes an object. *Him* is for objects.

2 **he.** Who managed to rub in the fact? *He managed to rub the fact. He* is a subject pronoun.

3 **she.** Someone has to do the thinking referred to in the sentence. Therefore you need a subject pronoun, *she*.

4 **I, me.** These two sentences illustrate the difference between subject and object pronouns. In the first sentence, you need *I* because it's a subject pronoun, the word that does the action (*think*). In the second sentence, you need an object pronoun (*me*) to receive the action (*help*).

5 **I.** You need a subject pronoun with the verb (*am*).

6 **she.** Did we confuse you with the choice of *herself?* You could say *she herself* for emphasis but you can't use *herself* on its own as an object pronoun in this sentence. The subject pronoun she is the correct choice.

7 **he.** You need the subject pronoun here, *he*.

8 **he.** You need the subject pronoun here, *he*.

9 **me.** You need an object pronoun here, and so you can rule out I because it's a subject pronoun. The pronoun *myself* works only for emphasis, leaving you with *me*, the correct choice.

10 **her, her.** You need two object pronouns here, after the preposition *with*.

11 **she, her.** The first pronoun needs to be a subject one and the second needs to be an object one. She is doing the action (*think*) and the object pronoun *her* is on the receiving end of another action (*let down*).

12 **me, I.** Two straightforward pronouns are need here – first an object one and then a subject one.

13 **he.** A word is missing but implied at the end of this sentence: *is*. If you insert the missing word after the pronoun, you hear it: *she was smarter than he is*. . . . The pronoun *he* is the subject of the implied verb *is*.

14 **him.** The correct choice here is an ordinary object pronoun.

15 **she.** *She* is the subject of the verb *said*.

16 **he.** The subject pronoun *he* is the doer of the action of the verb *saw*.

17 **him.** The object pronoun *him* is what's needed here.

18 **he.** This sentence is a bit tricky because the pronoun choice is camouflaged by other words (*they and*). If you isolate the pronoun, however, you see that it is: *he can figure out where the loot is stashed*. You need the subject pronoun *he*.

19 **I, they.** Two subject pronouns are needed here: *I* and *they*. In this sentence both pronouns are doers of verbs – *suggested* and *solved*.

20 **she herself, we.** Here you need two subject pronouns – one with *thought* and one with *figured out*. With the first pronoun, you also require an emphasis to show that Peyton thought differently from the writer. So the first pronoun is a reflexive one, *she herself*.

21 **who.** Focus on the part of the sentence containing the *who/whom* issue: *who/whom phoned in the tip-off.* The verb *phoned* needs a subject, and so *who* is the correct choice.

22 **who.** Somebody *was the president of Codebusters,* and so you need a subject pronoun. *Who* is the right choice.

23 **whoever.** The verb *was* needs a subject, and so *whoever* has to do the job.

24 **who.** Somebody *had access to millions,* and so you need the subject pronoun *who.*

25 **whom.** When you see the word *to* (a preposition), plump for the object pronoun, because prepositions are completed by object pronouns such as *whom.*

26 **whoever.** A subject pronoun such as *whoever* (rather than *whomever*) is right here because the verb *was* needs a subject.

27 **whom.** *Whom* is correct because the preposition *to* is completed by object pronouns such as *whom.*

28 **who.** The verb *knew* must have a subject (verbs are picky that way), and so here you need *who* not *whom.*

29 **whom.** Concentrate on the part of the sentence between the commas. Rearrange the words into the normal subject-verb order: *I didn't trust who/whom.* Now you can see that the answer has to be *whom.* The pronoun *I* is the subject, and *whom* is acted upon, not an actor.

30 **who.** The verb *have* needs a subject, and the subject pronoun *who* does the job.

31 **who.** The verb *can* needs a subject pronoun.

32 **whoever.** The verb *trusted* needs a subject and *whoever* is the right choice here.

33 **who.** The verb *was* needs a subject, and *who* is a subject pronoun – a match made in heaven.

34 **whoever.** This one is tricky. When you see the word *to* (a preposition), you may want to jump for the object pronoun, because prepositions are completed by object pronouns such as *whomever.* But in this sentence, the verb *is* needs a subject, and *whoever* fits the bill perfectly. For those who love grammar terminology (if it makes you quake, look away now), the object of the preposition *to* is the whole clause, *whoever is willing to help me do it.*

35 **whom.** The preposition *to* needs an object pronoun (*whom*).

36 **her.** *Promise* isn't a linking verb; it expresses action. After an action verb you need an object pronoun, and *her* fits the description.

37 **she.** *The rightful owner is she,* and *she is the rightful owner.* See how smoothly that reverses?

38 **I.** The subject pronoun *I* belongs after the linking verb *is.*

39 **he, he.** *He* is a subject pronoun and needs to appear twice here: once after the linking verb *is,* and once after the linking verb *was.*

40 **she.** *Walk* is a plain old action verb, not a linking one. Therefore, a subject pronoun (*she*) is required.

41 **whoever.** The verb *can be* is a linking verb. After a linking verb you need a subject pronoun (*whoever*).

42 **me.** *Let* is an action verb that must be followed by an object pronoun such as *me*.

43 **I.** The action verb *let* is still on duty, but this time it's looking for subject pronoun (*I*).

44 **we.** Peyton and Matt *know* (the action verb in this sentence), and so you need a subject pronoun in front of it.

45 **I.** This action verb (*lived*) needs a subject pronoun (*I*).

46 **he.** The verb *is* needs a subject pronoun *he*.

47 **us, whoever.** This question is a hard one; if you got it right, you deserve a medal. The pronoun *us* is the object of the preposition *behind*. But the preposition *at* is NOT completed by the pronoun *whomever*. Instead, *whoever* functions as the subject of the verb *comes*. The whole thing – *whoever comes too close* – is the object of the preposition *at*.

48 **whom.** Change the question to a statement and you get this one right away: *This dog is snarling at whom.* The preposition *at* is completed by the object *whom*.

49 **her.** The preposition *on* needs an object, and *her* is just right for the job.

50 **them.** *Around* is a preposition in this sentence, meaning that it takes the object *them*.

51 **me.** The preposition *to* needs an object, and so opt for *me*.

52 **him.** You can't write to *he,* because *he* is a subject pronoun, and the preposition *to* can't bear to be without an object pronoun.

53 **she.** This sentence makes a comparison, and comparisons often contain implied verbs. The missing word is *does,* as in *Spike loves letters even more than she does.* When you include the missing word, the answer is clear. You need *she* as a subject of the verb *does*.

54 **whoever.** The preposition *from* needs an object, but in this tricky sentence, the entire expression *whoever really wants to get his attention* is the object, not just the first word. The pronoun *whoever* functions as the subject of the verb *wants*.

55 **he.** This implied comparison omits the verb *is*. Add the missing verb and the answer leaps off the page: *My mum is as fond of meaty bones as he is.* You need the subject pronoun *he* to match with the verb *is*.

56 **his.** Mr Lawrence doesn't need help with a person; he needs help with a task (*scripting*). Whose *scripting* is it? *His.*

57 **their.** Mr Lawrence didn't hate the people at the agency. He didn't love *their sending* pronoun-challenged writers. The possessive pronoun shifts the focus to the action, where it belongs.

58 **her.** We sneaked this one in to see whether you're awake: *he saw her.* What was she doing? *Reading,* but the reading is a description tacked onto the main idea, which is that he saw *her.* A possessive isn't called for in this sentence, just a normal object pronoun.

59 **her.** The love isn't directed towards a person (*she*) but to an action (*insisting*).

60 **my.** This sentence is a straightforward subject-verb-object one with *I took my*, in which *my* is possessive.

61 **his.** The writer wanted to talk about his (Mr Lawrence's) filmmaking themes. *His* ensures that the reader's attention is focused on the *filmmaking*.

62 **him.** The *him* is the focus here, not the *swashbuckling* (which is an adjective that happens to end in *-ing*). You need an object pronoun (*him*) for the verb *told*.

63 **his.** The writer didn't admire Mr Lawrence, but the way he kept his resolve. The *his* draws attention to his stance, rather than to him.

64 **him.** What would be fun to watch him doing? *Eating.* The *eating* is a description added to the main idea (*it would be fun to see him*), and so you need an object pronoun (*him*) rather than a possessive one (*his*).

65 **he.** An easy one to finish. No possessives, nothing complicated, just a plain, old subject (*he*) is necessary to go with the verb (*was*).

Garage Sale for You

66 —— Last weekend, **my** brother cleared out the garage. His hard work has

67 —— given you – **our** neighbours – and ~~I~~ **me** a great opportunity (for a very limited —— 68

time) to bond over a few bargains. The merchandise, which, just between

69 —— **you** and ~~I~~ **me** is mostly rubbish, will go on sale tomorrow, for one day only. —— 70

71 —— ~~Him~~ **His** taking the initiative to earn a few quid will put money in

everyone's pocket as well! The gently used DVDs — a few surprises here for

72 —— ~~whomever~~ **whoever** looks really carefully at the subtitles — are priced to

73 —— sell! **I** recommend *For **Whom** the Dog Barks*. Why not buy it for your friends —— 74

and watch it with **them** and **their** pets? Other great items include a used —— 76
75 ——

fridge, given to Mum by **me** and my brother Doug, and recently repaired by

77 —— **our** dad and ~~I~~ **me**. It only leaks a tiny bit now. —— 79
78 ——

Come early to 38 Greenfield Road and make sure that your pockets are

stuffed with dosh, for it is **I who** will have to cart away unsold merchandise to —— 81
80 ——

the dump. I promise a free balloon to ~~whomever~~ **whoever** buys the most, —— 82

and **he** or ~~her~~ **she** may blow it up and then I'll pop it right on the spot! As I —— 84
83 ——

always say, 'Let ~~I~~ **me** have my way and then everyone's happy.'
85 ——

---

66 **correct.** *My* is a possessive pronoun and links the brother to the speaker.

67 **correct.** Another possessive pronoun, attached to the noun *neighbours*.

68 **me.** You need an object pronoun here, receiving the action expressed by the verb *has given*.

69   **correct.** The *you* is okay (*you* works in both subject and object positions).

70   **me.** *I* is a problem. For some reason the preposition *between* often entices people to put a subject pronoun (*I*) where an object pronoun (*me*) is needed.

71   **His.** The *-ing* noun *taking* is the real focus of the sentence, and the possessive pronoun keeps the reader's attention on the *taking*, not on *him*.

72   **whoever.** The preposition *for* may have tempted you to opt for an object pronoun, but the verb *looks* needs a subject, and so *whoever* is best. The object of the preposition, by the way, is the whole expression, *whoever looks*. . . .

73   **correct.** The subject pronoun *I* pairs with the verb *recommend*.

74   **Whom.** The preposition *for* requires the object pronoun *whom*.

75   **correct.** The object pronoun correctly follows the preposition *with*.

76   **correct.** The possessive pronoun *their* answers the pet-ownership question.

77   **correct.** The preposition *by* takes the object pronoun *me*.

78   **correct.** The possessive pronoun *our* clarifies the parent-child bond here.

79   **me.** *By I?* That doesn't sound right. You need the object pronoun *me*.

80   **I.** The linking verb *is* needs to be followed by a subject pronoun (*I*), not an object pronoun (*me*).

81   **correct.** The verb *will have to* needs a subject, and *who* fits the bill.

82   **whoever.** The verb *buys* takes the subject, *whoever*.

83   **correct.** The verb *may blow* is paired with the subject pronoun *he*.

84   **she.** You need a subject pronoun for the verb *may blow,* and so *she* is correct.

85   **me.** The verb *let* needs the object *me*.

Chapter 11

Choosing the Best Pronoun for a Tricky Sentence

In This Chapter

▶ Matching possessive pronouns

▶ Referring to organisations with pronouns

▶ Pairing *who*, *which* and *that* with verbs

▶ Avoiding vague pronoun references

Have you figured out that pronouns are the most annoying part of speech in the entire universe? Pronouns are the words that stand in for nouns – words that name people, places, things and ideas. English can't do without pronouns, but as regards error-potential, they're a minefield just waiting to blow up in your speech or writing.

We cover the basics of pronoun use in Chapter 3 and more advanced topics in Chapter 10. In this chapter we hit the big time, supplying information about pronouns that even your great-uncle – the one with a collection of antique grammar books that he actually reads – doesn't know. If you conquer everything in this chapter, give yourself a gold pronoun . . . er, star.

Nodding in Agreement: Pronouns and Possessives Come Head to Head

Pronouns substitute for nouns, but in a sincere effort to ruin your life, they also match up with other pronouns. For example, take a look at this sentence: 'When Charlie yelled at me, I smacked him and poured glue on his homework.' The pronoun *his* refers to the pronoun *him*, which stands in for the noun *Charlie*. This example sentence is fairly straightforward; unfortunately, not all pronoun-pronoun couples get together so easily.

'Everybody is here.' Doesn't that comment sound plural? So why do you need the singular verb *is*? Because *everybody* is a singular pronoun. So are *everyone, someone, anyone, no one, somebody, anybody, nobody, everything, something, anything, nothing, each, either* and *neither*. Chances are your ear for good English already knows that these pronouns belong in the singular box.

If you extend the logic and match another pronoun – such as a possessive – to any of the *every-, some-, any-* and other similar pronouns, you can come a cropper. You may decide that this sentence 'Everyone needs their lunch money' commits a serious crime against grammar because the singular *everyone* doesn't agree with the plural *their*. And you'd be right. And you'd be wrong.

On the one hand you're right because in some parts of Grammarland, making sure that all plurals match with other plurals and singulars with other singulars is a Very Big Deal. The only acceptable version of this sentence, for people inhabiting this particular part of Grammarland, is 'Everyone needs his or her lunch money.' On the other hand you're wrong to state categorically that 'Everyone needs their lunch money' is wrong, because the use of the singular *their* has a very long and noble tradition in English. For hundreds of years the words *they*, *them* and *their* were used (by Shakespeare, among others) to refer to both singular and plural nouns. But then some grammarians came along and decided that this usage was wrong. More recently a lot of grammarians have been coming back round to (or indeed never went away from) the idea that *they* is a useful (and perfectly correct) singular pronoun.

We see no reason why something as useful and natural-sounding as this convention (and with such a long unbroken history of use in the language) shouldn't be allowed, and so you have our permission to use it.

However, what if your boss, professor, teacher or lecturer is a hard-line *their*-can't-ever-be-used-for-the-singular kind of person? Well, you have a couple of options: use the clunky *he or she* construction or simply rewrite any sentence with *he or she* to make it fit with a plural *they*. The sentence above, for example, can easily be written as '*All students* need *their* lunch money'.

Of course, not every pronoun is singular. *Both, several, few* and *many* are plurals and can match with *their* or other plural words.

Scan the following example sentence and practice exercises and put a pronoun that makes sense in each blank. Where appropriate, you can use *he or she* or *they*, or you can rewrite the sentences to avoid the whole messy *he or she or they* issue altogether.

Q. Neither of Alan's aunts has a wart on _____ nose.

A. **her.** The singular pronoun *neither* must pair with another singular pronoun. True, the sentence refers to *aunts*, a plural. But the word *neither* tells you that you're talking about the aunts individually, and so you have to go with a singular pronoun. Because *aunts* are female, *her* is the word you want.

1. Alan and his brother Bertie can be easily found in a crowd because both have warts on _____ noses.

2. Bertie was born warty but Alan only recently achieved _____ wartiness through surgery.

3. Relieved that the procedure went well, everybody sent him _____ best wishes.

4. Many of the get-well cards had miniature warts drawn on _____ envelopes.

5. A few even had little handwritten messages beneath _____ illustrations.

6. Because Alan's surgery went so smoothly, someone else in his family is going to get _____ nose done too.

7. 'Doesn't everyone need more warts on _____ nose?' reasoned Alan.

8. Anybody who disagreed with Alan kept quiet, knowing that _____ opinion wouldn't be accepted anyway.

9. Each of Alan's implanted warts had _____ own unique shape

10. Several of his warts model _____ appearance on facial features of famous film stars.

11. Although someone said that _____ didn't like Alan's new warts, the crowd reaction at the National Gallery was generally positive.

12. Neither Adam nor Martin, Alan's cousins, opted for a similar procedure on _____ own beak.

13. Nothing Alan said could change _____ minds about nose-warts.

14. '_____ just went in one ear and out the other,' complained Alan to Bertie.

15. Alan was sure that they were jealous. He knew both of them would change _____ tune when they saw Alan's fabulous profile hung on the nation's gallery walls.

16. 'Lots of people will be asking _____ own doctors for cosmetic surgery after seeing your portrait,' said Bertie.

17. 'I'm sure millions will opt for _____ own version of wart enhancement,' predicted Bertie.

18. 'Although not everyone will want the same type of wart on _____ nose,' envisioned Alan.

19. Within a few weeks warts started to appear on lots of celebrities who wanted something dramatic for _____ publicity photos.

20. But Adam and Martin stuck to their guns. Neither of them would ever consider the tacky practice of putting warts on _____ nose, they insisted. Each opted for a tasteful cheek placement instead.

Tackling Pronouns for Companies and Organisations

Marks & Spencer (M&S), the National Health Service (NHS), the United Nations and a lot of other businesses or community groups are waiting for the chance to mess up your pronoun choices. How? They cleverly create names that sound plural, and unsurprisingly, many people pair them up with plural pronouns. However, a moment of logical thinking tells you that each is one organisation and therefore requires a singular pronoun. Here's what we mean:

Wrong: Harrods put their designer lingerie on sale last week.

Why the sentence is wrong: The pronoun *their* is plural, but *Harrods*, despite the letter *s* at the end of the name, is singular because it's one company.

Right: Harrods put its designer lingerie on sale last week.

Why the sentence is right: Now the singular possessive pronoun (*its*) matches the singular store name (*Harrods*).

Choose the correct pronoun for each of the following sentences. Just to keep you alert, we mix in a couple of sentences in which the pronoun doesn't refer to a singular company or organisation. The same principle applies: singular matches with singular, and plural matches with plural.

Q. Carrie patronised Debenhams because (she/they) liked (its/their) shoe department, which had a good supply of her favourite size-13 stilettos.

A. **she, its.** The first pronoun refers to Carrie, and so the singular *she* matches nicely. The second refers to the department store, which is singular also, and thus merits the singular *its*.

21. Almost every employee at Kipples Kakes had been stuffing (itself/himself or herself/themselves) silly for years with anything they could get their hands on in the factory.

22. However, Carrie believed that Kipples Kakes had a duty to give away (its/their) broken biscuits to feed 'starving' workers.

23. Carrie wrote to the World Sweetie Association (WSA) asking for (its/their) help to make her broken biscuit policy a global initiative.

24. The WSA answered Carrie's letter with a suggestion of (its/their) own.

25. 'Why don't you work locally to overcome starvation?' read the reply. 'If you take care of the employees at Kipple Kakes, the WSA will take care of (its/their) own staff.'

26. The letter continued, '(It's/ its) not the policy of WSA to get involved in local initiatives.'

27. The letter ended, 'Perhaps you should contact the UNPOCI (United Nations Pieces of Cake Initiative), to see if (it/they) would like to join forces with you.'

28. Carrie, depressed by her failure to secure a source of free sweet things, decided to visit Moos to sample (its/their) full range of chocolate-chip cookies.

29. About 5,000 calories later, Carrie was ready to take on the WSA again. 'The WSA needs to listen to me. (It knows/They know) I'm talking sense!' she screamed.

30. Suddenly, Carrie choked on the bit of Macadamia Crunch, which (she/it) had been saving for last.

31. 'I'll sue Moos and all (its/their) subsidiaries,' vowed Carrie, even as she struggled to breathe.

32. 'Sue all you like, just don't sue the NHS,' muttered the ambulance driver who had appeared, as if by magic, at her side to revive her. '(It doesn't/They don't) get enough funding as it is.'

33. 'I'm a supporter of the NHS,' declared Carrie hoarsely, because (she/it/they) still had a bit of biscuit in (her/its) throat.

34. 'However, because you failed to detect that I'm clearly allergic to the products here, I'm afraid I'm going to have to sue the NHS, Moos, all (its/their) employees and you,' she insisted.

35. 'I'm overworked and underpaid and you're overweight and under-grateful. Don't you think there's another kind of legal relationship that would suit us better?' said the driver. 'I do,' whispered Carrie. And they did. And we bet you'll never guess what kind of cake they had at (its/their) wedding.

Decoding Who, That and Which

Most pronouns are singular or plural, masculine or feminine or neuter, popular or unpopular, good at maths or barely passing arithmetic. Okay, we went a little too far, but you get the point. The characteristics of most pronouns are fixed. But a couple of pronouns change from singular to plural and from masculine to feminine without a moment's pause. *Who*, *which* and *that* take their meaning and characteristics from the sentences in which they appear. Here's what we mean:

- May, who was born in April, wants to change her name. (The *who* is feminine and singular because it replaces the feminine, singular *May*.)

- Her sisters, who were named after their birth months of June and August, support May's idea. (The *who* is feminine and plural because it replaces *sisters*.)

A change in the meaning of *who*, *which* or *that* would be an interesting but useless fact except for one issue. Whether a subject pronoun is singular or plural affects what sort of verb (singular or plural) is paired with it. In the preceding sample sentences, the *who* is paired with *was* when it represents *May* and with *were* when it represents *sisters*.

Sometimes, deciding singular/plural verb issues is especially tough:

- She is one of the few midfielders who (is/are) ready to join the premier league.

- She is the only midfielder who (is/are) negotiating with Sheffield Wednesday.

The key to selecting the correct verb in this sort of sentence is deciding what the pronoun represents. If *who* means *she*, of course you opt for a singular verb because *she* is a singular pronoun. But if *who* means *midfielders*, the verb must be plural, because *midfielders* is plural. Logic tells you the answers:

- She is one of the few midfielders who ***are*** ready to join the premier league.

- She is the only midfielder who ***is*** negotiating with Sheffield Wednesday.

How many are ready for the premier league? A few midfielders are ready. And she's one of them. The *who* in the first example clearly stands in for *midfielders*, a plural. In the second example just one person is negotiating – *she*. Therefore, *who* is singular and so is the verb paired with it.

Don't score any own goals here. Instead, kick as many correct verbs as you can into the opposition's net by selecting the correct singular or plural verbs from the brackets.

Q. Jalini, who (was/were) one of the many people from her office on the excursion that day, was desperate to catch a dolphin.

A. **was.** Jalini is only one person. Therefore, the *who* replaces the singular, and the singular verb *was* is needed to match the singular *who*.

36. The boss had made it clear that promotion was guaranteed for anyone brave enough to bag a dolphin. With only a few minutes left till anchors-away, Jalini's colleagues, who said they (was/were) only trying to be helpful, pointed out that she didn't have any bait.

37. A sun-kissed hippie who (was/were) sitting on the pier by a rickety old booth – The Sunshine Shack – was Jalini's only hope.

38. 'I've got sun-cream, flip-flops, and somewhere in here I've got my secret supply of dolphin-treats,' mumbled the hippie who (was/were) rummaging through the hut's entire stock.

39. 'I don't mean to be rude, but can you hurry up a tiny bit, please?' begged Jalini. She looked down the pier and saw the boat, which (was/were) the boss's pride and joy, begin is final pre-launch preparations.

40. 'Aha! Here is it. I think I'm the only person in the world who (believes/believe) that one in ten of our beautiful dolphins is vegetarian,' the hippie said, pressing a small, glass jar into Jalini's hand.

41. With no time to lose, Jalini, who never (forgets/forget) her manners, thanked the hippie, ran down the pier and jumped onto the ship, just as it was heading out to sea.

42. As she was trying to catch her breath, one of her many colleagues who (was/were) laughing exclaimed, 'Marmite? You can't catch a dolphin with Marmite!'

43. Just a few minutes later, a couple of dolphins that really (was/were) rather fond of the famous yeast extract, swam sweetly into Jalini's net.

44. Jalini smiled. The corner office, the one that (has/have) fabulous views of the whole city, was hers for the taking. But then she realised that wasn't what she was after at all.

45. All the office bods, who still (talks/talk) of what they saw that day, watched as Jalini released the dolphins, jumped overboard and swam with the lovely creatures towards her new life of hippie happiness at The Sunshine Shack.

Getting Down to Specifics: Avoiding Improper Pronoun References

The underlying principle of using pronouns is that one pronoun can replace one and only one matching noun. This rule bends only a tiny bit by allowing *they*, for instance, to take the place of more than one name. (*Eda, Maria and Pauline*, for example, can be replaced by *they*.) In everyday informal speech and writing, pronouns are sometimes sent to fill other roles. But if you're going for correct, formal English, don't ask a pronoun to break the rules for you.

A common error is to ask a pronoun to stand in for an idea expressed by a whole sentence or paragraph. (Pronouns can't replace verbs or noun/verb combinations) The pronouns *that*, *which* and *this* are often misused in this way.

Wrong: Jeffrey handed in a late, error-filled report, which annoyed his boss.

Why the sentence is wrong: The pronoun *which* improperly refers to the whole sentence. In formal English the pronoun can replace one and only one noun.

Right: Jeffrey's report, which annoyed his boss, was late and error-filled. (Now *which* refers to *report*, a noun.)

Also right: The fact that Jeffrey's report was late and error-filled annoyed his boss. (Sometimes the best way to fix one of these sentences is to eliminate the pronoun entirely.)

Another common mistake is to send in a pronoun that approaches in meaning, but doesn't match, the noun it's replacing:

Wrong: Jane's sports marketing course sounds interesting, but she doesn't want to be one.

Why the sentence is wrong: She doesn't want to be *one* what? *Sports marketing course*? We don't think so. The writer of the sentence wants *one* to replace *sports marketer*, but no *sports marketer* is in the sentence to match with *one*.

Right: Jane's sports marketing course sounds interesting, but she doesn't want to complete it. (Now *it* replaces *sports marketing course* – a better match.)

Also right: Jane is studying to become a sports marketer, but she doesn't want to be one. (Now *one* replaces *sports marketer*.)

Fix the pronoun problems in the following exercises. Some are correct as written and when you find one, write 'correct' in the blank. Rewrite the clunkers so that every pronoun refers to an appropriate noun. Remember that sometimes you have to drop the pronoun entirely in order to correct the mistake. Note that the incorrect sentences have more than one possible answer; in the following example, we show you two possibilities, but in the answers section we provide only one possible answer.

0. Jeffrey's dream job features a corner office, five-hour lunches and frequent 'research' trips to Tahiti, which is unlikely given that he has no skill whatsoever.

A. **Given that he has no skill whatsoever, Jeffrey is unlikely to get his dream job, which features a corner office, five-hour lunches and frequent 'research' trips to Tahiti.** The preceding sentence is just one possible solution, in which the pronoun *which* takes the place of *job*. Here's another: **The fact that Jeffrey has no skill whatsoever makes his dream job, which features a corner office, five-hour lunches and frequent 'research' trips to Tahiti, unlikely.** Any sentence that achieves the goal of one noun out, one pronoun in is fine. The original doesn't work because *which* replaces an entire sentence, *Jeffrey's dream job features a corner office, five-hour lunches and frequent 'research' trips to Tahiti.*

46. Jeffrey jogged for an hour in an effort to work off the flab he had gained during his last three-hour lunch, but this didn't help.

_____

_____

47. He's always admired the superhero's flat-ab look, but no matter how hard he tries, he can't be one.

_____

_____

48. The 15 sit-ups that were prescribed by his personal trainer didn't help at all.

_____

_____

49. Jeffrey's next fitness effort ended in disaster; that did not discourage him.

_____

_____

50. He simply ignored the police sirens, abandoned his bike and ran away; this was only a temporary solution.

_____

_____

51. Next, Jeffrey joined a gym, where he recited Shakespeare's sonnets, which helped him to stay focused.

_____

_____

52. The great poet inspired Jeffrey to study it too.

_____

_____

53. 'No, I didn't see the car when I directed my bicycle into the street,' testified Jeffrey, 'but that wasn't the cause of the accident.'

_____

_____

54. 'The driver was distracted by his mobile, which rang at the exact moment I started to ride,' explained Jeffrey.

_____

_____

55. The judge was not impressed by Jeffrey's testimony and fined him, and Jeffrey paid it.

_____

_____

56. When Jeffrey paid the fine, the court clerk quoted Shakespeare, which impressed Jeffrey very much.

_____

_____

57. 'I see you are a sonneteer,' said Jeffrey as he smiled and gave the clerk a romantic look; the clerk wasn't impressed by this at all.

_____

_____

58. 'Please pay your fine and leave the room,' the clerk roared, and that squashed Jeffrey's hopes for a date.

_____

_____

59. The clerk never goes out with anyone from work, which is a wise policy.

_____

_____

60. The clerk quotes poems in the hope of becoming a literary critic; Jeffrey studied it at university, and so in theory they are a good match for each other. He just needs to compose the right poem for the clerk. Then their romantic future will be assured.

_____

_____

Brain Strain: Extra Practice with Tricky Pronoun Situations

Figure 11-1 shows a field trip report written by a battle-weary teacher after a particularly bad day. Can you find ten pronoun errors that cry out for correction? Circle the mistakes and give a thought to how you would fix them.

Figure 11-1:
A field trip report, written by a teacher who doesn't use pronouns correctly (shame!).

Mr Levi Martin

Year 6 class teacher

Field Trip Report, 16 June 2010

I left school at 10:03 a.m. with three teaching assistants and 17 pupils, all of whom were excited about our visit to Adventure Land. The day passed without incident, which was a great relief to me. I sat in the Adventure Land Bar and Grill for five hours while the assistants and students visited Space Camp, Pirates' Mountain and other attractions that are overrated but popular. The pupils saw me eating and said they wanted one too, but I replied that everyone had their packed-lunch. This was a disappointment, and several students threw them at me. We got on one of the buses that was overdue for maintenance. The engine whirred loudly, and it scared the bus driver. We drove to a branch of Quick Fix Brake and Wheel Repairs because the driver said their expertise was what we needed. Quick Fix is also the only one of the many car mechanic outfits on the M62 to Great Sankey that take credit cards, which was helpful because I had spent all my money in the Adventure Land Bar and Grill.

Answers to Advanced Pronoun Problems

1   **their.** The plural pronoun *both* matches with the plural possessive pronoun *their*.

2   **his.** The singular possessive *his* works nicely here because we're talking about *Alan* – a singular male.

3   **his or her.** Or **their.** Technically you can answer 'his best wishes' and be grammatically correct, but we always opt for the more inclusive term 'his or her'. You can pair the plural *their* with the singular *everyone*, but if your boss disapproves of this usage, you can also rewrite the sentence to get round the awkward *his or her* or *their*, for example by taking out the pronoun completely: **Relieved that the procedure had gone so well, everybody sent him best wishes.**

4   **their.** The plural pronoun *many* is a good mate for the plural possessive *their*.

5   **their.** The pronoun *few* is plural, and so is *their*. A fine pair – they may even consider a Civil Partnership soon!

6   **his or her.** Or **their.** To avoid the *his or her* or the use of the singular *their*, you can rewrite the sentence in lots of ways. For example: **Because Alan's surgery went smoothly, someone else in his family is going to have the same operation too.**

7   **his or her.** Or **their.** Again, though, a rewrite can help you avoid the clunky *his or her* construction or the controversial singular *their*. For example, **'Doesn't every nose need more warts?' reasoned Alan.**

8   **his or her.** Or **their.** If you want to rewrite the sentence to avoid the *his or her* clumsiness or because your boss objects to the singular *their*, you can try: **Even if we disagreed with Alan, we kept quiet, knowing that our opinions wouldn't be accepted anyway.** Or **Even if people disagreed with Alan, they kept quiet, knowing that their opinions wouldn't be accepted anyway.**

9   **its.** Yes, the sentence refers to *warts*, but the *each* indicates that you're talking about one wart at a time. The singular *each* matches the singular possessive pronoun *its*.

   Don't confuse the possessive pronoun *its* with the shortened form of *it is* (*it's*). The possessive has no apostrophe.

10   **their.** The pronoun *several* moves you into plural territory, where *their* rules.

11   **he or she.** Or **they.** Again, a rewrite would make this sentence much less clumsy: **Although not everyone liked the warts, the crowd reaction was generally positive.** Or **Although someone said, 'I don't like the new warts,' the crowd reaction was generally positive.**

12   **his.** You know that the cousins are both male (because of their names), and so you can use the male singular pronoun (*his*) to talk about each one's *beak*.

13   **their.** The plural *minds* matches with the plural *their*.

14   **it.** The singular *nothing* of the previous sentence pairs with the singular pronoun *it* in this sentence.

15   **their.** The pronoun *both* is plural, making *their* the best choice.

16   **their.** The *lots* tells you that you're talking about more than one person, and so the plural pronoun *their* fits the bill here.

17 **their.** *Millions* is plural and matches with the plural pronoun *their*.

18 **his or her.** Or **their.** You can rewrite this sentence to get round the awkward *his or her* or the singular *their* issue, like this: **Although not everyone will want the same type of nose wart.**

19 **their.** The plural possessive pronoun *their* refers to *publicity photos*, a plural.

20 **his.** *Neither* calls for a singular pronoun. You know that both the cousins are male, and so the singular male pronoun *his* is perfect.

21 **themselves.** The pronoun refers to the members of staff who like to nibble on a sponge cake or two. Because lots of workers are involved, *themselves* is the best choice.

22 **its.** The possessive pronoun refers to the company, *Kipples Kakes*. Because the company is singular (despite its plural-sounding name), it needs to be matched with a singular possessive, *its*.

23 **its.** The possessive pronoun refers to *the WSA*, a singular organisation. The singular pronoun is the one you want.

24 **its.** We know, we know. The word that sounds correct here is *their*. Unfortunately, the correct word is *its*, the singular pronoun that matches the singular organisation.

25 **its.** The association is singular, and so pronouns referring to it must also be singular.

26 **It's.** We slipped this one in just to see whether you're still awake! You don't need a pronoun here at all. Instead you require the contraction of *It is: It's*.

27 **it.** The *UNPOCI* body is singular, and so pronouns referring to it must also be singular.

28 **its.** *Moos* is one business, and so it must pair up with the singular *its*.

29 **It knows.** Use logic to figure this one out. Carrie is referring to the WSA, and so *it knows* is appropriate. If she were referring to the staff, *they know* would work.

30 **she.** The singular feminine pronoun *she* refers to *Carrie*, a singular female.

31 **its.** The company is singular, and so pronouns referring to it must also be singular.

32 **it doesn't.** *The NHS*, an organisation, takes the singular pronoun *it* and a singular verb.

33 **she, her.** These two pronouns refer to *Carrie*, and so singular and feminine rule is the way to go, both times.

34 **its.** The company name sounds plural, but in reality we're talking about a singular entity, and *its* matches up correctly.

35 **their.** The pronoun *they* refers to two people, a plural, and so the plural pronoun *their* makes a match.

36 **were.** The clue here is *colleagues*, which is a plural noun that needs a plural verb.

37 **was.** The *sun-kissed hippie* is singular, and so you need the singular *was*.

38 **was.** The *hippie* is still singular, and so you still need the singular *was*.

39 **was.** The *boat* is a singular noun, and so the *which* is singular and takes a singular verb, *was*.

40   **believes.** The *only* tells you that you're talking about something or someone singular, and so the singular verb, *believes*, works just fine here.

41   **forgets.** Jalini is very polite, and singular too. The singular *forgets* is the right choice here.

42   **was.** Don't be fooled by the plural *colleagues*. Although many of them were laughing, you want to zoom in on *one* of them in particular. To do this, use the singular verb *was*.

43   **were.** How many dolphins swam sweetly into the net? Not just one, but two. The *that* is plural, as is the verb, *were*.

44   **has.** *The corner office* is a singular place with a fabulous view, and so the singular *has* is the way to go.

45   **talk.** The plural *office bods* calls for the plural *talk*.

46   **Jeffrey jogged for an hour in an effort to work off the flab he had gained during his last three-hour lunch, without success.** The easiest way to fix the pronoun problem (in the original sentence, *this* incorrectly refers to a complete sentence, not to a single noun) is to eliminate *this*. You can dump *this* with any number of rewrites, including the one given here.

47   **He's always admired the superhero with flat abs, but no matter how hard he tries, he can't be one.** Now the pronoun *one* refers to *superhero*. In the original, the noun *superhero* doesn't appear, just the possessive *superhero's*, which doesn't match the nonpossessive pronoun *one*.

48   **correct.** The pronoun *that* replaces one word: *sit-ups*.

49   **The fact that Jeffrey's next fitness effort ended in disaster did not discourage him.** Eliminate the pronoun and you eliminate the problem, which is the pronoun *that*. *That* can't refer, as it does in the original sentence, to a whole sentence (*Jeffrey's next fitness effort ended in disaster*).

50   **As a temporary solution, he simply ignored the police sirens, abandoned his bike and ran away.** The pronoun *this* needs a one-word reference, but in the original, *this* replaces everything that appears before the semicolon. As usual, an easy fix is to rewrite without a pronoun.

51   **correct.** Surprised? The pronoun *which* refers to sonnets. One word out, one in and you're fine.

52   **The great poet inspired Jeffrey to study poetry too.** The original doesn't make clear what *it* means. The solution is to insert a noun (*poetry*) and get rid of the pronoun.

53   **'No, I didn't see the car when I directed my bicycle into the street,' testified Jeffrey, 'but my distraction wasn't the cause of the accident.'** One possible fix is to cut *that* and insert a specific word. We choose *distraction*, but you can also use *blindness*, *lack of awareness* or something like that.

54   **correct.** The pronoun *which* correctly refers to *mobile*.

55   **The judge was not impressed by Jeffrey's testimony and fined him, and Jeffrey paid the £50.** Okay, you can pick any amount you want, just so long as you dump the *it*. Why is *it* wrong? The original sentence has no *fine*, just the verb *fined*. A pronoun has to replace a noun, not a verb.

56   **When Jeffrey paid the fine, he was impressed by the court clerk, who quoted Shakespeare.** The problem here is the pronoun *which*. In the original sentence, the *which* refers to the fact that the court clerk spouted sonnets while Jeffrey counted out his money. In this suggested rewrite, the *which* is dropped altogether.

57 **'I see you are a sonneteer,' said Jeffrey as he smiled and gave the clerk a romantic look; the clerk was not impressed by Jeffrey's efforts at all.** The original sentence contains a vague pronoun (*this*). You can eliminate this vagueness in a couple of different ways; just write a noun instead of *this* and you're all set.

58 **'Please pay your fine and leave the room,' the clerk roared, squashing Jeffrey's hopes for a Saturday night date.** To create a correct sentence, simply rewrite the sentence to omit the vague pronoun *that*.

59 **The clerk wisely never goes out with anyone from work.** You can eliminate the vague pronoun *which* in several different ways. Another possible correction is **The clerk's policy never to date anyone from work is wise.**

60 **The clerk quotes poems in the hope of becoming a literary critic; Jeffrey studied literary criticism at university, and so in theory they are a good match for each other. He just needs to compose the right poem for the clerk. Then their romantic future will be assured.** The original sentence didn't make clear what *it* refers to. Jeffrey didn't study *literary critic* (the expression in the original); he studied *literary criticism*, an expression that replaces *it* in the corrected sentence.

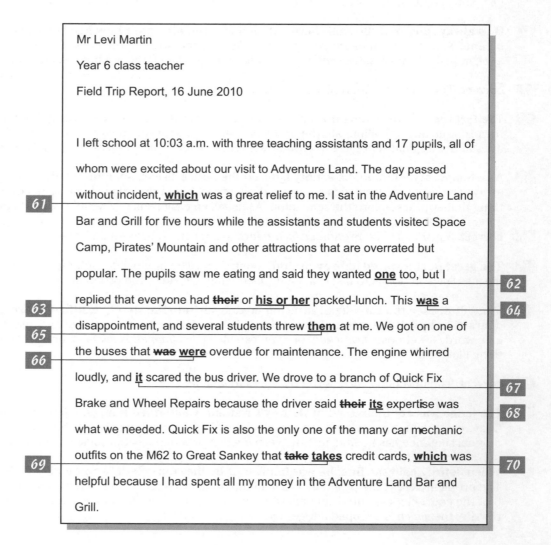

Mr Levi Martin

Year 6 class teacher

Field Trip Report, 16 June 2010

I left school at 10:03 a.m. with three teaching assistants and 17 pupils, all of whom were excited about our visit to Adventure Land. The day passed without incident, **61** **which** was a great relief to me. I sat in the Adventure Land Bar and Grill for five hours while the assistants and students visited Space Camp, Pirates' Mountain and other attractions that are overrated but popular. The pupils saw me eating and said they wanted **62** **one** too, but I replied that everyone had **63** ~~their~~ or **his or her** packed-lunch. This **64** **was** a disappointment, and several students threw **65** **them** at me. We got on one of the buses that **66** ~~was~~ **were** overdue for maintenance. The engine whirred loudly, and **67** **it** scared the bus driver. We drove to a branch of Quick Fix Brake and Wheel Repairs because the driver said **68** ~~their~~ **its** expertise was what we needed. Quick Fix is also the only one of the many car mechanic outfits on the M62 to Great Sankey that **69** ~~take~~ **takes** credit cards, **70** **which** was helpful because I had spent all my money in the Adventure Land Bar and Grill.

61 In the original sentence, *which* refers to the fact that *the day passed without incident*. A pronoun can't replace an entire sentence. One possible fix is *The fact that the day passed . . . was a great relief to me*.

62 *One* what? The pronoun has no noun to refer to, just the verb *eating*. Reword to add some food (*. . . saw me eating an ice-cream cone*) and the *one* will make sense.

63 The pronoun *everyone* is singular, and so it must be paired with *his or her*, not *their*. That's the verdict from the hard-line school of grammar. A more liberal approach says that this sentence doesn't contain a mistake at all, because *their* is an acceptable match for *everyone*. The fence-sitting, don't-want-to-offend-anyone school of grammar says, 'Why not just go for a rewrite and avoid the entire controversy?' and offers this as a compromise: 'I replied that *all of them* had *their* packed-lunches.'

64 The pronoun *this* needs one noun to replace, not a whole sentence. Substitute the pronoun and the verb *was* with something like *The packed-lunches were. . . .*

65 In the original, the pronoun *them* refers to nothing. Add *theirs* or *their lunches* or *their sandwiches* and you're in business.

66 The sentence should read *one of the buses that were*, not *one of the buses that was*. The pronoun *that* is a stand-in for *buses*.

67 What does *it* mean? The engine didn't scare the driver; the whirring sound scared her. But *it* needs to replace a noun. Fix this problem by saying that *the driver was scared* or something similar.

68 *Their* shouldn't refer to a company. Try *its* instead.

69 This sentence should say that the shop was *the only one of the many that takes*. When you get into 'only one of ____' territory, you know that the pronoun is singular and needs a singular verb.

70 What does *which* mean? The fact that the car mechanic outfit takes credit cards. The pronoun can't replace all those words, and so rewrite to eliminate the pronoun with something like *It was helpful that Quick Fix accepted credit cards because. . . .*

Chapter 12

Travelling in Time: Tricky Verb Tense Situations

*H*ave you ever noticed that *The Terminator* films and ordinary English verbs have quite a lot in common? No? Well, in Terminator's world, characters can travel through time and English verbs let writers and speakers do the same. You may not have a protective metal friend from the future to help you with verbs, but we can help you negotiate not only the grammar of the future but also some of the tense rules of the past and present. For example, did Arthur say that he *has* or *had* a cold? *Did* or *does* Mars qualify as a planet? And what effect do verbals – hybrid forms that are part verb, part another speech form – have on the timing of events in a sentence?

If you're not completely sure of all these aspects of grammar, you're in exactly the right place. So, pull up a chair and we can explore this exciting frontier together.

Telling Tales of the Past

Everybody loves to gossip, and if your day is anything like ours it's probably filled with lots of little stories of what other people have said or written (summaries, in other words). Because you're telling (actually, retelling) something that already happened, your base of operations is the past. Note the past tense verbs in italics in the following:

> She *caught* Arthur with Stella, but he *told* her that he *was* only helping Stella with her necklace and not nibbling her neck. Then she *said* that Arthur *brought* her a box of chocolates with a note saying that no one else *had* eyes like hers.

What's wrong with the preceding example? Nothing, apart from the fact that Arthur was indeed nibbling Stella's neck. The verb tenses are all in the past because that's the correct form when you're summarising speech. So even if Stella still *has* incomparable eyes, in this paragraph the verb *had* is better. (One important exception to the stay-in-past-tense-for-speech-summary rule is explained in the next section, 'Communicating the Unchanging Universe: When You're Stuck in the Present'.)

A common error is to switch from one tense to another with no valid reason. Can you spot the mistakes in some of the following italicised verbs?

So she *sat* home and *waited* for the phone to ring. He finally *called*. Then he *says* that the big dance *is* a waste of time and they *will skip* the whole thing!

If she *sat* and *waited* until he *called* (all past tense verbs), the next three verbs (*says*, *is* and *will skip*) should be in the past tense too (*said*, *was* and *would skip*).

Take a crack at selecting the right verb from the options in brackets – circle your answer. Just to be sure that you're paying attention, we sneak in a few verbs that aren't summary of speech and so shouldn't be in the past tense.

Q. During yesterday's auditions for the new reality show, *Grammarian Idol Factor*, Roberta (tells/told/will tell) the producer that she (likes/liked/will like) selecting pronouns while dangling 60 metres feet above the ground.

A. **told, liked.** The first answer is easy. If the auditions were yesterday, Roberta's chat with the producer has to be in past tense. *Told* is past tense. The second part is trickier. She may always *like* selecting pronouns, but in summary of speech, past tense (*liked*) is the way to go (with one exception, which we look at in the next section, 'Communicating the Unchanging Universe: When You're Stuck in the Present').

1. The director of *Grammarian Idol Factor* explained to the candidates that he (has/had/will have) to select a maximum of 30 contestants.

2. All the contestants said that they (want/wanted/would want) to make the final 30.

3. Roberta, who (is/was/had been) ultra-competitive, screamed at the director that he (doesn't/didn't) have the faintest idea how to select the best applicants.

4. Michael Hooper, a guy who didn't get selected, told me Roberta (is/was) the clear favourite when she won all three audition challenges – the noun toss, the pronoun shuffle and the verb race.

5. But then he also told me something surprising: Roberta (fails/failed) the psychological screening.

6. Last week when the psychologist (asks/asked) Roberta her feelings about various parts of speech, Roberta said that linking verbs (pose/posed) a problem for her.

7. 'Why (don't/didn't) you like linking verbs?' probed the psychologist.

8. Roberta explained that any form of the verb *to be* (annoys/annoyed) her.

9. 'I always (try/tried) to avoid any sentence with that sort of verb,' added Roberta.

10. She went on to say that adjectives (are/were/had been) her favourite part of speech.

11. The psychologist later reported that he (is/was) worried about Roberta's reaction to punctuation.

12. Roberta apparently said that commas (are/were/had been) 'out to get her'.

13. She added that exclamation marks also (threaten/threatened) her.

14. The psychologist nodded in agreement. He said that he felt (hem/hemmed) in by quotation marks.

15. Roberta and the psychologist disagreed, however, when Roberta said that the semicolon (is/was) the best punctuation mark.

16. This morning the director said that he (doesn't/didn't) know what to make of Roberta's punctuation obsession.

17. The assistant director said that Roberta (is/was) too unstable for a show that relies heavily on question marks.

18. The make-up artist chipped in that Roberta (is/was) probably faking a punctuation phobia just to attract attention.

19. The camera operator added that she (knows/knew) lots of people who (are/were) terrified by commas and apostrophes.

20. The director thanked the psychologist for his report and all the crew for their input but declared that a publicity hungry grammar-phobe – fake or real – would be a huge ratings success. Roberta (is/was) in!

Communicating When You're Stuck in the Present

Verb tenses express the march of time: past, present and future. But some things don't march; they stay in one, unchanging state forever. When you talk about these things, the present tense is the only one that makes sense, no matter what else is going on in the sentence. Take a look at the following example:

> **Wrong:** Theresa told the class that the earth was a planet.

> **Why this sentence is wrong:** What is the earth now, a bagel? The unchanging fact, that the earth is a planet, must be expressed in the present tense, even though all the other summarised speech in the sentence is in the past tense. (See the preceding section 'Telling Tales of the Past' for more information on summarising speech.)

> **Correct:** Theresa told the class that the earth is a planet.

Choose the correct verb from the brackets in the following sentences. To complicate your life, we mix 'eternal truths' with changeable information. The eternal truths get present tense treatment no matter what, but with the other stuff . . . you're on your own.

Q. Although even Bradley Patterson, the slowest boy in the class, knew that 10 plus 10 (equals/equalled) 20, the new teacher wrote '15' on the board last week.

A. **equals.** In maths, 10 added to 10 always makes 20. No change is possible, and so you need the present tense here.

21. Theresa won't last very long as a schoolteacher if she keeps telling her class that each molecule of water (has/had) three hydrogen atoms.

22. Science has never been Theresa's best subject. Yesterday she explained that water (covers/covered) nine tenths of the planet.

23. Her teaching assistant, Jacqueline, whispered to her that land (makes/made) up about a quarter of the earth's surface.

24. Theresa sniffed. She wasn't being rude to Jacqui. It was just that she (has/had) a cold. Theresa thanked Jacqui for her suggestion but said that she couldn't think about the earth anymore. It was time for lunch.

25. Jacqui suggested that they went out for a snack (bagels and cream cheese) at VeggieMight, a café that had just opened near the school. Theresa promptly told Jacqui that she had lots of allergies. Theresa said she couldn't eat the cheese because it (is/was) a dairy product.

26. 'Not the way they make it here,' Jacqui replied, pointing out that the product (is/was) completely artificial.

27. Did anyone actually like Vegan Cheesy Smile, Theresa wondered, and why (is/was) it on my bagel when I ordered peanut butter?

28. Theresa put on her best science teacher's voice and intoned, 'Cheese (comes/came) from milk. I may be violently ill any second now.'

29. 'Don't you know that the ingredients of Vegan Cheesy Smile (are/were) not naturally found in dairy?' Jacqui asked.

30. Theresa shook her head. She decided to figure out the bill instead of being sick. She declared, 'One pound eighty, divided by two (is/was) one pound eighty.' Then she got out her calculator to check her sums.

31. Jacqui asked if Theresa wanted some strawberries and ice-cream before they (go/went) back to school.

32. Theresa declined Jacqui's offer. Theresa has never liked strawberries because they (have/had) seeds.

33. Theresa once counted all the seeds on a strawberry before deciding not to eat it; there (are/were) 45.

34. Jacqui said she was surprised that Theresa even (knows/knew) how to count that far.

35. Theresa said Jacqui should keep her smart alec comments to herself if she wanted to continue to assist the best teacher in the universe. The universe, of course, which (include/includes) Mars, Milky Way and Polo Mints.

Tackling the Timeline: Verbals to the Rescue

In Chapter 1 we looked at the basic and 'perfect' tenses of verbs (past, present, future, past perfect, present perfect and future perfect). Here we drop you into a vat of boiling grammar as you choose the best tense for some complicated elements called *verbals*. As the name implies, verbals have a link with verbs, but they also have something in common with other parts of speech (nouns, adjectives and adverbs). Verbals never act as the verb in a sentence, but they do influence the sense of time that the sentence conveys. Here are the three types of verbals:

✔ **Gerunds** look like the *-ing* form of a verb but function as a noun; that is, a gerund names a person, place, thing or idea. ('I like smiling,' said Alice, who had just had her braces removed. In this sentence, *smiling* is a gerund.)

✔ **Infinitives** are what you get when you add 'to' to the base form of a verb. Infinitives may function as nouns or they may take a descriptive role. ('To be safe, Alice packed a few hundred packets of chewing gum.' In this sentence, *to be* is an infinitive.)

✔ **Participles** are a verb form used to describe something, not as the verb of the sentence. Created using *-ing*, *-ed* or an irregular form (*driven*, *seen* or *drunk*, for example), participles often give you background information about when something happened. For example, 'Having driven across the desert, she stopped for a drink.' *Having driven* is a verb form but it describes the subject *she*. *Stopped* is the verb of the sentence.

Two types of participles exist: past participles (*driven, played, talked, gone* and so on) and present participles (*singing, writing, watching* and so on). You can use a past participle to show an action is complete before another begins: 'Having driven across the desert, she stopped for a drink' (in this sentence the driving happened before the stopping). On the other hand, if you want to show two actions happening simultaneously, you need a present participle: 'Screaming his head off, the boss demanded last week's report'. Here, the present participle *screaming* tells us that the screaming and the demanding happened at the same time.

The same logic applies with infinitives; they can be used to show actions happening simultaneously or at different times. In 'He screamed and started to run', both the actions are taking place more or less at the same time. In 'He appears to have seen a ghost', the seeing took place earlier and so the experience shows on his face now.

When choosing between a present and past participle you need to decide whether the events are simultaneous, at least in the grammatical sense. To start, figure out how important the timeline is. If the events are so closely spaced as not to matter, go for the present participle (*-ing*) form. If it matters to the reader/listener that one event followed or is going to follow another, go for a past participle (*having + verb -ing*).

Circle the correct verbal form from the brackets in this example and in the practice sentences that follow.

0. (Delivering/Having delivered) the new product, the chemists asked the boss to conduct some market research on the funny little earth creatures.

A. **Having delivered.** The two events occurred in the past, with the chemists' request closer to the present moment. The event expressed by the verbal (a participle) *having delivered* attributes another action to the chemists. The perfect form (*having* + the past participle *delivered* tells you that you're in perfect-land) places the act of *delivering* before the action, *asked*, which is the main verb in the sentence.

36. (Peering/Having peered) at each interview subject's mouth, the researchers checked for discoloration.

37. One interview subject blushed a pretty crimson on (hearing/having heard) the interviewer's comment about 'teeth as white as the moon'. She didn't look so happy when the interviewer insisted she therefore needed some of his colour enhancement product.

38. (Refusing/Having refused) to open her mouth again, she glared silently at the interviewer.

39. The market research on Emerald Smile (completed/having been completed), the team tabulated the results.

40. The tooth greener (being distributed/having been distributed), no further research is scheduled.

41. The researchers actually wanted (to interview/to have interviewed) 50 per cent more subjects after Emerald Smile's debut, but the legal department objected.

42. Additional interviews will be scheduled if the legal department succeeds in (getting/having got) participants to sign a 'will not whinge, will not moan, will not sue' pledge.

43. '(Sending/Having sent) free tubes of Emerald Smile to every home in the land means that I'm sure that it works,' said the captain of the friendly mission to earth.

44. (Seeing/Having seen) the tears of joy from the first earthlings to join the ranks of the civilised, the scientists and researchers knew they had done a good job.

45. '(Managing/Having managed) to get the funny little people's teeth to look almost normal, I suppose we now have to get to work on centring their eyes and removing those useless secondary ones they all have,' said the chief scientist with a weary green smile.

Brain Strain: Extra Practice with Verb Tenses

You need to know how to summarise speech, allow for unchangeable facts and create a timeline with verbals in order to edit the accident report in Figure 12-1, filed by a security guard. Read the report and circle the correct verbs or verbals in the brackets.

GMT Industries

Incident Report

Date: 29/8/10   Time: 1:10 a.m.

Place: Loading dock   Guard on duty: P. Samuels

(Proceeding, Having proceeded) from the locker room where *Grammarian Idol Factor* was on television, I noticed smoke (coming, having come) from a doorway that leads to the loading dock. (Knowing, Having known) that no deliveries were scheduled, I immediately became suspicious and took out my two-way radio. I alerted the other guard on duty, M. Faulkner, that trouble might be brewing. Faulkner, not (turning, having turned) off the television, couldn't hear me. Upon (screaming, having screamed) into the radio that I needed him right away, I crept up to the door.

I noticed that the smoke was not hot. As I waited, (touching, having touched) the door to see whether it was getting hot, I sincerely wished (to find, to have found) Faulkner and (to strangle, to have strangled) him for not (replying, having replied) when I called. (Arriving, Having arrived), Faulkner apologised and explained that the adverb competition (is, was, had been) his favourite. 'It was just heating up when you called,' he said. He also said that he (has, had) a clogged ear that he (has, had) not been able to clean out, no matter how many toothpicks he (uses, used).

'(Speaking, Had spoken) of heating up,' I remarked, 'I don't sense any heat from this door.' I reminded him that fire (is, was) hot, and where there's smoke, (there is, there was) fire. Then Faulkner and I, (hearing, having heard) a buzz from the other side of the door, ran for shelter. I told Faulkner that the buzz (is, was) not from a bomb, but neither of us (being, having been) in the mood to take chances, we headed for the locker room. We did not put the television on again, *Grammarian Idol Factor* (being, having been) over for more than ten minutes, but we did plug in a CD as we waited for the police to arrive, (calling, having called) them some time before. Therefore we didn't hear the director yell, 'Cut!' In no way did we intend (to disrupt, to have disrupted) the film crew's work or (to ruin, to have ruined) the dry ice that caused the 'smoke'. (Respecting, Having respected) Hollywood for many years, Faulkner and I wish Mr Scorsese only the best with his next film.

Answers to Advanced Verb Tense Problems

1. **had.** The tip-off is the verb *explained*, which tells you that you're summarising speech. Go for the past tense *had*.

2. **wanted.** *Said* is a clue that you're summarising speech, and so *wanted*, the past tense, is best.

3. **is, didn't.** The first choice has nothing to do with summary of speech and is a simple statement about Roberta. The present tense works nicely in this spot. The second choice is a speech summary (well, a scream summary, but the same rule applies), and so the past tense verb *didn't* fits the bill.

4. **was.** The sentence tells you what Michael Hooper said. The past tense works here for summary of speech.

5. **failed.** If Michael *told* me, the sentence is summarising what he said, and so the past tense *failed* is the right option.

6. **asked, posed.** The first answer comes from the fact that the psychological test was in the past. The second is summary of speech (Roberta's words) and calls for past tense.

7. **don't.** Give yourself a pat on the back if you answered this one correctly. The quote marks indicate that the words are exactly what the psychologist said. The speech isn't summarised; it's quoted. The present tense makes sense here because the tester is asking Roberta about her state of mind at the current moment.

8. **annoyed.** Straight summary of speech is used here, indicated by the verb *explained*. Therefore, you want the past tense.

9. **try.** This statement isn't a summary, but a direct quote from Roberta. She's speaking about her habits, and so the present tense fits.

10. **were.** Roberta's comments are summarised, not quoted, and so the past tense is appropriate.

11. **was.** The psychologist may still be worried (you would be too, if you were treating Roberta!), but the summary of what he said should be in the simple past tense.

12. **were.** The brackets contain two past tense verbs, *were* and *had been*. You can use the *had* form to place one event further in the past than another, but that isn't needed here. When you're simply summarising what someone is saying and not placing events in order, go for the simple past tense.

13. **threatened.** Roberta's remark about exclamation marks is summarised speech calling for the past tense.

14. **hemmed.** The psychologist's comments should be reported in the simple past tense.

15. **was.** Some more summarised speech, and so use the simple past tense.

16. **didn't.** *The director said* is your cue to chime in with in the simple past tense, because you're reporting his speech.

17. **was.** *The assistant director said* tells you that you're reporting the words she used. The past tense is the way to go.

18 **was.** The words *chipped in* are key here because they indicate summarised speech, which calls for in the simple past tense.

19 **knew, were.** Your intuition may point you towards the present tense in this sentence because the camera operator may still be hanging around with people who can't handle punctuation marks. However, summarised speech needs past tense.

20 **was.** This sentence is a summary of what the director said, and so the simple past tense is what you want here.

21 **has.** The composition of water doesn't change, no matter how wrong Theresa is about the number of hydrogen atoms in H_2O. Present tense is called for here.

22 **covers.** Theresa has apparently tried to change the amount of water on the planet, but in reality the amount of water is constant and so merits present tense.

23 **makes.** The amount of land doesn't change; go with present tense.

24 **had.** Colds come and go; they aren't unchangeable conditions. The summary of speech rule doesn't change, and so you want the past tense. (See the earlier section 'Telling Tales of the Past' for more details.)

25 **is.** For once, Theresa is correct. Cheese is a dairy product and can't change into anything else. For an eternal truth, present tense is correct.

26 **was.** Product composition can change, and the speaker is summarising what was said. Past tense makes sense.

27 **was.** What's on the bagel doesn't fall into the eternal truth category, and Theresa's wondering happened in the past. The past tense verb *was* is the one you want.

28 **comes.** The definition of 'cheese' doesn't change (although the makers of Vegan Cheesy Smile may disagree), and so the present tense works best here.

29 **are.** This directly quoted remark refers to something that doesn't change. Vegan Cheesy Smile doesn't contain dairy products unless someone's been tampering with Mother Nature. Present tense works for an unchangeable fact.

30 **is.** Maths doesn't change, and so the present tense is appropriate.

31 **went.** *Asked* is your clue here. If you're summarising what Jacqui asked and you're not dealing with eternal truths, the past simple tense is best.

32 **have.** Because strawberries and seeds are linked for eternity, go for the present tense.

33 **were.** One particular strawberry had 45 seeds, but another strawberry may have a different number. Because this sentence expresses a changeable and not an eternal truth and because the sentence as a whole is in the past tense, past tense is appropriate for the verb *were* as well.

34 **knew.** Theresa (contrary to the opinion of every other teacher in her school) can learn, and so this statement expresses a fact that may change. The past tense works best here because it's a summary of what Jacqui said.

35 **includes.** Theresa may be mistaken but she's talking about eternal truths here (the composition of the universe), and so the present tense is needed.

36 **Peering.** Here the two actions take place at the same time. The researchers check out the subjects' teeth and look for trouble. The perfect form (with *having*) is for actions at different times.

37 **hearing.** Again, two actions take place at the same time. Go for the non-perfect, *-ing* form, *hearing*.

38 **Refusing.** The 'not on your life will I open my mouth' moment is simultaneous with an 'if looks could kill' glare, and so the non-perfect, *-ing* form is best.

39 **having been completed.** The non-perfect, *-ing* form *completed* would place two actions (the completing and the tabulating) at the same time. Yet common sense tells you that the tabulating follows the completion of the research. The perfect form (with *having*) places the completing before the tabulating.

40 **having been distributed.** The decision to stop market research is based on the fact that it's too late; the tooth product, in all its glory, is already being manufactured. Because the timeline matters here, and one action is clearly earlier, the perfect form is needed.

41 **to interview.** The *have* form, *to have interviewed*, places the action of interviewing before the action expressed by the main verb *objected*. But the legal department objected first, and so you need the infinitive form, *to interview*.

42 **getting.** The two actions to concentrate on here are *succeeding* and *getting*. They take place at the same time, because the minute somebody signs a legal paper, the lawyers are successful. Because it expresses a simultaneous action, the verbal without *having* is appropriate.

43 **Sending.** The captain's statement places two things, sending and being sure, at the same time, and so the *-ing* form without *have* is the best option here.

44 **Seeing.** The people's happiness and scientists' knowledge of a job well done happen at the same time, and so the *-ing* form without *have* is correct.

45 **Having managed.** Two events are occurring at different times (the successful change in tooth colour was in the past and the beginning of realigning eyes is in the future). The event expressed by the participle, *having managed*, places the act of managing before the future action of having to begin the eye-centring work.

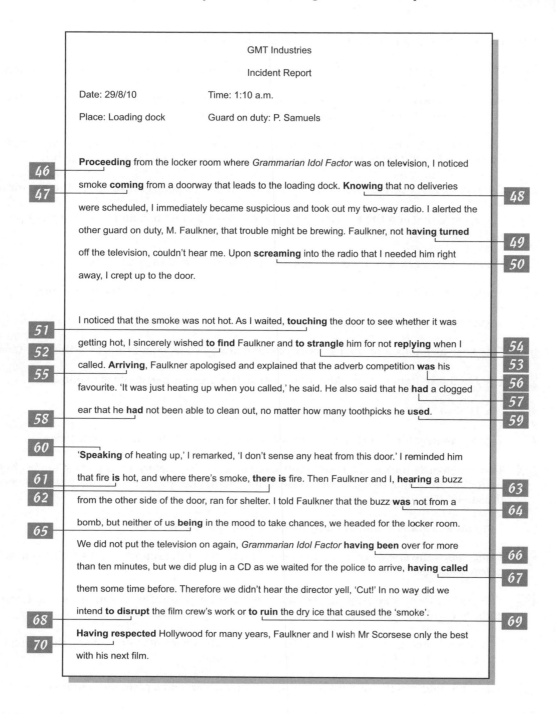

GMT Industries

Incident Report

Date: 29/8/10   Time: 1:10 a.m.

Place: Loading dock   Guard on duty: P. Samuels

46 **47** **Proceeding** from the locker room where *Grammarian Idol Factor* was on television, I noticed smoke **coming** from a doorway that leads to the loading dock. **Knowing** that no deliveries **48** were scheduled, I immediately became suspicious and took out my two-way radio. I alerted the other guard on duty, M. Faulkner, that trouble might be brewing. Faulkner, not **having turned** **49** off the television, couldn't hear me. Upon **screaming** into the radio that I needed him right **50** away, I crept up to the door.

51 **52** **55** I noticed that the smoke was not hot. As I waited, **touching** the door to see whether it was getting hot, I sincerely wished **to find** Faulkner and **to strangle** him for not **replying** when I **54** called. **Arriving**, Faulkner apologised and explained that the adverb competition **was** his **53** **56** favourite. 'It was just heating up when you called,' he said. He also said that he **had** a clogged **57** ear that he **had** not been able to clean out, no matter how many toothpicks he **used**. **58** **59**

60 **61** **62** **65** 'Speaking of heating up,' I remarked, 'I don't sense any heat from this door.' I reminded him that fire **is** hot, and where there's smoke, **there is** fire. Then Faulkner and I, **hearing** a buzz **63** from the other side of the door, ran for shelter. I told Faulkner that the buzz **was** not from a **64** bomb, but neither of us **being** in the mood to take chances, we headed for the locker room. We did not put the television on again, *Grammarian Idol Factor* **having been** over for more **66** than ten minutes, but we did plug in a CD as we waited for the police to arrive, **having called** **67** them some time before. Therefore we didn't hear the director yell, 'Cut!' In no way did we intend **to disrupt** the film crew's work or **to ruin** the dry ice that caused the 'smoke'. **68** **69** **70** **Having respected** Hollywood for many years, Faulkner and I wish Mr Scorsese only the best with his next film.

46 The proceeding and the noticing took place at roughly the same time, and so you want the present participle *proceeding*.

47 The noticing and the coming of the smoke were more or less simultaneous, and so go for the *-ing* form here. The perfect form would place one action earlier than another, which is contrary to the intended meaning.

48 The suspicions arose from the knowledge that no deliveries were scheduled, and so the knowing and the act of suspecting are simultaneous, calling for the *-ing* form.

49 This sentence emphasises the order of events. Because the television wasn't turned off first, Faulkner was unable to hear. The perfect form – *having turned off* – works to distinguish the earlier action.

50 The screaming and the creeping are simultaneous; go for the *-ing* form.

51 The touching of the door and the waiting are simultaneous, calling for the present participle.

52 Samuels wished to find Faulkner, and the wishing and finding are more or less simultaneous. The infinitive places both actions at around the same time.

53 The infinitive *to strangle* is appropriate because the guard wished *to find and to strangle* Faulkner all at the same time. The actions are presented equally, not in time order.

54 The calling and replying are presented as simultaneous acts, and so go for the *-ing* form.

55 The apologising and the arriving are going on at the same time, and so the present participle *-ing* form is best.

56 This verb expresses summarised speech, and so you need the past tense.

57 Another speech summary is expressed by this verb, and so go for the past tense.

58 In summarising this speech, opt for the past tense.

59 This verb also falls into the category of summarised speech and thus take the past tense.

60 The *I* in the sentence is speaking now, and so the present participle is needed.

61 Fire is always hot, indicating that the present tense works here.

62 This unchangeable fact (fire is never without smoke) calls for the present tense.

63 The two guards took off at exactly the same time as they heard a buzz – no time lag here! The perfect form would indicate two consecutive events, but these events were simultaneous and thus need the *-ing* form.

64 Summarised speech, indicated by *told*, calls for the past tense.

65 *Being* keeps the speakers in the moment. The writer of the report is not placing one action before another.

66 The perfect form is appropriate because the guard is putting events in order. First, the show ends. Second, they put on a CD.

67 In hopes of saving his job, the guard emphasises the order of events, using the perfect form to place the calling of the police earlier on the timeline.

68 The intending and the disrupting are simultaneous, and so a plain old infinitive is best.

69 Another infinitive works here because the intending and the ruining occur at the same time.

70 Here the writer is emphasising a longstanding respect for the film world. The perfect form shows the respectful feeling started in the past and continues into the present.

Chapter 13

Getting Your Verbs in the Right Mood

• •

In This Chapter

▶ Understanding the different moods of verbs

▶ Choosing verbs for various types of sentences

• •

*N*o, they're not pregnant or having a mid-life crisis, but verbs do have mood swings. One minute they're *indicative* – the regular, plain, just-the-facts sort of verb. (The dishes *are* dirty. No one *has washed* them. Little colonies of mould *established* themselves all over the sink a couple of days ago.) Suddenly they're issuing orders in the *imperative* mood. (*Wash* the dishes. *Stop* whining. *Don't think* your pocket money is off-limits to me!) And when you least expect a change, the *subjunctive* pops up. (If I *were* rich enough to hire a maid, I wouldn't ask for your dishwashing help. I'm not a millionaire, and so I request that 7 p.m. *be* the official washing-up hour.)

Got the idea? Of the three verb moods, you're probably the most familiar with the indicative. Every statement of fact is in the indicative mood, as are nearly all the sentences in this book. The imperative mood gives commands, usually to an understood *you* who doesn't appear in the sentence. The subjunctive, the one designed to give you a headache, shows up in condition-contrary-to-fact sentences and in certain command/wish sentences. In this chapter we take you through all three moods, with a little extra attention to the hard one, the subjunctive.

Stating the Obvious: Indicative Mood

Do you want to see some samples of indicative verbs? No problem. Every verb in this paragraph is in the indicative mood. In fact, just about everything we say about verbs in this book applies to indicative verbs, which, as the name implies, indicate facts. Indicative mood is the one you use automatically, stating action or describing states in any tense and for any person.

Indicative verbs change according to the time period you're talking about (the tense) and, at times, according to the person doing the action. We cover these issues in Chapters 1 and 2.

Now that you're in the mood, circle the indicative verb that works best in each of the following sentences. The verb options are in brackets.

Q. The boss (holds/held) a performance review every June.

A. **holds.** Both options are indicative, but the present tense works better. You use the present simple tense to talk about habits, and the expression *every June* is the clue that these reviews are a habit.

1. So, every year, each employee (is/was) summoned to Gwyneth's office for what she calls 'our little annual chat'.

2. All the workers (know/will know) that the 'chat' is all on Gwyneth's side.

3. Gwyneth (likes/like) to discuss the economy, and the reasons no one (will/would) get a raise.

4. '(Is/Was) business good these days?' she asks.

5. She always (mentions/will mention) that she too may have to make personal sacrifices to save the company.

6. Sacrifices! She (means/meant) that she (takes/will take) home only a million instead of two million next year!

7. Maybe she (replaced/will replace) the linen napkins in the executive dining room with paper ones.

8. After the chat, we always (go/will go) out for some conversation of our own.

9. (Does/Do) we review Gwyneth's performance in the most candid way?

10. Yes, if you (think/thinks) candid performance feedback means belting out 'Take this job and shove it' in a karaoke bar at two in the morning.

Taking Command: Imperative Mood

When you study another language, you can develop a major headache right around the time you come to the imperative mood. Languages such as French, Italian, Russian and Japanese each have a lot of rules on how to form commands – plus irregulars! English is much kinder. In English, the command (also known as the imperative mood), is the same whether you're talking to one person or 20, to a peasant or a queen, or to a woman or a man. The English command form is the infinitive minus the *to*. In other words, the unchanged, plain form of the verb. Negative commands are slightly different. They take the infinitive-minus-to and add *do not* (or *don't*), as in *do not say a word, do not blink* and *don't blubber*.

Here are some examples, with the imperative verb in italics:

- ✔ *Stop* snivelling, Harry.
- ✔ *Pull* yourself together and *face* your new in-laws.
- ✔ *Don't mention* our engagement.
- ✔ *Prepare* to die if they find out we're getting married!

Fill in the blanks with commands for Harry, who is meeting his prospective in-laws. The base verb you're working with appears in brackets at the end of each sentence.

Q. _____ quietly on the couch, Harry, while I fetch Daddy. (to sit)

A. **Sit.** The command is formed by dropping the *to* from the infinitive.

11. Harry, _____ my lead during the conversation. (to follow)

12. If Mummsie talks about Paris, _____ your head and _____ interested. (to nod/to look)

13. You know I adore your funny little voices but Daddy hates comedy accents, and so _____ your 'zut alores' French routine. (to do, negative command)

14. _____ them to show you their footage of last year's trip to Normandy. (to ask)

15. _____ asleep during Daddy's director's cut DVD extras! (to fall, negative command)

16. _____ some of Mummsie's tripe, even if it's cold. (to eat)

17. _____ the mould on the bread or the risk of food poisoning. (to mention, negative command)

18. When she serves you a huge plate of bread, dripping and tripe, just _____ that a little touch of food poisoning never killed anyone. (to remember)

19. _____ them good night and _____ them for a lovely evening. (to wish/to thank)

20. _____ that we won't visit them very often after the wedding. (to remember)

Telling Lies or Being Passive: Subjunctive Mood

The subjunctive is a very big deal in some languages, for example German and Spanish. Fortunately for you, in English the subjunctive pops up in only two situations: conditions that are contrary-to-fact and indirect commands.

Condition-contrary-to-fact means that you're talking about something that isn't true:

✔ If I *were* famous, I would wear sunglasses day and night.

✔ *Had* I *known* the secret password, the bouncer would have let me in.

✔ If I *had* not *punched* the police office, I would have avoided jail.

Notice that the subjunctive changes some of the usual forms. In the indicative, the pronoun *I* is paired with *was* (see the earlier section 'Stating the Obvious: Indicative Mood' for more detail). The switch to *were* in the first sample sentence tells you that you're in fantasy land. In the second and third sample sentences, the *had* does more than its usual indicative job, which is to place events earlier in the past than other past-tense events. (See Chapter 1 for more details on this use of *had*.) Instead, in a subjunctive sentence the *had* also means that the person didn't know the secret password and did punch the police officer. Note also the difference in word order – with the helping verb *had* coming before the main verb *known*.

In some regions of Britain, as well as in informal English, the condition-contrary-to-fact form *I was* is acceptable. For example, If *I was* a rich girl, I'd buy everything.

Condition-contrary-to-fact sentences always feature a *would* form of the verb. In standard English, the *would* form never appears in the part of the sentence that is untrue (that's usually the part that has the *if* in it. For example: *If* I knew you were coming, I *would have* baked a cake.)

Subjunctive verbs also express commands indirectly, as in these sentences, in which the subjunctive verb is italicised:

✔ The bouncer requested that she *remove* herself from the queue as soon as possible.

✔ The club owner declared that guests wearing unfashionable clothes *be* denied entry.

Subjunctive, indirect commands are formed by dropping the *to* from the infinitive. In the first sample sentence, the pronoun *she* normally (that is, in the indicative mood) pairs with *removes*. In the subjunctive, the infinitive *to remove* loses the *to* and becomes *remove*. In the second sample, *guests* pairs with *be*, which is created by dropping *to* from the infinitive *to be*. The indicative form would be *guests are*.

Write the correct verb in the blank for each exercise in this section. The verb you're working with appears in brackets after each sentence. Just to keep you honest, we tuck in a few sentences that don't require the subjunctive. Keep your eyes open.

0. If Ellen _____ for her turn at the wheel, she wouldn't have wrapped her car around that telephone pole. (to prepare)

A. **had prepared.** The *had* expresses a condition-contrary-to-fact here, because Ellen didn't prepare for her driving test.

21. The driving test examiner asked that Ellen _____ ready for her exam at 9 a.m. (to be)

22. The test would have gone better if Ellen _____ a morning person. (to be)

23. 'If it _____,' explained her driving instructor, 'you will be required to take the test as soon as the roads are cleared.' (to snow)

24. If the gritter _____ the entire route, Ellen would have passed. (to cover)

25. Unfortunately, the supervisor of the gritting crew declared that the motorways _____ cleaned first. (to be)

26. Terrified of ice, Ellen requested that the examiner _____ her test. (to postpone)

27. If he _____, Ellen would have taken the test on a sunny, warm day. (to refuse, negative form)

28. If Ellen _____ about the examiner, the Driver and Vehicle Licensing Agency would have investigated. (to complain)

29. If an examiner _____ unfair, the DVLA schedules another test. (to be)

30. The department's policy is that if there _____ a valid complaint, they dismiss the examiner promptly. (to be)

31. If Ellen _____ the test fives times already, she would have been more cheerful about failing this time. (to take, negative form)

32. If in the future Ellen _____ somewhere else to take her test, she may have more luck. (to go)

33. Not every testing centre cares if the driver _____ into a tree. (to skid)

34. If only Ellen _____ to Pluto, she would have a licence already. (to travel)

35. Plutonian law apparently requires that a driver _____ 'reasonable competency' and nothing more. Ellen reckons she'd pass with flying colours in outer space. (to demonstrate)

Brain Strain: Extra Practice with Moody Verbs

Now that you're in control of these three moods (cranky, irritable, ready to bite someone's head off!), try your hand at this exercise. The progress report in Figure 13-1 has some serious mood problems. Check out the underlined verbs, circle the ones that are correct, and cross out and correct the ones that are in the wrong mood.

Progress Report: Coffee Break Control

From: Mr Bell, Coffee Break Coordinator

To: Ms Schwartz, Department Head

Re: Coffee Break Control

31 July 2010

As you <u>know</u>, I <u>were</u> now in charge of implementing the new directive that every

employee <u>submits</u> to a coffee-residue test. If a test <u>were</u> given at a time when coffee-

sipping <u>were</u> not <u>authorised</u> and the results <u>were</u> positive, the policy <u>require</u> that the

member of staff '<u>donates</u>' a large pack of coffee to the staff lounge.

<u>Do not asked</u> me to describe the union's reaction to this directive. If I <u>would tell</u> you

what the shop steward <u>would have said</u>, you <u>had blushed</u>. All I <u>would say</u> is that the

steward <u>were</u> not happy.

<u>Would</u> you <u>have known</u> about the reaction before issuing the directive, you <u>would have</u>

<u>had reconsidered</u>. One more thing: the coffee stains on my shirt, if you <u>were to notice</u>

them, please don't <u>thought</u> that I <u>were drinking</u> coffee outside of the official break time.

These stains <u>are</u> the result of coffee being thrown at me.

Figure 13-1:
This progress report contains some verbs that are in the wrong mood.

Answers to Verb Mood Problems

1 **is.** The sentence speaks of habit (*our little annual chat*), and so the present tense is best.

2 **know.** The workers have been through this 'chat' many times, and so the act of knowing isn't in the future but in the present.

3 **likes, will.** The present tense form for talking about someone (*Gwyneth*, in this sentence) is *likes*. The future tense verb *will* explains that in the coming year employees will be shopping in the bargain basement.

4 **Is.** The expression *these days* is a clue that you want a present tense verb.

5 **mentions.** If an action always occurs, present tense is the best choice.

6 **means, will take.** The boss is talking about the future (the clue is *next year*). The talking takes place in the present (so you want *means*), but the earning is in the future (hence, *will take home*).

7 **will replace.** The *maybe* creates a hypothetical situation, wondering what the boss *will* do in the future.

8 **go.** A habit (and the clue is *always*) calls for the present tense.

9 **Do.** The subject *we* calls for the plural form.

10 **think.** *You* can be either a singular or plural pronoun. Whichever way you use it, it requires the plural verb, *think*.

11 **follow.** The command is formed by stripping the *to* from the infinitive.

12 **nod, look.** Drop the *to* and you're in charge, commanding poor Harry to act interested even if he's ready to call off the engagement rather than listen to one more story about French wine.

13 **don't do** or **do not do.** The negative command relies on a form of *do*.

14 **Ask.** Poor Henry! He has to ask, which in command form is *ask*.

15 **Don't fall** or **Do not fall.** Take *to* from the infinitive and add one *don't* or *do not,* and you have a negative command.

16 **Eat.** Henry's in for a long evening with tripe on the menu. To make the command, *Eat*, drop *to* from the infinitive.

17 **Don't mention** or **Do not mention.** The negative command needs a form of *do* or it dies.

18 **remember.** Drop the *to* from the infinitive and you're in imperative mood.

19 **Wish, thank.** The imperative verbs are created by subtracting *to* from the infinitives.

20 **Remember.** Somehow we doubt that Harry is going to forget this fact, but to order him, take *to* from the infinitive.

21 **be.** The subjunctive is needed for this indirect command, expressed by the verb *asked.*

22 **were.** Ellen likes to sleep until mid-afternoon, and because she's not a morning person, the subjunctive verb *were* expresses condition-contrary-to-fact. The verb *were* is better than *had been* because Ellen is still not a morning person.

23 **snows.** Surprise! This example isn't subjunctive. The instructor is talking about a possibility, not a condition that didn't occur. The normal indicative form, *snows*, is what you want.

24 **had covered.** The gritter didn't finish (the clue here is *would have passed*), and so the subjunctive is needed.

25 **be.** An indirect command is created by the verb *declared*. The subjunctive *be* fits nicely.

26 **postpone.** The indicative (the normal, everyday form) of *to postpone* is *postpones*, when the verb is paired with *examiner*. Here the indirect command created by *requested* calls for the subjunctive *postpone*.

27 **had not refused** or **hadn't refused.** The examiner stood firm: take the test or else. Thus the first part of this sentence is condition-contrary-to-fact and calls for the subjunctive.

28 **had complained.** Ellen said nothing, as revealed by the conditional *would have investigated* in the second part of the sentence. The subjunctive is the way to go.

29 **is.** Did we fool you here? The possibility expressed in the *if* portion of the sentence calls for a normal, indicative verb (*is*). Stay away from subjunctive if the statement could be true.

30 **is.** The first part of this sentence is not condition-contrary-to-fact. It expresses a possibility and thus calls for the normal, indicative verb (*is*).

31 **had not taken** or **hadn't taken.** She has taken it five times, and so the statement isn't true and needs a subjunctive.

32 **goes.** Here the sentence expresses a possibility. She may go and she may have more luck. Stay away from subjunctive if the sentence could be true.

33 **skids.** As in sentence 32, this one talks about something that is true (or may be true). Go for the normal indicative and give the subjunctive a rest.

34 **had travelled.** She didn't travel, and she (thank goodness) doesn't have a licence. This condition-contrary-to-fact sentence needs the subjunctive.

35 **demonstrate.** The verb *requires* tips you off to the fact that subjunctive is appropriate for the indirect command.

Progress Report: Coffee Break Control

From: Mr Bell, Coffee Break Coordinator

To: Ms Schwartz, Department Head

Re: Coffee Break Control

31 July 2010

36 As you **know**, I ~~were~~ **am** now in charge of implementing the new directive

37 that every employee ~~submits~~ **submit** to a coffee-residue test. If a test

38 ~~were~~ **is** given at a time when coffee-sipping ~~were~~ **is** not **authorised** and the **40**

39 results ~~were~~ **are** positive, the policy ~~require~~ **requires** that the member of **42**

41 staff ~~'donates'~~ **'donate'** a large pack of coffee to the staff lounge.

43 **Do not** ~~asked~~ **ask** me to describe the union's reaction to this directive. If I

44 ~~would tell~~ **were to tell** you what the shop steward ~~would have~~ **said**, you **46**

45 ~~had blushed~~ **would blush**. All I ~~would say~~ **will say** is that the steward **48**

47 ~~were~~ **was** not happy.

49 ~~Would~~ **Had** you ~~have~~ **known** about the reaction before issuing the directive, **50**

you **would have** ~~had~~ **reconsidered**. One more thing: the coffee stains on **51**

my shirt, if you ~~were to notice~~ **noticed** them, please don't ~~thought~~ **think** **53**

52 that I ~~were drinking~~ **drink** coffee outside of the official break time These **54**

stains **are the result of** coffee being thrown at me. **55**

---

36 Correct.

37 The indicative is called for here because the sentence expresses a truth, not a condition-contrary-to-fact or a command.

38 This part of the sentence expresses an indirect command, *that every employee submit*. The indicative verb that matches the singular subject *every employee* is *submits*, but the subjunctive form (*submit*) is needed here.

39 A normal indicative verb works here because giving *a test* is a real possibility, not a condition-contrary-to-fact.

40 The indicative *is* works best in this sentence, which expresses a real possibility and not a condition-contrary-to-fact.

41 Because the possibility exists, the indicative is called for.

42 This statement is simply a fact, and so the indicative is needed.

43 The second part of the sentence is an indirect command (*the member of staff 'donate'*) and needs the subjunctive.

44 The imperative mood, the command, calls for the infinitive minus the *to*, and because this command is negative, *do not* is added. In the original, the *-ed* at the end of *ask* is wrong.

45 The writer is *not* telling, and so a subjunctive verb form is needed to express a condition-contrary-to-fact.

46 The report referred to concerns what was actually *said*, and so the indicative works here.

47 In a sentence expressing a condition-contrary-to-fact, the 'untrue' portion needs to be subjunctive, with the 'would' statement in the other part of the sentence. Other possible corrections are *Had I told you . . . you would blush* or *If I told you . . . you would blush*.

48 A plain indicative verb is needed for this statement.

49 The original has a subjunctive (*were*) but the indicative is called for in this simple statement.

50 The sentence expresses a condition-contrary-to-fact, and so you need a subjunctive. The corrected sentence is *Had you known about the reaction. . . .*

51 The original has two 'would' statements. The 'would' doesn't belong in the 'untrue' portion of the sentence. Replace the first with a *had* statement and you're in business: *Had you known . . . you would have reconsidered.*

52 This sentence doesn't express a condition-contrary-to-fact. Instead, it talks about a possibility, and so go with the indicative, not the subjunctive.

53 Stay in the indicative present here, not past.

54 The indicative present is correct here.

55 Correct.

Part IV

All You Need to Know about Descriptions and Comparisons

'To make sure he's going to a good home, I'm going to have to give you an English grammar test.'

In this part . . .

Listen to a toddler and you hear language at its most basic: *Jake want apple. Daddy go shop? No nap!* These 'sentences' – nouns and verbs and little else – communicate effectively but once you've passed the sandpit stage, you need a bit more. Enter descriptions and comparisons. Also enter complications because quite a few common errors are associated with these elements.

In this part you can practise your navigation skills, steering around such potholes as the choice between adjectives, adverbs and articles. (*Sweet* or *sweetly? Good* or *well? A* or *an?* Chapter 14 explains all.) This part also tackles the placement of descriptions (Chapter 15) and the proper way to form comparisons (Chapters 16 and 17). Getting the hang of all these topics lifts you out of the sandpit and places you permanently in the big school of grammar.

Chapter 14

Writing Good or Well: Adjectives, Adverbs and Articles

In This Chapter

▶ Choosing between adjectives and adverbs

▶ Managing tricky pairs: *good/well* and *bad/badly*

▶ Selecting *a, an* or *the*

Do you write *good* or *well* – and what's the difference? Do you munch on *a apple* or *an apple* or even *the apple*? Do you wear *a, an* or *the* uniform? If you're puzzling over these questions, never fear. This chapter is specifically designed to help you. Here you can practise choosing between two types of descriptions – adjectives and adverbs. This chapter also helps you decide whether *a, an* or *the* is the right choice in any given situation.

Distinguishing Between Adjectives and Adverbs

In your writing or speaking, of course, you don't need to stick labels on adjectives and adverbs. But you do need to send the right word to the right place to get the job done: the job being to communicate your meaning to your reader or listener. Also important is to punctuate strings of adjectives and adverbs correctly. (For help with that topic, have a look at Chapter 5.) A few really hard-working words (*fast, short, last* and *likely,* for example) function as both adjectives (that's a *fast* car) and adverbs (they work *fast*), but for the most part, adjectives and adverbs aren't interchangeable.

Adjectives describe nouns – words that name a person, thing, place or idea. They also describe pronouns, which are words that stand in for nouns (such as *she, they, it, other, someone* and similar words). Adjectives usually go before the word they describe, but not always. In the following sentence, the adjectives are italicised:

> The *rubber* duck with her *little orange* bill sailed over the *murky, shallow* water (*rubber* describes duck; *little* and *orange* describe bill; *murky* and *shallow* describe water).

An adverb, on the other hand, describes a verb, usually telling how, where, when or why an action took place. Adverbs also indicate the intensity of another descriptive word (for example, *incredibly* happy) or add information about another description. In the following sentence, the adverbs are in italics:

> The boat rocked *furiously* while the duck *violently* flapped her wings (*furiously* describes rocked; *violently* describes flapped).

Most adverbs end in *-ly*, but some vary, and adjectives can end with any letter in the alphabet, except *Q* or *Z* (unless you can think of any!). If you're not sure which form of a word is an adjective and which is an adverb, check the dictionary. Most definitions include both forms with handy labels telling you what's what.

Here's a description dilemma for you: which word is correct? The brackets contain both an adjective and an adverb. Put a circle round the right one.

Q. The water level rose and fell (dramatic/dramatically) as the (intense/intensely) altercation between the boat and the duck the rumbled on.

A. **dramatically, intense.** How did the water drop? The word you want from the first set of brackets must describe an action, and so the adverb *dramatically* wins the prize. Next up is a description of an *altercation*, a thing, meaning that the adjective *intense* does the job.

1. The boat, a (loyal/loyally) member of the Talking Bath Playthings Union, (real/really) didn't like the duck being so close to the taps.

2. 'Can't you just stay out of my (personal/personally) sailing area once and for all?' asked the boat (reasonable/reasonably).

3. 'I'm not going to tell you again,' snapped the duck. 'He says we both work here. Stop being so (defensive/defensively) about the water supply and just get over it!'

4. The two creatures (swift/swiftly) circled each other, both looking for a (clear/clearly) advantage.

5. 'You seem (extreme/extremely) territorial about these taps. Is there some kind of childhood trauma that you'd like to talk about? Didn't Mummy Boat give you enough water to play in when you were a baby?' whispered the duck (menacing/menacingly).

6. The boat retreated (fearful/fearfully) as the duck quacked (sharp/sharply).

7. 'You leave my mother out of this,' whimpered the boat (sad/sadly).

8. The duck, relishing the prospect of tears before bedtime, pressed her advantage. 'The reason I have the prized position near these (glorious/gloriously) taps is . . . oh, I really shouldn't say. He told me not to tell you.'

9. 'Not tell me what?' asked the boat, as he heard his heart pound (loud/loudly) in his ears.

10. 'Oh you wouldn't understand,' said the duck (curt/curtly).

11. 'I will. Tell me. Please,' begged the boat. He hated hearing that (pleading/pleadingly) tone creep into his voice.

12. 'Promise me you won't cry,' demanded the duck (ominous/ominously).

13. 'Promise,' said the boat, trying (hard/hardly) to stop his voice quivering.

14. 'No blubbering?' The only sound in the bathroom was the water lapping (gentle/gently) and the boat's laboured breathing.

15. 'No blubbing. I give you my word,' said the little (heroic/heroically) boat.

16. 'Okay. He said I'm guard of the taps because, of all the (cute/cutely) bathing accessories, I'm the one he trusts the most. He told me not to tell you but . . . he says he loves me the best.'

17. One big fat tear (slow/slowly) trickled down the (miserable/miserably) boat's chubby little face.

18. 'Crybaby! Crybaby! You big blubbering baby boat,' jeered the duck (happy/happily).

19. The boat sobbed (quiet/quietly) but (uncontrollable/uncontrollably). The duck's taunts only became louder.

20. (Sudden/Suddenly) a creature dressed in a shabby, moth-eaten dressing gown appeared in the doorway.

21. The human whipped out a megaphone that was (near/nearly) two metres in length.

22. 'Listen!' he shouted (forceful/forcefully). 'Can't a man turn his back for a second without this whole *Waterworld* thing kicking off?'

23. The boat and the duck were (complete/completely) speechless. 'And now that I've got your attention,' he said, as he put the megaphone down (careful/carefully) on the bathroom floor, 'I'd like to introduce you to my new friends.'

24. 'This is Ms Vanilla Bean Candle, Mr Pot Pourri and their friends the Incense-Stick family. I really do believe they'll help me find the peace and enlightenment I'm (constant/constantly) craving.'

25. 'And best of all,' he said, 'they've promised me my very own (personal/personally) nirvana in return for burning just a couple of bits of brightly-coloured plastic. Now, where do you think I can find two things like that?'

Asking How It's Going: Choosing Between Good/Well and Bad/Badly

Adjective and adverb pairs (especially *good* and *well*, *bad* and *badly*) can cause quite a bit of trouble to quite a few people. How often have you heard sports stars say that they 'played aggressive'? Use this quick guide on how to use these pairs, and you won't find yourself fluffing your soundbites in your post-match interviews. *Good* and *bad* are adjectives, and so they have to describe nouns (people, places, things or ideas). *Well* and *badly* are adverbs used to describe actions. They can also be attached to other descriptions. In the expression *a well written essay*, for example, *well* is attached to the word *written*, which describes *essay*.

Well can also be an adjective in one particular circumstance: health. When someone asks how you are, the answer (we hope) is *I'm well* or *I feel well*. You can also – and we hope you do – feel *good*, especially when you're talking about your mental state, although this usage is a bit more informal. Apart from health questions, however, *well* is a permanent member of the adverb team. In fact, if you can insert the word *healthy* in a particular spot, *well* works just as well (as it were).

A few special verbs take the adjectives *good* and *bad*. They are verbs of being (the state a person is in) or verbs of the senses, such as *feel, look, smell, taste* and so on. You may think that examples such as, 'that shirt looks good on you' or 'this food smells bad' are wrong, but actually they're right. The verbs *look* and *smell* are unusual in that they don't use the adverbs *well* and *badly* but the adjectives *good* and *bad* instead.

Note that the adverb *badly* exists but it has a different meaning when you pair it up with the sense verbs. *He smells badly* implies he has something wrong with his nose and he's having trouble differentiating between different aromas. *He smells bad* means that you want him to shower a bit more often after playing a sweaty game of football.

Take a look at these judgement words in action:

- ✔ I gave a good report to the boss this morning. (The adjective *good* describes the noun *report*.)

- ✔ In my opinion, the report was particularly well written. (The adverb *well* is attached to the verb *written*.)

- ✔ Smokey, the bad cat, snaffled up the entire fish stew that was left cooling in the kitchen. (The adjective *bad* describes the noun *cat*.)

- ✔ Smokey slept badly after his fish feast. (The adverb *badly* describes the verb *slept*.)

When a description follows a verb, danger lurks. You have to decide whether the description gives information about the verb or about the person/thing doing the action or being. If the description tells you more about the verb, go for an adverb. If it describes the noun (a person or thing), opt for the adjective.

Put on your judge's robes and pass sentence on these sentences. Circle the correct word in each set of brackets.

Q. Nipper's trainer works (good/well) with all types of dogs, especially those that don't outweigh her.

A. **well.** How does the trainer work? The word you need must be an adverb because you're giving information about an action (*work*), not a noun.

26. Nipper barks when she runs (good/well) during her daily race with the postie.

27. The postie likes Nipper and feels (bad/badly) about beating her almost every day in their morning sprints.

28. Nipper insists that she's not a (bad/badly) loser. On the other hand, she does bite the poor bloke's ankles whenever the race doesn't turn out (good/well) for her.

29. Although Nipper likes dog biscuits (good/well) enough, her real weakness is postie leg and feet parts.

30. The postie thinks Nipper's little nibbles on his ankles aren't too (bad/badly), actually.

31. He often wonders what his ankles taste like. The postie hopes they don't taste too (bad/badly) to his four-legged friend.

32. If only he knew. The taste of his ankles isn't what makes Nipper want to throw up on a daily basis; it's the smell of his feet. They smell so (bad/badly), Nipper often thinks she's going to faint when she's near them.

33. Last week, Nipper could eat only a tiny morsel of ankle, before the stench of cheesy feet completely ruined her appetite. Nipper didn't feel (good/well) afterwards and had to be taken to the vet.

34. Patti the vet recognised all the classic symptoms of Postie Nasal Irritation Syndrome in Nipper. 'Have you been sniffing round that malodorous postal carrier again? (Bad/Badly) dog!'

35. She told Nipper, 'I'm afraid there's only one solution if you want to be (good/well) again – a Post Pursuer's Schnozzle Occluder.' That's a clothes peg to you and me.

Mastering the Art of Articles

Three little words known as articles – *a, an* and *the* – crop up in just about every English sentence. Which one you need depends on the situation, and so sometimes selecting the right one is a matter of interpretation. Here are some pointers to help you decide which article is correct in a particular context:

✔ *The* refers to something specific. When you say that you want *the book*, you're implying one particular text, even if you haven't named it. *The* can refer to both singular and plural words.

✔ *A* and *an* are more general in meaning, and they work only with singular nouns. If you want *a book*, you're willing to read anything, or at least to browse the bookshelves a bit. *A* goes before words beginning with consonants and *an* goes before words beginning with vowels – or rather, before words that begin with a vowel *sound*. For example, *university* begins with a vowel (*u*) but the correct usage is *a university* not *an university*, because *university* begins with a *y* sound, a consonant and not a vowel. In other words, you want *a* book, specifically *an encyclopedia* because you want to read about *a UFO*.

If you want a general term but you're talking about a plural, try *some* or *any* instead of *a* or *an*, because these last two articles can't deal with plurals.

Write the correct article in each blank in the following sentences.

Q. When Louise asked to see _____ wedding pictures, she didn't expect Rachel to put on _____ eight-hour slide show.

A. **the, an.** In the first half of the sentence, Louise is asking for something specific. Also, *wedding pictures* is a plural expression, and so *a* and *an* are out of the question. In the second half of the sentence, something more general is appropriate. Because *eight* begins with the vowel *e*, *an* is the article of choice.

36. Although Louise was mostly bored out of her mind, she did like _____ picture of Rachel's Uncle Josh that caught him snoring in the back of the synagogue.

37. _____ nearby guest, one of several attempting to plug up their ears, can be seen poking Uncle Josh's ribs.

38. At Rachel's wedding, Uncle Josh wore what he thought was _____ antique bow tie that he'd bought from his favourite shop, *Buy Smart*.

39. _____ sales assistant at *Spy Smart* (Uncle Josh's eyesight wasn't what it once was) inserted _____ microphone and _____ miniature radio transmitter into Uncle Josh's tie. These surveillance items come as standard with _____ 407H Spy Tie.

40. Uncle Josh's snores were broadcast to _____ Secret Agents' Annual Conference in . . . well, we can't tell you where. If we did, we'd have to kill you. Sorry.

41. Rachel, who hadn't wanted to invite Uncle Josh in the first place, had placed _____ buzzer under his seat, before anyone arrived for _____ nuptials.

42. Rachel's plan was for him to get zapped whenever he snored too loudly; unfortunately, Uncle Josh chose _____ different seat. Mrs McClusky, _____ old family friend, decided to sit in the place Rachel had prepped for Uncle Josh.

43. _____ wedding flowers (lilies and roses) triggered Mrs McClusky's allergies. Her sneezing set off the buzzer, which made her jump a metre in _____ air.

44. One of _____ two flower girls, distracted by Mrs McClusky's gymnastics, dropped _____ basket of roses that she was supposed to scatter over _____ bride and groom when they made their vows. She burst out crying and no one could get her to stop.

45. Rabbi Gluckman shortened _____ ceremony in _____ effort to avoid any further upstaging of _____ happy couple by tantrums, sudden movements or nasal issues.

Brain Strain: Extra Practice with Descriptors

Show off the knowledge you gained from the sections in this chapter by finding the mistakes in the excerpt from a clothing catalogue shown in Figure 14-1. Twenty descriptive words are underlined, but only some of them are wrong. Look for adjectives trying to do an adverb's job (and vice versa) or the wrong sort of articles. When you find an error, correct it. If the description is okay, leave it alone.

Smooth Styles: Cheap Fashion That Looks 'It'

A–D. <u>Surprising</u> <u>comfortably</u> suits for work and leisure. <u>Easily</u>-to-clean polyester in <u>real</u> varied colours takes you from the <u>office</u> grind to the <u>extreme</u> <u>hip</u> club scene without a pause!

A. <u>Fast</u>-track jacket. Stun your colleagues with <u>a</u> <u>astonishingly</u> elegance of <u>deeply</u> purple. <u>Gently</u> curves follow <u>an</u> <u>real</u> natural outline to accentuate your figure. The <u>silkily</u> lining, in <u>delightful</u> loud shades of orange, gives <u>a</u> <u>strong</u> message: I am woman! Hear me roar!

B. <u>Softly</u>, woven trousers coordinate with <u>a</u> jacket described above — and with everything in your wardrobe. In purple, orange, or purple-orange tartan.

Figure 14-1: Clothes catalogue exercise.

Answers to Adjective and Adverb Problems

1 **loyal, really.** What kind of member is the boat? A *loyal* member. Because you're describing a noun (*member*), you need the adjective *loyal*. In the second part of the sentence, the adverb *really* explains how intensely the boat *didn't like* the duck's presence.

2 **personal, reasonably.** In the first part of the sentence, *personal* describes a thing (*sailing area*). How did the boat ask? *Reasonably*. The adverb describes the verb, *asked*.

3 **defensive.** The adjective *defensive* describes *you* when the duck is talking to the boat.

4 **swiftly, clear.** The adverb *swiftly* describes the action of *circling*. The adjective *clear* explains what kind of *advantage* the creatures were seeking.

5 **extremely, menacingly.** The adverb *extremely* clarifies the intensity of the adjective *territorial*. The adverb *menacingly* describes how the duck *whispered*.

6 **fearfully, sharply.** Both of these adverbs tell how the actions (*retreated* and *quacked*) were performed.

7 **sadly.** The adverb *sadly* gives information about the verb *whimpered*.

8 **glorious.** The adjective *glorious* tells us more about the noun *taps*.

9 **loudly.** The adverb *loudly* describes the verb *pound*.

10 **curtly.** The adverb *curtly* tells how he *said*, a verb.

11 **pleading.** That *tone* is a noun. Adjectives describe nouns, and so *pleading* does the trick here.

12 **ominously.** *Demand* is a verb and if you want to describe how the duck *demanded*, an adverb (*ominously*) is just what you need.

13 **hard.** This word is an irregular adverb. The adverb *hardly* means *only just* ('she so rich she *hardly* has to work at all'). But you want the meaning of *using a lot of effort* (as in 'the boat used a lot of effort to stop his voice quivering'), and so the irregular adverb *hard* is the one you want.

14 **gently.** The verb *lapping* must be described by an adverb, and *gently* fits the bill nicely.

15 **heroic.** The *boat* is a noun, which may be described by the adjective *heroic* but not the adverb *heroically*.

16 **cute.** You need an adjective and *cute* is as good as any other to describe the nouns that are the *accessories*.

17 **slowly, miserable.** The adverb *slowly* describes the verb *trickled* and the adjective *miserable* describes the noun *boat*.

18 **happily.** To describe the verb *jeered*, you need an adverb such as *happily*.

19 **quietly, uncontrollably.** Both these adverbs describe the verb *sobbed*.

20 **Suddenly.** This adverb is used to describe how the creature *appeared*.

21 **nearly.** This question is a tough one, and if you got it right, treat yourself to a spa day. The expression *two metres* is a description of the *megaphone*. The adverb *nearly* gives additional information about the description *two metres in length*.

22 **forcefully.** The adverb *forcefully* tells how he *shouted*, a verb.

23 **completely, carefully.** The first adverb describes the adjective *speechless* and the second one describes the verb *put down*.

24 **constantly.** The adverb *constantly* tells you about the verb *craving*.

25 **personal.** If you're describing *nirvana*, a noun, you need an adjective, which in this case is *personal*.

26 **well.** The adverb *well* tells you how Nipper *has run*.

27 **bad.** This sentence illustrates a common mistake. The description doesn't tell you anything about the postie's ability to feel (touching sensation). Instead, it tells you about the letter carrier's state of mind. Because the word is a description of a person, not of an action, you need an adjective, *bad*. To *feel badly* sounds like you're wearing gloves and can't feel anything through the thick wool

28 **bad** and **well.** The adjective *bad* describes the noun *loser* and the adverb *well* is attached to the verb *turn out*.

29 **well.** How does Nipper like dog biscuits? She likes them *well*. The adverb is needed because you're describing the verb *likes*.

30   **bad.** The description *bad* applies to the noun *nibbles*, and so you need an adjective here.

31   **bad.** *Bad* describes *taste* and *taste* is a sensing verb, and so you need the adjective *bad*. *Taste badly* is wrong because ankles aren't able to taste anything.

32   **bad.** The adjective *bad* means *unhealthy* when attached to the verb of sense – *smell*.

33   **well.** The best response here is *well*, an adjective that works for health-status statements. *Good* can do at a pinch, but *good* is better for psychological or mood statements.

34   **Bad.** The adjective *bad* applies to the noun *dog*.

35   **well.** This phrase is another health statement, and so *well* is the right choice here.

36   **the.** The sentence implies that one particular picture caught Louise's fancy, and so *the* works nicely here. If you chose *a*, no problem. The sentence would be a bit less specific but still acceptable. The only one that doesn't work here is *an*, which goes before most words beginning with vowels – a group that doesn't include *picture*.

37   **A.** Because the sentence tells you that several guests are nearby, *the* doesn't fit here. The more general *a* is best to express 'one of many'.

38   **an or the.** You can use *an* (because *antique* begins with the vowel *a*) or *the*. Usually *a* or *an* is used when introducing something for the first time, as here with his *bow tie*. If everyone knows about Uncle Josh's famous (and only) bow tie, however, *the* works just as well.

39   **The, a, a** and **the.** Lots of blanks in this question! The first one is most likely about a particular sales assistant, and so *The* fits well. The next two blanks imply that the assistant selected one from a group of many, not a particular microphone or transmitter. Therefore the more general article *a*, which precedes words beginning with consonants, is correct here. The final blank needs *the* because you're now not talking about just any tie, but a specific one – the *407H*, to be exact.

40   **the.** Only one of these conferences is likely to take place each year, and so *the* is the right option. If, however, you think that loads of spy conferences are held every year, and you used the article *a*, don't worry: that article can work here as well.

41   **a** and **the.** The word *buzzer* doesn't begin with a vowel, and so you have to go with *a*, not *an*. The more definite *the* can work, implying that the reader knows that you're talking about a particular buzzer, not just any buzzer. In the second blank, because the reader already knows that you're talking about a wedding, the article *the* communicates which particular wedding ceremony you're talking about.

42   **a, an.** He chose any old seat, not a particular one, and so *a* is what you want. To introduce one of many family friends, *an* works because it come before the word *old* (which starts with the vowel, *o*).

43   **the, the.** *Flowers* is a plural word which needs the article, *the*. Only one *air* exists, and so you need *the*, which is more specific.

44   **the, the** and **the.** In these three blanks, you're discussing particulars, and so *the* fills the bill.

45   **the, an** and **the.** Only one *ceremony* and one *happy couple* exists in this case, and so *the* does the job for the first blank and the third blank. In the second blank, *an* effort is being made – an example of *effort* in general.

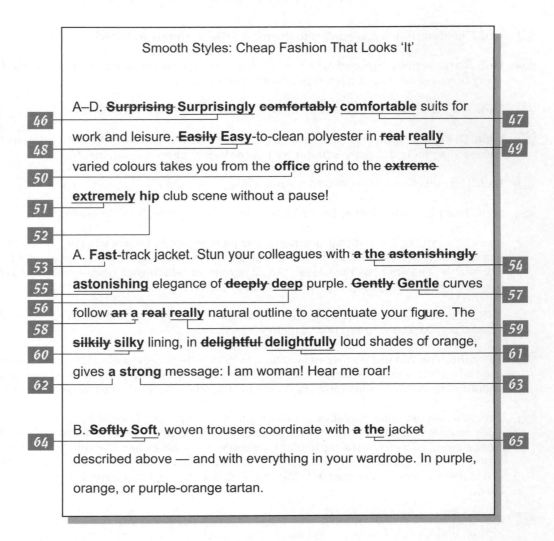

Smooth Styles: Cheap Fashion That Looks 'It'

A–D. ~~Surprising~~ Surprisingly ~~comfortably~~ comfortable suits for _46_ _47_

work and leisure. ~~Easily~~ Easy-to-clean polyester in ~~real~~ really _48_ _49_

varied colours takes you from the **office** grind to the ~~extreme~~ _50_

extremely hip club scene without a pause! _51_

_52_

A. **Fast**-track jacket. Stun your colleagues with ~~a~~ the ~~astonishingly~~ _53_ _54_

astonishing elegance of ~~deeply~~ deep purple. ~~Gently~~ Gentle curves _55_ _57_ _56_

follow ~~an~~ a ~~real~~ really natural outline to accentuate your figure. The _58_ _59_

~~silkily~~ silky lining, in ~~delightful~~ delightfully loud shades of orange, _60_ _61_

gives **a strong** message: I am woman! Hear me roar! _62_ _63_

B. ~~Softly~~ Soft, woven trousers coordinate with ~~a~~ the jacket _64_ _65_

described above — and with everything in your wardrobe. In purple,

orange, or purple-orange tartan.

---

46 The description *comfortable* must be intensified by the adverb *surprisingly*, not by the adjective *surprising*.

47 The adjective *comfortable* describes the noun *suits*.

48 *Polyester* is a noun and must be described by an adjective. *Easy*, which is part of the combo description *easy-to-clean*, describes the noun nicely.

49 The description *varied* is intensified by the adverb *really*.

50 In this sentence *office* is an adjective describing *grind*, a noun here.

51 The adverb *extremely* intensifies the descriptive word *hip*.

52 The adjective *hip* describes the *club scene*, a noun.

53 That hard-working word *fast* can be an adjective or an adverb. Here it functions as an adjective describing the noun *track* (although the finished product *fast-track* is an adjective that describes *jacket*).

54 A particular sort of *elegance* is being discussed, and so you need the definitive *the*.

55 *Elegance* is a noun, and so the adjective *astonishing* is the best description.

56 Purple is a colour, which is a thing and therefore a noun. To describe a noun, you need the adjective *deep*.

57 To describe the noun *curves*, go for the adjective *gentle*, not the adverb *gently*.

58 *An* can only precede words beginning with vowels, and *real* (or *really*) begins with a consonant.

59 *Natural* is a descriptive word and so must be described by an adverb, *really*.

60 The noun *lining* is described by the adjective *silky*.

61 The adverb *delightfully* attaches to another description, *loud*. Descriptions are always described by adverbs, not by adjectives.

62 You need the article *a* to precede a word beginning with a consonant.

63 The adjective *strong* describes the noun *message*.

64 This sentence is tricky. You may have thought that *softly* described *woven*, but the meaning indicates otherwise. You're not talking about how the weaver created the cloth. Instead, you have two separate words (the comma gives you the clue) describing the noun *trousers*. *Soft* is an adjective, appropriate for noun descriptions.

65 Clearly you're talking about one particular item, the tastefully patterned jacket described as item A. *The*, which goes well with particulars, is better here than the more general *a*.

Chapter 15

Going on Location: Placing Descriptions Correctly

● ●

In This Chapter

▶ Placing *even, only, almost* and similar words

▶ Dodging dangling, misplaced or confusing descriptions

● ●

*1*f you watch any of the property shows on TV, you know that the real deal-clincher isn't the size, shape or colour of a house, but where the property is situated. Location is everything. That statement is also true for descriptive words: plop a descriptive word in the wrong spot and your meaning can sink like a stone.

Descriptions in English can be composed of one word or, if you like to pour it on, 20 or more. Regardless of length or form, descriptive elements fall into one of two huge categories:

  ✔ They belong to the **adjective** family if they describe people, places, things or ideas (that is, nouns or pronouns).

  ✔ They belong to the **adverb** clan if they describe verbs (that is, action or being words) or other descriptions.

See Chapter 14 for a host of practice exercises with basic adjectives and adverbs.

The general principle guiding the placement of descriptions is simple: descriptive words need to relate clearly to what they describe. Some sentences give you a bit of leeway – move a descriptive word a little and the meaning still comes across – but other words require precision.

In this chapter you can practise that precision and, like presenters from property shows, concentrate on location, location, location.

Situating 'Even', 'Only' and Similar Words: Little Words Mean a Lot

Have you ever seen those T-shirts with slogans such as, 'My granny went to London and only bought me this lousy T-shirt'? Doesn't it make your blood boil? Not because your grandmother's a bit mean on the present-buying front, but because the descriptive term *only* is misplaced. The sentence as written means that Granny did nothing at all in London except buy one T-shirt – no West End musicals, no Buckingham Palace visit – just T-shirt buying.

Little words – *only, even, almost, just, nearly* and *not* – can hijack the meaning of your sentence if you put them in the wrong spot. Each of these descriptions must go before the word being described. Take a look at these examples:

Even Clare knows that song. (Clare generally sticks to Radio 4, but the song is so popular that she recognises it.)

Clare knows *even* that song. (Clare has thousands of songs on her mp3 player. She knows every musical work ever written, including the one to which the sentence refers.)

Got the idea? Now take a look at the following sentences. If you find a misplaced description, rewrite the sentence as it should be. If everything is fine and dandy, write 'correct' in the blank.

Q. Every afternoon Mrs Lovat says that 15 hours of homework may seem excessive but she only wants what's best for us.

A. **Every afternoon Mrs Lovat says that 15 hours of homework may seem excessive but she wants only what's best for us.** If she *only* wants, she doesn't do anything else – just *wants*. In the corrected version of the sentence, Mrs Lovat has considered all the options available and refuses to settle for what's second or third best. She has chosen the very best, and *only* the very best, option for us.

1. Because she was celebrating an important birthday last week, Mrs Lovat only gave us ten hours of homework.

_____

_____

2. The first task nearly seemed impossible: to write an essay about the benefits of eating sensibly.

_____

_____

3. After I had almost done two pages, I heard my phone beep, and so I got up from my computer.

_____

_____

4. I even thought that Mrs Lovat, the strictest teacher on the planet, would understand the need to take a screen break.

_____

_____

5. I picked up my phone and wandered down to the kitchen. Because I didn't want to ruin my appetite, I only ate six chocolate digestives and ignored the rest of the packet, which seemed to murmur, 'Eat me'.

_____

_____

6. My mum says that she nearly put on two kilograms last week just from eating chocolate digestives. She's back on her special diet this week to help shift the weight. She has to eat crisps, ice-cream and deep-fried Mars Bars to remind herself how tasty carrots and lettuce really are.

_____

_____

7. My mum, my three brothers and I love chocolate digestives, but all of us do not eat them; Mum and I can't resist.

_____

_____

8. My mum even draws the line somewhere, and she hardly ever looks at a chocolate biscuit when she's sleeping.

_____

_____

9. My phone beeped again and that made me stop thinking about food, but only for a second.

_____

_____

10. The text was from Lizzie asking if I fancied going for pizza later. I texted back '4sure', went back upstairs to my homework and found I only had five tasks left.

_____

_____

11. Not all the work was boring, and I actually liked the history assignment.

_____

_____

12. I had to read two chapters about an empire that almost covered half the known world. I made it more interesting by thinking about an empire that almost covered half the known world in chocolate.

_____

_____

13. I read that the conquerors even invaded countries that had superb defence systems. (I imagined that to hold off a chocolate attack, the countries must have had vast quantities of toffee-covered popcorn and enormous vats of strawberry cheesecake ice-cream.)

_____

_____

14. The next day I overheard Mrs Lovat telling the head that she had almost chosen 3C as her favourite class in the whole school, but then she decided it was actually 4B. I was so proud! She liked us the best.

_____

_____

15. But I felt sorry for one girl when Mrs Lovat said, 'I nearly love all students, except that messy one – whatshername? – who's always eating digestives and leaving chocolate smears all over her work. I can't stand her.'

_____

_____

Avoiding Misplaced Descriptions: It Must Be Here Somewhere!

If you're in a bakery and want to _buy a cupcake from the woman who works there with a cherry on top_, you're in the right place. Unfortunately, the description – _with a cherry on top_ – isn't, because its current place attaches it to the woman and so indicates a lady with an interesting hairdo, not a cake with a small, bright red fruit popped on top of the icing.

This section deals with long descriptions (for the grammar obsessed: prepositional phrases, verbals and clauses) that sometimes stray from their appointed path. For info on short descriptions – simple adjectives and adverbs – take a look at Chapter 14. To keep you on the straight and narrow, be sure that long descriptions stay close to the word they describe.

Except for a few place or time descriptions, nearly every multiword description directly follows the word it describes, as in these sentences:

I want to buy a cupcake with a cherry on top from the woman who works in the bakery. (The description *with a cherry on top* describes *cake*.)

The bread that Naomi baked yesterday is as hard as the rock of Gibraltar. (*That Naomi baked yesterday* refers to *bread*.)

The leaf shimmering in the sunlight bothers Joe's light-sensitive eyes. (The expression *shimmering in the sunlight* describes *the leaf*.)

These descriptions quickly become absurd if they move slightly. (Imagine the sentence, *The bread is as hard as the rock of Gibraltar that Naomi baked yesterday*.)

When you move a misplaced description, take care not to make another error. For example, if you change *I put a conker in my pocket that I found in the park* to *I put a conker that I found in the park in my pocket*, you have a problem. In the original sentence, you found a pocket in the park. In the changed sentence, you have a park in your pocket. The solution is to place a description at the beginning of the sentence: *In my pocket I put a conker that I found in the park*.

Have a look at the following sentences. If all the descriptions are where they should be, write 'correct' in the blank. If anything is misplaced, rewrite the sentence in the blanks provided, dropping the description into the right spot.

In addition to moving descriptions, you may have to reword in certain places to create a sentence that makes sense.

0. Even before he passed his driving test, Mark bought a leather licence holder that was given only twice a month.

A. **Even before he passed his driving test, which was given only twice a month, Mark bought a leather licence holder.** The licence holder is available all the time in a leather goods shops, but the test shows up only twice a month. Move the description closer to *test* and you're all set.

16. Mark passed the eye examination administered by a very near-sighted official with flying colours.

_____

_____

17. The theory test asked about manoeuvres for cars skidding on ice.

_____

_____

18. Another question asked about defensive driving, which Mark thought required an essay rather than a simple multiple-choice response.

_____

_____

19. Soon after the theory test, the driving school sent Mark a letter suggesting a date for the driving test lacking sufficient postage.

_____

_____

20. Mark asked his sister to drive him to the testing centre before the letter arrived.

_____

_____

21. Mark's examiner, a nervous man whose foot kept slamming onto an imaginary brake pedal, constantly wrote notes on an official form.

_____

_____

22. The first page contained details about Mark's turning technique, which was single-spaced.

_____

_____

23. Mark hit only two pedestrians and one tree in the middle of a zebra crossing.

_____

_____

24. The examiner relaxed soon after Mark's test in his aunty's house in Aberfeldy.

_____

_____

25. Mark wasn't surprised to hear that he'd failed his test, but the pedestrians' lawsuit was a shock because the examiner had fainted when the speedometer hit 80.

_____

_____

Hanging off a Cliff: Dangling Descriptions

The most common structure in an English sentence is a subject (the person or thing you're talking about) followed by a verb (a statement of being or action about the subject), in that order (head to Chapter 19 for tips about making subject-verb agreements more exciting). This structure is a good workhorse to carry your meaning to the reader, but it can become boring if overused. To spice up your writing, you can begin some sentences with extra information – introductory descriptions that resemble verbs, but aren't verbs. Usually a comma separates these introductory statements from the main portion of the sentence. Here are a couple of examples, with the introductory description italicised:

> *Dazzled by the reflection from Tiffany's new diamond ring*, Mari reached for her sunglasses. (The introductory description gives more information about *Mari*.)

> *To block out all visible light*, Mari's glasses have been coated with a special plastic film. (The introductory description gives more information about the *glasses*.)

A variation of this sort of introduction is a statement with an implied subject:

> *While wearing these glasses*, Mari can see nothing at all, and so she's constantly walking into walls. (The implied statement is *While Mari is wearing these glasses*.)

All these introductory elements must follow one important rule: the subject of the sentence must be what the introduction describes. In the preceding examples, *Mari* is the one who is *dazzled*, *Mari's glasses* are what *block out light* and *Mari* is the one *wearing* the sunglasses.

A common error is to detach the introduction from the subject, resulting in a sentence with flawed logic, what grammarians call a *dangling modifier* or simply a *dangler*. Here are some examples of those dangerous danglers:

> *Perched on her nose*, the red light was invisible to Mari's eyes.

> *Before buying them*, the glasses carried a clear warning, which Mari ignored.

In the first sample sentence the *red light* is on *her nose* – not a pretty picture and also not what the writer is trying to say. In the second sample sentence, if you expanded the sentence it would read *Before the glasses were buying them*. Illogical! These corrections tether the danglers safely:

> *Perched on her nose*, Mari's glasses made the red light invisible.

> *Before buying them*, Mari read a warning about the glasses and chose to ignore it.

See whether you can find danglers in these sentences, and rewrite them if necessary. If everything is securely attached, write 'correct' in the blank. Your rewritten sentence may differ from the suggested answer. That's no problem, as long as the introductory information refers to the subject.

Q. After waiting for the green man, the road filled with people rushing to avoid Mari and her speeding skateboard.

A. **After waiting for the green man, people rushed into the road to avoid Mari and her speeding skateboard.** In the original sentence, *the road is waiting for the green man*. The rewritten sentence has the *people waiting for the green man*.

26. To skateboard safely, kneepads help.

_____

_____

27. Sliding swiftly across the pavement, a tree smashed into Mari.

_____

_____

28. Although bleeding from a cut near her nose, a change of sunglasses was out of the question.

_____

_____

29. To look fashionable, a certain amount of sacrifice is necessary.

_____

_____

30. While designing her latest skateboard, a small camera attached to the frames of her glasses seemed like a good idea.

_____

_____

31. Covered in rhinestones, Mari made a fashion statement with her glasses.

_____

_____

32. Discussed in the fashion press, many articles criticised Mari's choice of eyewear.

_____

_____

33. Coming to the rescue, Tiffany grabbed the offending glasses and lectured Mari on the irrelevance of such fashion statements.

_____

_____

34. To pacify Tiffany and the pedestrians' lawyers, the glasses eventually went into the rubbish bin.

_____

_____

35. Being reasonable, Mari opted for a wraparound stainless steel helmet with UV protection, but only because she thought it made her look like a really frightening Terminator.

_____

_____

Being Dazed and Confused: Vague Descriptions

The general rule governing descriptions is that they need to be near the word they're describing to avoid confusion. If you place a description an equal distance from two words that it can describe, however, you may present your reader with a puzzle, such as the following example:

>   Protesting successfully scares politicians.

Which word does _successfully_ describe? _Protesting_ or _scares_? You can't tell. Now look at these corrections:

>   Successful protests scare politicians.

>   Protests scare politicians successfully.

The one you use depends on what you want to say. The point is that each of these sentences is clear, and clarity is a great quality in writing, if not in politics.

Read the following sentences and decide whether they're clear or unclear. If they're clear, write 'correct' in the blanks. If not, rewrite them.

_Q._ The MP speaking last week voted against the Clarity Bill.

_A._ **The MP speaking now voted against the Clarity Bill last week.** Or, **The MP who spoke last week is the one who voted against the Clarity Bill.** You may find still other variations. As long as your sentence indicates whether _last week_ is attached to _speaking_ or _voted_, you're fine.

36. Going through a red light once earned a stiff fine.

_____

_____

37. Driving away from the police officer swiftly caused a reaction.

_____

_____

38. The ticket the MP got last summer was a blot on his spotless driving record.

_____

_____

39. The judge said that when the case came to trial she would punish the driver severely.

_____

_____

40. The liaison officer from the driving-infraction department soon arrived on the scene.

_____

_____

41. Speaking to the driver forcefully made the point.

_____

_____

42. The MP charged with reckless driving recently went to court.

_____

_____

43. The driver education course redesigned a year ago won an award.

_____

_____

Brain Strain: Extra Practice Placing Descriptions

Breathing deeply, check out the yoga instruction manual in Figure 15-1 and look for ten errors caused by vague, misplaced or dangling descriptions. After you find the clunkers, correct them by crossing out misplaced words, inserting words or revising whole sentences if necessary. Note that the errors have several possible corrections, but in the answers section we show only one correction for each error.

Yoga and You: An Excerpt

If you only learn one yoga posture, this should be it. Beginners can even do it. To form the 'Greeting Turtle Posture', the mat should extend from knees to armpits freshly laundered and dried to fluffiness. While bending the right knee up to the nose, the left ankle relaxes. You should almost bend the knee for a minute before straightening it again. Throw your head back now extending each muscle to its fullest, only breathing two or three times before returning the head to its original position. Tucking the chin close to the collarbone, the nose should wiggle. Finally, raise the arms to the sky and bless the yoga posture that is blue.

Figure 15-1: Instruction manual exercise.

Answers to Description Placement Problems

1. **Because she was celebrating an important birthday last week, Mrs Lovat gave us only ten hours of homework.** You know, from the sentence before this one, that Mrs Lovat usually gives 15 hours. Because the number of hours is the issue, the *only* belongs in front *of ten hours*, not in front of *gave*.

2. **The first task seemed nearly impossible: to write an essay about the benefits of eating sensibly.** If it *nearly* seemed, it didn't *seem* – just approached that state. But that's not what you're trying to say here. Instead, the task approached *impossible* but stopped just short, still in the realm of possibility. So, the *nearly* describes *impossible* and needs to go before that word.

3. **After I had done almost two pages, I heard my phone beep, and so I got up from my computer.** How many pages had you written? That's what the sentence discusses. When the *almost* is in the right place, you had written about a page and a half or a bit more. In the original sentence, you had nothing at all on paper because the sentence says that you *had almost written* (you had approached the action of writing but then stopped).

4 I thought that even Mrs Lovat, the strictest teacher on the planet, would understand the need to take a screen break. Clearly the sentence compares this particular teacher with all others, and so the *even* belongs in front of her name.

5 I picked up my phone and wandered down to the kitchen. Because I didn't want to ruin my appetite, I ate only six chocolate digestives and ignored the rest of the packet, which seemed to murmur, 'Eat me'. This sentence compares the number of chocolate digestives eaten (six) with the number available (the rest of the packet). The *only* belongs in front of the number, not in front of the action (*ate*).

6 My mum says that she put on nearly two kilograms last week just from eating chocolate digestives. She's back on her special diet this week to help shift the weight. She has to eat crisps, ice-cream and deep-fried Mars Bars to remind herself how tasty carrots and lettuce really are. One word – *just* – is in the appropriate place, but *nearly* needs to be moved. The *nearly* tells you that the gain was a bit less than two kilograms, and the *just* tells you the reason (nibbling daintily on all those choccy bickies).

7 My mum, my three brothers and I love chocolate digestives, but not all of us eat them; Mum and I can't resist. To correct this sentence you have to play around with the verb a little, because you don't need the *do* in the new sentence. Here's the logic: if Mum and I eat the biscuits but they don't tempt the brothers, *some* but not *all* the family eat biscuits. The original sentence illogically states that no one eats the chocolate treats and then goes on to talk about the mother and daughter giving in to the biscuit temptation.

8 Even my mum draws the line somewhere, and she hardly ever looks at a chocolate biscuit when she's sleeping. The *even* shouldn't go before *draws* because two actions aren't being compared. Instead, *mum* is being singled out.

9 correct. She doesn't often stop thinking about food, but in this case she does, briefly.

10 The text was from Lizzie asking if I fancied going for pizza later. I texted back '4sure', went back upstairs to my homework and found I had only five tasks left. The sentence comments on the amount of remaining homework (only *five tasks*, not six or seven). Hence the *only* properly precedes *five tasks*.

11 correct. Some work made her yawn and some didn't. Logic tells you that you need *not all*.

12 I had to read two chapters about an empire that covered almost half the known world. I made it more interesting by thinking about an empire that covered almost half the known world in chocolate. If the chapters *almost covered*, they didn't *cover* at all, they just approached the act of covering. If the empire covered *almost* half, it spread over maybe 40 to 45 per cent *of the known world*, a much more logical meaning.

13 I read that the conquerors invaded even countries that had superb defence systems. (I imagined that to hold off a chocolate attack, the countries must have had vast quantities of toffee-covered popcorn and enormous vats of strawberry cheesecake ice-cream.) The conquerors were willing to go up against the best (countries with superb defenses), and that's where the *even* belongs. In front of the verb, you get an implied comparison of action (*even invaded* – didn't just threaten).

14 correct. In this one Mrs Lovat *almost* chose one class, but then changed her mind.

15 But I felt sorry for one girl when Mrs Lovat said, 'I love nearly all students, except that messy one – whatshername? – who's always eating digestives and leaving chocolate smears all over her work. I can't stand her.' Whom does Mrs Lovat love? *Nearly all*, with one notable exception. If *nearly love* is what she does, she feels affection that never reaches the level of love. Because the sentence compares *all students* with *all students* minus one, the *nearly* belongs in front of *all*.

16 **With flying colours, Mark passed the eye examination administered by a very near-sighted official.** Although you can easily see what's wrong with the original sentence, fixing it can be tricky. If you move *with flying colours* so that it follows *examination*, you solve one problem but create another because then the *colours* are *administered* by *a very near-sighted official*. You can place *with flying colours*, as we have, at the beginning of the sentence or, if you prefer, *after passed*. In both spots the description is close enough to the verb to tell you how *Mark passed*, and that's the meaning you want. You can also add a couple of extra commas and the words *which* and *was* to create this sentence: *The eye examination, which Mark passed with flying colours, was administered by a very near-sighted official.*

17 **correct.** The two descriptions, *theory* and *for cars skidding on ice*, are close to the words they describe. *Theory* describes *test* and *for cars skidding on ice* describes *manoeuvres*.

18 **Another question, which Mark thought required an essay rather than a simple multiple-choice response, asked about defensive driving.** Defensive driving techniques don't include essays, but test questions do. The description belongs after *question* because that's the word being described.

19 **Soon after the theory test, the driving school sent a letter lacking sufficient postage and offering Mark an appointment for his driving test.** The *letter* is described by *lacking sufficient postage*, and so that description must follow *letter*. Inserting *and* after *postage* clarifies that the letter, not the postage, offered Mark his appointment. The *and* attaches both expressions (*lacking sufficient postage* and *giving Mark an appointment for the driving test*) to the same word, *letter*.

20 **Before the letter arrived, Mark asked his sister to drive him to the testing centre.** This sentence mentions two actions: *asked* and *drive*. The time element, *before the letter arrived*, tells you when Mark asked, not when he wanted his sister to drive. The description needs to be closer to *asked* than to *drive* because *asked* is the word it describes.

21 **correct.** The description is where it needs to be. The information about the examiner's foot is near *nervous man*, and he's the one with the fidgety foot.

22 **The first page, which was single-spaced, contained details about Mark's turning technique.** The *page* is described by *single-spaced*, not Mark's three-point turn, which always sends him into a skid.

23 **Mark hit only two pedestrians in the middle of a zebra crossing and one tree.** Common sense tells you that the tree isn't in the zebra crossing, but the pedestrians are. The description *in the middle of the zebra crossing* must follow the word it describes, in this case, *pedestrians*.

24 **The examiner relaxed in his aunty's house in Aberfeldy soon after Mark's test.** The relaxing took place *in his aunty's house in Aberfeldy*. The driving test took place on the roads of Pitlochry. Move the description closer to the word it describes.

25 **Because the examiner had fainted when the speedometer hit 80, Mark wasn't surprised to hear that he'd failed his test, but the pedestrians' lawsuit was a shock.** The *because* statement must be closer to *wasn't surprised*, because that expression is being described. You may have been tempted to move *because the examiner had fainted when the speedometer hit 80* to the spot after *test*. Bad idea! If you put the *because* information after *test*, it looks as if he failed *because the examiner had fainted*. Yes, the examiner fainted, but the *because* information relates to Mark's lack of surprise and therefore needs to be near *wasn't surprised*.

26 **To skateboard safely, you may find kneepads helpful.** In the original sentence, no one is skateboarding. A person must be inserted into the sentence. We've chosen *you*, but *skaters*, *people* and other terms are also okay, as long as some sort of potential skater is in the sentence.

27 **Sliding swiftly across the pavement, Mari smashed into a tree.** Mari is doing the *sliding*, not the tree, and yet the original sentence implies that the tree is sliding across the pavement.

28 **Although Mari was bleeding from a cut near her nose, a change of sunglasses was out of the question.** The original sentence has *a change of sunglasses bleeding*. The easiest way to correct a sentence with the wrong implied subject is to insert the real subject, which is *Mari*. Another correct revision: **Although bleeding from a cut near her nose, Mari said that a change of sunglasses was out of the question.**

29 **To look fashionable, you must sacrifice a certain amount.** Who is looking fashionable? In the original sentence, no one. Add a person: *you*, *everybody*, *one* or something similar.

30 **While designing her latest skateboard, Mari thought it would be a good idea to attach a small camera to the frames of her glasses.** Mari has to be doing the designing, but in the original sentence, *a small camera* is *designing her latest skateboard*. Another way to correct this sentence is to insert *Mari* into the first part of the sentence, making her the subject: *While Mari was designing. . . .*

31 **Covered in rhinestones, Mari's glasses made a fashion statement.** Mari's glasses are covered in rhinestones, not Mari herself. *Mari's glasses* must be the subject of the sentence.

32 **Discussed in the fashion press, Mari's choice of eyewear was criticised in many articles.** What was discussed? The eyewear, not the articles.

33 **correct.** Tiffany's *coming to the rescue*, and so the sentence is fine.

34 **To pacify Tiffany and the pedestrians' lawyers, Mari eventually threw the glasses into the rubbish bin.** The glasses can't *pacify*, but *Mari* can.

35 **correct.** Okay, you may not think that wearing a stainless steel helmet is reasonable, but grammatically this sentence is fine.

36 Several corrections are possible. Two examples: **A single red-light violation earned a stiff fine. Going through a red light earned a stiff fine at one time.** The problem word is *once*, which must be more clearly attached to *going through* or *earned*. Here you have to reword and drop the *once* in order to be perfectly clear whether you're talking about *at one time* or *a single time*, both of which are meanings of *once*.

37 Several corrections are possible. Two examples: **Driving swiftly away from the police officer caused a reaction. Driving away from the police officer caused a swift reaction.** Here *swiftly* causes problems unless it is moved closer to *driving* or, changed to *swift*, it describes *reaction*.

38 **correct.** No one would hear this sentence and attach *last summer* to *was*, and so this one passes the clarity test.

39 Several corrections are possible. Two examples: **When the case came to trial, the judge said that she would punish the driver severely. The judge said that she would punish the driver severely when the case came to trial.** The problem with the original is subtle but nevertheless worthy of attention. The expression *when the case came to trial* may be when the judge made her statement or when the judge intended to wallop the drivers. Move the expression and clarity reigns.

40   **correct.** The description *soon* can describe only *arrived*. The word preceding the description, *department*, doesn't logically attach to a time element, and so the sentence is okay as written.

41   Several corrections are possible. Two examples: **Speaking forcefully to the driver made the point. Speaking to the driver made the point forcefully.** The problem with the original is that *forcefully* can describe *speaking* or *made*. To clarify the meaning, you have to move *forcefully* closer to one of those words.

42   Several corrections are possible. Two examples: **The MP recently charged with reckless driving went to court. The MP charged with reckless driving went to court recently.** *Recently* is a description that, like all descriptions, likes to nestle next to the word it describes. If you place it between two possible descriptions, it has a nervous breakdown.

43   Several corrections are possible. Two examples: **The redesigned driver education course won an award a year ago. The driver education course was redesigned a year ago and has won an award.** The problem with the original sentence is that *a year ago*, placed between *redesigned* and *won*, can describe either word. Fixing this sentence is a bit tricky; you have to reword to express a clear meaning.

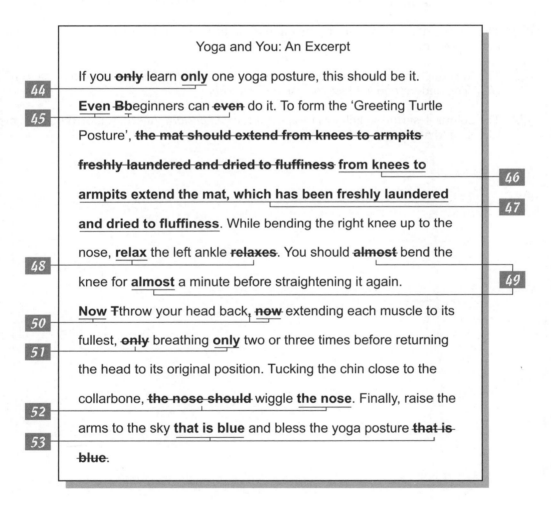

Yoga and You: An Excerpt

44 If you ~~only~~ learn **only** one yoga posture, this should be it.

45 **Even** ~~B~~beginners can ~~even~~ do it. To form the 'Greeting Turtle Posture', ~~the mat should extend from knees to armpits freshly laundered and dried to fluffiness~~ **from knees to armpits extend the mat, which has been freshly laundered and dried to fluffiness**. **46** **47** While bending the right knee up to the nose, **relax** the left ankle ~~relaxes~~. You should ~~almost~~ bend the knee for **almost** a minute before straightening it again. **48** **49**

50 **Now** ~~T~~throw your head back, ~~now~~ extending each muscle to its fullest, ~~only~~ breathing **only** two or three times before returning the head to its original position. **51** Tucking the chin close to the collarbone, ~~the nose should~~ wiggle **the nose**. Finally, raise the arms to the sky **that is blue** and bless the yoga posture ~~that is blue~~. **52** **53**

44   The description *only* applies to the number, not to the act of learning.

45   The description *even* is attached to *beginners* to show how easy this posture is.

46 The sentence begins with a verb form (*To form the 'Greeting Turtle Posture'*), and so the subject of the sentence must be the person who is supposed to do this ridiculous exercise. In the corrected sentence, an understood *you* fills that need.

47 The laundry description belongs to *mat*, not to *armpits*, though fluffy armpits are nice, don't you think?

48 In the original sentence the subject of *bending* is implied, not stated, and so by default the other subject in the sentence (*the left ankle*) takes that role. But the *left ankle* can't bend the right knee, meaning that the logic is flawed. Changing the second half of the sentence to 'relax the left ankle' makes the subject *you* (understood), and '*you*' works as the understood subject you want for the first half of the sentence. Another possible solution is to change the first half of the sentence to *While you are bending. . . .*

49 The description *almost* applies to *minute*, not to *bending*.

50 In the original sentence *now* is equidistant from *throw* and *extending*, creating a vague statement. Moving the description clarifies the meaning. When you've moved *now*, add a comma between *back* and *extending* to help the reader separate these two actions.

51 The description *only* applies to the number of times one must breathe, not to the number of actions one needs to do.

52 The introductory verb form must be an action done by the subject, and the *nose can't tuck the chin*. The understood subject *you* can *tuck the chin*.

53 The colour description belongs to *sky*, not to *yoga posture*. Another, more concise correction is to delete 'that is blue' and simply say, 'blue sky'.

Chapter 16

Forming Comparisons: For Better or Worse

Does Nellie have a bigger ice-cream cone? Whose cold is worse? Who do you think is the most attractive, strongest and richest star in Hollywood? If human beings didn't compare their circumstances with other people's situations, life – and grammar – would be a lot easier.

You can express comparisons with one word (*higher*, *farther* or *sooner*) or two words (*more beautiful*, *most annoying* or *least sensible*). Sometimes many words are necessary (*as much electricity as possible*). We look at extended comparisons in Chapter 17, but in this chapter we concentrate on giving you practice in creating and placing one- or two-word comparisons to make your meaning come through loud and clear.

Visiting the -ER (and the -EST): Creating Comparisons

We know, we know! In the UK, this section should really be called Visiting the A&E, but what with George Clooney and his fabulous doctor routine on the telly, we thought we'd risk the 'ER' gag. Mind you, you know what they say, if you have to explain a joke. . . .

Anyway, adjectives (words that describe people, places, things or ideas) and adverbs (describing actions, states of being or other descriptions) are the basis of comparisons. Regular unadorned adjectives and adverbs are the base upon which two types of comparisons may be made: the comparative and the superlative. *Comparatives* (*faster*, *cleverer*, *neater*, *more interesting*, *less comfortable* and so on) deal with only two elements. *Superlatives* (*the faster*, *the cleverest*, *the neatest*, *the most interesting*, *the least comfortable* and so on) identify the extreme in a group of three or more. To create comparisons, follow these guidelines:

✔ Put -*er* onto the end of a one-syllable descriptive word to create a comparative form showing a greater or more intense quality (for example, *softer*). Use *the* before the adjective and add -*est* to make a superlative of one-syllable words in order to express superiority (for example, *the softest*). Employ *less* to make a comparative that shows inferiority, and create superlatives expressing inferiority with the words *the least*.

✔ Use *-er/the -est* or *more/the most* for many two-syllable adjectives (for example, *cleverer* or *more clever, the likeliest* or *the most likely*). The choice is a matter of taste.

✔ Avoid using *-er* or *-est* for descriptions of long adjectives (three syllables or more) because the result can sound awkward: *the expensivest* just sounds wrong, doesn't it? Generally, create comparatives and superlatives of long words by adding *more* or *the most* in front of the description, such as *more expensive* and *the most spectacular*.

✔ Change the *y* to *i* and add *-er* or *-est* to two-syllable adjectives ending in *-y* (for example, *nastier* or *the messiest*).

✔ Use only *more/the most* or *less/the least* for two-syllable adjectives ending in *-ing, -ed, -ful* and *-less*. For example, *hopefuller* doesn't work, and so you use *more hopeful*.

✔ To compare two people or things, put *than* at the end of your comparative adjective – *Carmel's brighter than Bruce*. If you don't mention what you're comparing someone or something to, you don't need *than*, for example, *Jack's taller*.

✔ Check the dictionary if you're unsure of any word's correct form. The entry for the plain adjective or adverb normally includes the comparative and superlative forms, if they're single words. If you don't see a listing for another form of the word, take the *less/more, least/most* option.

As you may have guessed, a few comparatives and superlatives are irregular. We discuss these in the next section, 'Going from Bad to Worse (and Good to Better): Irregular Comparisons'.

Ready for some comparison shopping? Insert the comparative or superlative form, as needed, into the blanks for each question. Remember that you may need to add *than* or *the* to complete your answer. The base word is in brackets at the end of the sentence.

Q. Pete thinks he's _____ of all the staff in his office. (sophisticated)

A. **the most sophisticated** or **the least sophisticated.** The sentence compares Pete to other staff in the office. Comparing more than two elements requires the superlative form. Because *sophisticated* is a long word, *the most* and *the least* create the comparison. Which one you choose depends on what you think Pete's opinion of his own sophistication is.

1. As soon as the boss announced there was an overseas transfer in the offing, no one was _____ Pete. (excited)

2. On Monday, in his bid to show he was _____ anyone else, he insisted that his name was now Pierre. (cosmopolitan)

3. Courtney, on the other hand, thought that being seen to be a hard worker was _____ consideration in deciding who should be sent to Paris. (important)

4. Courtney pointed out the efficiency measures she had introduced last year. These proved she was _____ employee in the company. (diligent)

5. Natalie, feeling an argument brewing between the two of them, tried desperately to keep the peace. She said _____ advice she'd ever heard about efficiency was from Charles Lamb. Apparently when his boss pointed out how late he'd arrived at the office, he said, 'Yes, but see how early I leave.' (pertinent)

6. Over lunch on Wednesday Pierre declared, while the boss was walking by, that _____ thing he'd ever eaten was frogs' legs. (delicious)

7. Not to be outdone, Courtney said that she thought a meal of French soup, followed by French toast was _____ Pierre's slimy suggestion. (tasty)

8. Natalie, not getting the hang of this French bragging thing, said, '_____ meal for me is anything I share with friends.' (lovely)

9. Courtney didn't think she'd ever heard anything _____ that. (vomit-inducing)

10. On dress-down Friday, Pierre wore a cravat. He was sure that made him _____ guy in the office. (cool)

11. However, when Courtney turned up in a beret and Eiffel Tower earrings she was sure she looked even _____ Pierre. (fashionable)

12. Poor old Natalie, not _____ penny in the bank, wore jeans and a checked shirt. (bright)

13. 'That must be _____ outfit ever to have graced this office,' said Pierre to Courtney at the water cooler. (stylish)

14. The boss called the three of them into her office and said, 'From what I've seen and heard over the last few days there's clearly one of you who's _____ for this overseas assignment.' (suitable)

15. 'This person will stay in _____ hotel in the city. This person will. . . .' (posh)

16. 'Could this announcement be any _____?' quipped Pierre to Courtney. 'Why can't she just get on with it?' (slow)

17. 'I heard that Peter,' said the boss. 'This person will dine in _____ restaurants and sing along to some of _____ music the world has ever heard.' (fancy, heart-breaking)

18. 'I was with her with the hotel and the restaurants, but you can't describe French music as _____ in the world. What's she on about?' whispered Courtney. (sad)

19. 'Natalie, I'm delighted to tell you that you passed my test with _____ marks possible,' said the boss. (high)

20. Natalie, clearly a lot _____, geographically speaking, than Courtney and Pierre, grinned and said, 'It's Paris I'm off to but not as you know it. Paris, Texas, here I come. Yeehaw!' (smart)

Going from Bad to Worse (and Good to Better): Irregular Comparisons

A couple of basic descriptions form comparisons irregularly. Irregulars don't add *-er* or *more/less* to create a comparison between two elements, or tack on *the* plus *-est* or *most/least* to make superlatives that indicate the top or bottom of a group of more than two – turn to the preceding section, 'Visiting the -ER (and the -EST): Creating

Comparisons', for more information on comparatives and superlatives.) Instead, irregular comparisons follow their own strange path, as you can see in Table 16-1.

Table 16-1	Forms of Irregular Comparisons	
Description	*Comparative*	*Superlative*
Good or well	Better	Best
Bad or ill	Worse	Worst
Much or many	More	Most

Time for some practice. Put the correct form of the description (which you can find in brackets at the end of each sentence) in the blank.

O. Annie's notebook, which contains detailed observations from her course 'Watch Repair for Beginners', is _____ example of a boring book that I've ever seen. (good)

A. **the best.** When you mention the top or bottom experience of a lifetime, you're in the superlative column. Because *goodest* isn't a word, you want *best*.

21. Annie explains her notes in _____ detail than anyone would ever want to hear. (much)

22. I think _____ item in her notebook is about a set of gears, which Annie can discuss for hours. (bad)

23. On the upside, everyone knows that Annie's watch repair skills are _____ any jeweller's. (good)

24. Last week Annie became sick; a few hours later she felt _____ and her mum had to call the doctor. (ill)

25. 'I've known you for years and you look _____ I've ever seen you before,' said the doctor. (bad)

26. 'I felt bad this morning but I feel even _____ now. What's wrong with me doc? My left hand won't keep still,' said Annie. (bad)

27. 'That's _____ impersonation of a windmill I've seen outside of the Netherlands,' observed the doctor. (good)

28. 'My right hand is _____ my left one, but even so, every now and then my right hand isn't too steady either,' said Annie worriedly. (good)

29. 'Have you noticed that one of her hands is now slightly bigger than the other one? I think she's getting _____ by the minute,' whispered Annie's mum to the doctor. (bad)

30. 'Well, the bad news is that this is _____ case of The Watchmaker's Tick that I've ever seen,' said the doctor. 'The good news is that with her big hand moving so smoothly and her little one moving just once every 60 minutes, you won't need to phone the speaking clock to find out the right time.' (bad)

Using Words That Are Incomparable (Like You!)

You bought this book, and so we assume that you're perfect. Therefore you can't be compared to anything or anyone else because the word *perfect* – as well as *unique*, *round*, *circular*, *right*, *mistaken* and a few other terms – is an absolute. Logic, which pops up from time to time in English grammar, is the basis for this rule. If you reach an absolute state, you can't go any further, which means that an expression such as *more circular* or *really unique* is a no-no. You can, however, approach an absolute, and so *nearly* or *almost round* is okay.

Words for direction and shape tend to be absolutes. You can turn *left* and but not *lefter* or *more left*. Nor can something be *the squarest* or *most square* of them all, at least when you're discussing a four-sided figure.

Check out the following sentence pairs and indicate the correct sentence. Just to keep you awake, we throw in some pairs in which both sentences are wrong or both sentences are right. (For those sentences, just write 'both wrong' or 'both right' in the margin.)

0. Sentence A: The design of that vase is very unique, and I expect to pay serious money for it.

Sentence B: The design of that vase is unique, and I expect to pay serious money for it.

A. **Sentence B is correct.** The vase is either one-of-a-kind or not, an idea that sentence B expresses. If you want anything less than unique, use the word *rare* or *uncommon*, as in, 'The design of the vase is quite uncommon, and I expect to pay serious money for it.'

31. Sentence A: The base of it was almost round, so I knew right away it was better than the other, cheaper vases in the shop that were rounder.

Sentence B: The base of it was round, so I knew right away it was better than the other, cheaper vases in the shop that were almost round.

32. Sentence A: The antiques dealer said that the top of the vase was circular, but I got my special round measuring tape out and proved that he was more mistaken than any other antiques dealer I'd ever met before.

Sentence B: The antiques dealer said that the top of the vase was nearly circular, but I got my special round measuring tape out and proved that he was mistaken.

33. Sentence A: I didn't entirely trust him, and so I decided to drive to another village, about an hour west of there to find a better antiques dealer.

Sentence B: I didn't entirely trust him, and so I decided to drive to another village, about an hour more west of there to find a better antiques dealer.

34. Sentence A: That's where I found a dealer who sold Victorian buttons. I thought the buttons were some of the most unique gift items I'd ever seen.

Sentence B: That's where I found a dealer who sold Victorian buttons. I thought the buttons were some of the most unusual gift items I'd ever seen.

35. Sentence A: The reasonably circular shape of the buttons was surprising, given that the buttons were so old.

Sentence B: The very circular shape of the buttons was surprising, given that the buttons were so old.

36. Sentence A: The dealer had obtained the buttons from an extremely elderly widow.

Sentence B: The dealer had obtained the buttons from an elderly widow.

37. Sentence A: The widow had told him, 'I will sell you my antiques when the time is very right.'

Sentence B: The widow had told him, 'I will sell you my antiques when the time is just right.'

38. Sentence A: I decided there and then to buy one of the buttons that was almost perfect.

Sentence B: I decided there and then to buy one of the buttons that was surprisingly perfect.

39. Sentence A: I thought I'd sell it online for a huge profit, but my plans were more mistaken than I'd assumed.

Sentence B: I thought I'd sell it online for a huge profit, but my plans were very mistaken.

40. Sentence A: Before I'd even switched on the computer, my sister 'liberated' the button, claiming that it was uniquely suited to her personal style.

Sentence B: Before I'd even switched on the computer, my sister 'liberated' the button, claiming that it was uncommonly suited to her personal style.

Brain Strain: Extra Practice with Bad Comparisons

Political campaign literature is heavy with comparisons – and none more so than the election manifesto from one of the candidates in the marginal seat of Green Park primary school. The year 5 race is really heating up. Steven and Sally are both running for the coveted position of Teacher's Pet/General Bosser Arounder (When the Teacher's not Looking). Look at Sally's campaign leaflet in Figure 16-1 and find and correct ten errors in comparisons. To correct the errors, you may have to rewrite an entire sentence or phrase.

Vote for Sally!

She will be the most unique Teacher's Pet our class has ever had!

Here is Sally's campaign platform:

- ✓ Our dining hall is the dirtiest than River Road Primary School.

- ✓ Sally is gooder at organising school events than her opponent.

- ✓ Sally will collect your homework and deliever it to the teacher's desk most efficiently than Steven.

- ✓ Steven is very wrong when he says that Sally only wants to collect the homework so she can copy it if she needs to.

- ✓ The head teacher likes Sally's ideas because compared to Steven's, hers are best.

- ✓ Steven is most frequently absent, and the class should choose the candidate who will attend all school events.

- ✓ Sally's plan for the school playing field will make it more square and add really unique seats all the way around.

- ✓ Steven's face is unattractiver than Sally's, and you'll have to look at him all day if he is Teacher's Pet.

Figure 16-1:
Political campaign literature riddled with errors.

Answers to Comparison Problems

1 **more excited than.** Comparing two elements, in this case Pete and all the other staff in the office, calls for a comparative form. *Excited* has three syllables, and so the comparative needs *more* and *than*.

2 **more cosmopolitan than.** Here the sentence compares Pierre's level of sophistication to that of everyone else, and so the comparative is correct. *Cosmopolitan*, a long word, takes *more* or *less*. In the context of this sentence, *more* makes sense.

3 **the most important.** The superlative form is the way to go because Courtney is thinking about which factor needs to be at the top of the pile out of them all.

4 **the most diligent.** Of all the staff in the company, Courtney is something very special as far as hard work goes, and so you need a superlative. *Diligent* is a long adjective. Add *the most* to create the superlative.

5 **the most pertinent.** Often when you see the word *ever*, you know that you're in superlative territory, and that's certainly true here. Because *pertinent* is a long adjective, you need to add *the most* to it to create the correct superlative.

6 **the most delicious.** Pierre is talking about all the meals he's eaten in his life – more than two you'd think! So the superlative is correct here.

7 **tastier than.** Courtney is comparing two elements (Pierre's choice of meal and her own). Change the *y* to *i* and add *-er,* add *than* and you're in business.

8 **The loveliest.** Natalie's talking about all the meals she's had in her entire life, and so go for superlative, which is created by adding *the* and changing the *y* to *i* and adding *-est*. Most two-syllable words rely on *the most* or *the least* but adjectives ending in *-ly* are an exception. If you aren't sure how to form the comparative of a particular word, check the dictionary.

9 **more vomit-inducing than.** Because *vomit-inducing* is a long adjective, you need to add *more* before it. Add *than* after it and you create a perfect comparison.

10 **the coolest.** When comparing Pierre's wardrobe to that of the other people in the office, you need a superlative because you know that at least three people are in the office – four, if you count the boss, though we've never meet a boss we thought was a person!

11 **more fashionable than.** You're comparing two people's clothes, and so you need a comparative. Because *fashionable* is a long word with four syllables, you create the comparative with *more* (or *less*, depending on how trendy you reckon Courtney thinks her outfit is) and *than*.

12 **the brightest.** When compared to all the other pennies, Natalie isn't top of the shiny class. You need a superlative and because *bright* has only one syllable, adding *the* and *-est* works here.

13 **the least stylish.** Pierre is thinking about all the outfits he's seen in the office, and so you require a superlative. As far as Pierre is concerned, Natalie's dress sense is the most inferior and so *the least* is the option to go for here.

14 **the most suitable.** The boss is choosing from three candidates and so you need a superlative. The length of the adjective *suitable* indicates that you need to add *the most* to make the correct superlative.

15 **the poshest.** The boss is talking about all the hotels in the city and picking out one of them in particular, meaning that a superlative does the job. *Posh* is a short adjective, and so you just have to add *the* and *-est* and your work is done.

16 **slower.** Pierre is comparing what he's hearing now with all the other announcements he's ever heard before. You may think that leads to a superlative, but actually he's comparing only two things – this announcement and all the others – and so you require a comparative, and *slower* is just right.

17 **the fanciest, the most heart-breaking.** Again, the boss is talking about the top of the scale and so you need two superlatives here. The first is a two-syllable adjective that ends in *y*, and so change the *y* to *i* and add *-est*. For the second one, because *heart-breaking* has three syllables, add *most* to create the correct superlative. Both these superlatives need *the* to complete them.

18 **the saddest.** Courtney is picking out one type of music from all the types in the world. When you talk about the extreme at one end of a scale, you need a superlative.

19 **the highest.** Choosing one out of all the scores the boss has seen, calls for a superlative.

20   **smarter.** Natalie is being compared to the group that is made up of Courtney and Pierre, and so the comparative *smarter* is the correct answer.

21   **more.** Two elements are being compared here: the amount of detail Annie uses and the amount of detail people want. When comparing two elements, use the comparative form.

22   **the worst.** The superlative form singles out the extreme (in this case the most boring) item in the notebook.

23   **better than.** The sentence compares two elements – the skills of Annie and those of jewellers in general – and so you want the comparative form.

24   **worse.** *Ill* is one of those irregular adjectives and its comparative form is *worse*.

25   **worse than.** The doctor is comparing two things – her appearance now, and her appearance all the other times he's seen her – and so the irregular comparative *worse* is the right choice here.

26   **worse.** The comparative deals with two times – this morning and now.

27   **the best.** To single out the top or bottom rank from a group of more than two (here, of all the windmill impressions the doctor has seen outside the Netherlands), go for the superlative form.

28   **better than.** The sentence compares Annie's left and right hands. The comparative form works for two elements.

29   **worse.** You need a comparative here because Annie's mum is comparing two times – now and every minute that passes.

30   **the worst.** The doctor has seen lots of cases (more than two), and so you know he needs the superlative *the worst* to talk about Annie.

31   **Sentence B.** Because *round* is absolute, the term *rounder* isn't standard English.

32   **Sentence B.** You're either *mistaken* or *not*. *More mistaken* is wrong.

33   **Sentence A.** The direction *west* is absolute. You can't go *more west* or *wester*.

34   **Sentence B.** *Unique* is an absolute term, indicating that *most unique* is illogical. *Unusual*, on the other hand, isn't absolute, and so *most* can be attached to it.

35   **Both wrong.** The shape is either *circular* or not. The *reasonably* in sentence A is a no-no, as is the *very* in sentence B.

36   **Both right**. We try to trick you here by sneaking in a non-absolute, *elderly*. You can be *very*, *extremely*, *really* and *not-so elderly*, depending upon your birth certificate and/or your degree of truthfulness.

37   **Sentence B.** *Right* is an absolute, and so you're either *right* or *wrong*, not *very right* or *wronger*. You can, however, be *just right*, implying that you've reached the absolute state.

38   **Both right.** *Perfect* is an absolute, but *almost* expresses an approach to the absolute (which is fine) and *surprisingly* deals with the opinion of the speaker, not with a degree of perfection (also fine).

39   **Both wrong.** *Mistaken* is an absolute, and so *more mistaken* and *very mistaken* are wrong.

40 **Both right.** If the button is *uniquely suited*, nothing else in the universe is suited in the same way. No problem. *Uncommonly* means that more than one item may be suited, but this button fits to a rare degree. Also, no problem.

Vote for Sally!

41 She will be ~~the most unique~~ **a unique** Teacher's Pet ~~our class has ever had~~!

Here is Sally's campaign platform:

42 ✓ Our dining hall is ~~the~~ **dirtier than** ~~dirtiest~~ River Road Primary School.

43 ✓ Sally is ~~gooder~~ **better** at organising school events than her opponent.

✓ Sally will collect your homework and deliver it to the **44** teacher's desk ~~most~~ **more** efficiently than Steven.

45 ✓ Steven is ~~very~~ **wrong** when he says that Sally only wants to collect the homework so she can copy it if she needs to.

✓ The head teacher likes Sally's ideas because **46** compared to Steven's, hers are ~~best~~ **better**.

47 ✓ Steven is ~~most~~ **more** frequently absent, and the class should choose the candidate who will attend all school events.

✓ Sally's plan for the school playing field will make it **more nearly square** and add ~~really~~ unique seats all **48** the way around.

49 ✓ Steven's face is ~~unattractiver~~ **more unattractive 50** than Sally's, and you'll have to look at him all day if he is Teacher's Pet.

41 *Unique* is an absolute and can't be compared.

42 When comparing two elements, use the comparative (*dirtier*).

43 *Better* is an irregular comparison. *Gooder* isn't a word in standard English.

44 When comparing two items (the way Sally gets the homework from her classmates and the way Steven does), go for the comparative, not superlative, form.

45 *Wrong* is an absolute and can't be compared.

46 The comparative form (*better*) works for a two-element comparison.

47 The implied comparison here is between two attendance records, and so you want the comparative form *more*.

48 *Square* is an absolute and can't be compared. You may, however, state how close to the absolute a particular form comes.

49 The absolute term *unique* can't be compared.

50 A four-syllable word such as *unattractive* becomes a comparative or superlative with the addition of *more/less* or the *most/least*.

Chapter 17

Apples and Oranges: Improper Comparisons

In This Chapter

▶ Avoiding incomplete or illogical comparisons

▶ Handling double comparisons

According to the old saying, you can't compare apples and oranges, but that error is only one of many common comparison mistakes. Imagine that you're sitting on Centre Court at Wimbledon during the tennis tournament and you hear a fan compare Andy Murray to 'the British players'. In your best grammar umpire's voice, we hope that you shout 'Out!' and gently explain that the spectator should, of course, have compared Andy to 'the other British players'.

Chapter 16 explains one- or two-word comparisons, but this chapter takes you through more complicated situations, including illogical comparisons, such as the Andy Murray comment and incomplete comparisons. You can also practise double comparisons, a sentence construction for people who like to hedge their bets. So, as they say in tennis, time to get out the new balls and play!

Ensuring That You Complete Comparisons: No One Likes to Feel Incomplete

By definition, a comparison discusses two elements in relation to each other, or singles out the extreme in a group and explains exactly what form the extremism takes: for example, 'She throws more pies than he does' or 'Of all the clowns, she throws the most pies'. A comparison may also examine something in relation to a standard, as in 'Her pie throwing was so accurate that they were still washing custard out of their hair a week after they visited the circus.'

So may also mean *therefore*, in which case it doesn't pair with *that*. In informal speech, *so* may also be the equivalent of *very*, as in *I was so tired*. In formal English, however, *so* should be paired with *that* when it creates a comparison.

A comparison can be any of these things, but what it can't be is partially absent. If someone says, 'The snapper wasn't as fresh' or 'The sea bass is most musical', you're all at sea. As fresh as what? Most musical in comparison to whom? You have no way of knowing.

Of course, in context these sentences may be perfectly all right:

> I considered the snapper but in the end went with the flounder. The snapper wasn't as fresh.

In the preceding example, you understand that the second sentence is a continuation of the first. Also, some words in a comparison may be implied, without loss of meaning. Take a look at this sentence:

The snapper makes fewer snotty comments than a large-mouth bass *does*.

The italicised word in this sentence may be left out – and frequently is – without confusing anybody. And that's the key: the reader must have enough information to understand the comparison.

Read the following sentences and see whether you can find any incomplete comparisons. If the sentence is correct, write 'correct' in the blank. If not, rewrite the sentence to complete the comparison. You may come up with thousands of possible answers, a further illustration of why incomplete comparisons make for poor communication. We give two suggested answers for the example, but only one suggested answer for the exercises that follow, because we can't cover everything! Check if your answer is correct by determining whether your comparison is clear and complete.

0. 'There are more fish in the sea,' muttered the grouper to herself as she searched for her pals.

A. **'There are more fish in the sea than you know,' muttered the grouper to herself as she searched for her pals.** Or, **'There are more fish in the sea than birds in the air,' muttered the grouper to herself as she searched for her pals.** The key here is to define the term *more*. More than what? If you answer that question, you're fine.

1. Terry the trout, who is wealthier, spends a lot of money on seascape CDs.

_____

_____

2. Squidgy the octopus has almost as few friends but prefers to keep Wilma the whale at arm's length.

_____

_____

3. Whales are the most adept at financial planning.

_____

_____

4. Mermaids are less competent at buying kitten heels.

_____

_____

5. Not many people realise that mermaids' tail fins are as sensitive.

_____

_____

6. Whales are as fashion-challenged at shoe and accessory selection.

_____

_____

7. Suddenly the phone rang. It was the editor. 'I'm looking at Chapter 17 right now and do you know what I think? This whole under-the-sea theme has become more boring.'

_____

_____

8. He didn't give us any time to explain ourselves. He just went straight into, 'The marine jokes are so uninteresting.'

_____

_____

9. We promised to try harder at formulating new, wittier and more sophisticated storylines.

_____

_____

10. Then we put down our pens, went round his plaice (geddit?) and slapped him round the head with a kipper. We pray, gentle reader, that you find this ending more than satisfying.

_____

_____

Being Smarter Than Yourself:
Illogical Comparisons

If you say that your favourite British tennis player, Jamie Murray, is *cuter than the British players* or *better at playing doubles than the Brits*, you're making an error that's a lot worse than Jamie's occasional double faults. Why? Because Jamie is one of the British players. According to the logic of those statements, Jamie would have to be *cuter* or *better* than himself. The solution is simple. Insert *else*, *other* or a similar expression into the sentence. Then Jamie becomes *cuter than anyone else on the team* or *better at playing doubles than the other Brit players*.

Don't insert *other* or *else* if the comparison is between someone in the group and someone outside the group. You can correctly say that *Jamie is cuter than the American players* because Jamie isn't an American player and he *is* cute.

Another form of false logic that pops up in comparisons is overkill: the use of both *-er* and *more* or *less* or *-est* and *most* or *least*. You can be either *sillier* or *more silly*, but not *more sillier*.

Time for some comparison shopping. Check out the following sentences. If the comparison is logical, write 'correct' in the blank. If the comparison is faulty, rewrite the sentence in the space provided. Because some sentences may be corrected in more than one way, your answer may differ from ours. Just be sure that your answers are logical.

Q. The average pigeon is smarter than any animal in London.

A. **The average pigeon is smarter than any other animal in London.** Pigeons are animals, and pigeons flap all over London. Without the word *other*, pigeons are smarter than themselves, which makes no sense! The insertion of *other* restores logic and order to the sentence.

11. Spotting a pigeon waiting for the tube doors to open is no odder than anything you see on an average day in a major city.

_____

_____

12. Even though they don't use travelcards, pigeons are no worse than any tube passenger.

_____

_____

13. One day Boris saw a woman shampooing her hair in the rain, in the middle of Piccadilly Circus, an experience that was more weirder than anything else he'd seen in his life.

_____

_____

14. Singing with a thick Cockney accent, she appeared saner than Londoners.

_____

_____

15. The most strangest part of the whole shampooing incident was the lone pigeon that kept staring at the woman with its beady little eyes.

_____

_____

16. Pigeons are more curious than flying creatures. Boris reckoned this one just wanted to know what kind of shampoo the woman was using.

_____

17. Apparently pigeons have a keener interest in people's heads and shoulders than birds, Boris says.

_____

_____

18. Pigeons worry about anti-dandruff shampoo more than almost any other human grooming product.

_____

19. But the hair-care product that's the most scariest for pigeons hasn't come onto the market yet.

_____

_____

20. A rumour circulating among pigeons says that _DamnPoo_ – the world's most effective urban particle repellent – is going to be in the shops soon. Boris says that, until then, we should be sure to enjoy every lucky deposit our friendly pigeons shower on us.

_____

_____

Doubling Up Trouble: A Sentence Containing More Than One Comparison

Do you have trouble making up your mind? Well, yes and no. If this statement sounds like something you'd say, you may be prone to employing double (but perfectly correct) comparisons, such as the following:

The new sculpture is as fragile as the old one, if not more fragile.

Eleanor is almost as annoying as Julie, if not equally annoying.

Celeste's speech on tariff reduction was as complicated as, if not more complicated than, Jessica's oration.

The preceding examples are correct because each falls into one of two categories:

✔ **The first comparison is completed before the second begins.** The first two sentences (_The new sculpture is as fragile as the old one. . ._ and _Eleanor is almost as annoying as Julie. . ._) follow this pattern.

✔ **The beginning of both comparisons may be logically completed by the phrase at the end of the sentence.** The first comparison in the third sentence begins with the statement _as complicated as_. If you tack that statement onto the conclusion of the comparison, _Jessica's oration_, you have a complete and logical comparison: _as complicated as Jessica's oration_. The second comparison begins with _more complicated than_ and is completed by the same statement, _Jessica's oration_. Thus the second comparison is complete: _more complicated than Jessica's oration_. Because both comparisons are completed by the same phrase, the third sentence is also correct.

The most common mistake in double comparisons is to omit part of the first comparison:

Wrong: Celeste's speech on tariff reduction was as complicated, if not more complicated than, Jessica's oration.

Why the sentence is wrong: Each comparison must be completed by the same phrase at the end of the sentence. In the preceding sample sentence, the first comparison isn't completed by the phrase at the end of the sentence. The comparison currently reads *as complicated Jessica's oration*. The second *as* is missing.

Right: Celeste's speech on tariff reduction was as complicated as, if not more complicated than, Jessica's oration.

Also right: Celeste's speech on tariff reduction was as complicated as Jessica's oration, if not more complicated.

Double comparisons are so annoying that you may be tempted to make up your mind and go for one statement only. We applaud that decision. But if you must give two alternatives, ensure that each is correct. Here's an example and a set of exercises. If you find an error, rewrite the sentence. Note that more than one correction is possible with this sort of error. Just pick one way to rewrite.

Q. Celeste put as many people, if not even more people, to sleep as Jessica, even though Celeste's speech was five minutes shorter.

A. **Celeste put as many people to sleep as Jessica, if not even more than Jessica, even though Celeste's speech was five minutes shorter.** The two comparisons need to be logically completed by the same phrase, but in the original sentence, the second comparison is faulty. The first comparison, *Celeste put as many people to sleep as Jessica*, is okay. The second comparison in the original sentence, *if not even more people to sleep as Jessica*, is illogical. The word *than* is missing. The corrected version supplies two complete comparisons.

21. Celeste described every, or even more than, the monetary implications of the Snooty-Harvey Tariff Law.

_____

_____

22. Jessica concentrated on one of the most, if not the most important, loopholes of the law.

_____

_____

23. Celeste's choice of subject matter was equally, if not more important, than Jessica's.

_____

_____

24. Jessica insisted on the same amount, or even more time, as Celeste.

_____

_____

25. Celeste's request for some tax-deductible, pink jellybeans to nibble on during her lecture was as justifiable, if not more justifiable, than Jessica's demand for a ten-minute standing ovation every time she said the words 'avoidance strategy'.

_____

_____

Brain Strain: Extra Practice with Improper Comparisons

Figure 17-1 is an excerpt from a restaurant review. Be on the lookout for incomplete, illogical and messed-up double comparisons, as well as undercooked sausages and snobby waiters. You should find ten mistakes in comparisons and about a million reasons not to eat at this establishment. Correcting the errors may involve adding, removing or rearranging quite a few words. Note that often more than one correction is possible. We offer you one answer for each error in the following section, but your answer may differ slightly and still be correct.

The Pembroke: You Won't Go Broke, but You Won't Eat Well Either

A recent meal at The Pembroke was the most distressing. First of all, the tables are as close together, if not closer together, than bus passengers during rush hour. I truly did not want to hear my neighbours' conversation about their grandchildren, who are, they claim, so clever. Nor did I want to chew each bite of steak for ten minutes because the steak was tougher than any meat I've eaten in my life. The wine list of The Pembroke is the least interesting. I am, I admit, a wine snob, but even people who drink wine only once a year will have a hard time finding something that is as watery, if not more watery, than the house red. I was surprised to realise that I was less impressed than the diners munching happily in the restaurant. Surely The Pembroke can do better! The potato was much more inedible and more expensive. I recommend that you find a place with better food. The Pembroke must revise its menu and its layout immediately, or the restaurant will be so unpopular.

Figure 17-1:
A poorly
written
restaurant
review.

Answers to Complicated Comparison Problems

1   **Terry the trout, who is wealthier than the president of a Swiss bank, spends a lot of money on seascape CDs.** The problem with the original is that you can't tell what or who is being compared to Terry. The missing element of the comparison must be supplied.

2   **Squidgy the octopus has almost as few friends as Wilma the whale but prefers to keep the trout at arm's length.** The original sentence begins the comparison nicely (*almost as few friends as*) and then messes up the ending (*almost as much money as* what or who?). Supply an ending and you're fine.

3   **Whales are the most adept at financial planning of all marine mammals.** The original comparison doesn't specify the group within which mermaids excel. Your answer must provide context.

4   **Mermaids are less competent at buying kitten heels than other creatures in the sea.** In the original, the reader is left to wonder about the basis of comparison. In the corrected sentence, the mermaids are compared to other sea creatures. Now the comparison is complete.

5   **Not many people realise that mermaids' tail fins are as sensitive as ducks' feet.** The original sentence contains an incomplete comparison. As sensitive as what? Who knows? The suggested answer supplies another sensitive object to finish the comparison.

6   **Whales are as fashion-challenged at shoe and accessory selection as mermaids.** Don't worry about how you finish the comparison, as long as you finish it. In the suggested answer we put in *mermaids*, but you can just as easily place something or someone else. You decide.

7   **Suddenly the phone rang. It was the editor. 'I'm looking at Chapter 17 right now, and do you want to know what I think? This whole under-the-sea theme has become more boring than a lecture on the economics of pen nibs.'** Finish the comparison with your favourite example of excruciating boredom.

8   **He didn't give us any time to explain ourselves. He just went straight into, 'The marine jokes are so uninteresting that I may never go to the beach again.'** Although in informal English the original sentence is fine, in formal, standard English the *so* statement must be completed by some sort of *that* statement.

9   **correct.** Normally a comparison (*harder*, in this sentence) must be placed in context. In this sentence, however, the context is implied (*harder* than we did before).

10   **correct.** The phrase *more than satisfying* compares the ending to an ideal state (*satisfying*). The comparison is complete.

11   **Spotting a pigeon waiting for the tube doors to open is no odder than anything else you see on an average day in a major city.** The *else* serves an important purpose in this sentence; it shows the reader that the pigeon waiting for the tube is being compared to *other* events in a major city. Without the *else*, the sentence is irrational because then the sentence means that seeing pigeons in a city is no odder than what you see in a city.

12   **Even though they don't use travelcards, pigeons are no worse than any other tube passenger.** The context makes clear that pigeons sometimes travel by tube. Without the *other*, pigeons are no worse than themselves, an impossible situation.

13 **One day Boris saw a woman shampooing her hair in the rain, in the middle of Piccadilly Circus, an experience that was weirder than anything else he's seen in his life.** *More weirder* is overkill. Drop the *more* and you're all set.

14 **Singing with a thick Cockney accent, she appeared saner than other Londoners.** If she's got a Cockney accent, she's a Londoner. Without the word *other*, you're saying that she's saner than herself. Not possible!

15 **The strangest part of the whole shampooing incident was the lone pigeon that kept staring at the woman with its beady little eyes.** *Most strangest* is over-egging the pudding. Drop the *most* and your dish is just right.

16 **Pigeons are more curious than other flying creatures.** Pigeons are flying creatures, and so without the *other*, you're saying that pigeons are more curious than themselves.

17 **Apparently pigeons have a keener interest in people's heads and shoulders than other birds, Boris says.** To correct this sentence, just like the one before, you have to add the word *other*. This one extra word means that pigeons aren't now being compared to themselves.

18 **correct.** With the inclusion of the word *other*, no confusion exists here. The *shampoo* is being compared, not to itself, but to other *grooming products*.

19 **But the hair-care product that's the scariest for pigeons hasn't come onto the market yet.** In standard English something can either be *the scariest* or *the most scary*, but it can't be *the most scariest*.

20 **correct.** *The most effective* is the correct superlative here.

21 **Celeste described every monetary implication of the Snooty-Harvey Tariff Law, and even more.** The original sentence muddles two comparisons, braiding them together inappropriately. The first comparison is incomplete because it says *Celeste described every the monetary implication of the Snooty-Harvey Tariff Law*. You can easily see that doesn't make sense because of the extra *the*. The second comparison is in better shape. Separated from the other parts of the sentence, it reads *Celeste described even more than the provisions of the Snooty-Harvey Tariff Law*. One complete and one incomplete comparison isn't a good idea. The corrected version presents two complete comparisons.

22 **Jessica concentrated on one of the most important, if not the most important, loopholes of the law.** Or, **Jessica concentrated on one of the most important loopholes of the law, if not the most important.** The original is faulty because the first comparison can't be completed logically by the words supplied in the sentence. In the original sentence, the first comparison reads *one of the most loopholes of the law*. The word *important* is missing. The two corrections supply *important*.

23 **Celeste's choice of subject matter was equally important, if not more important than Jessica's.** In the original sentence, the first comparison is incomplete. In the rewritten version, each separate comparison makes sense. Comparison one: *equally important*. Comparison two: *more important than Jessica's*.

24 **Jessica insisted on the same amount of time as Celeste, or even more time than Celeste.** In the original sentence the second comparison is incomplete as written: the *than* is missing. In the corrected version each of the two comparisons works separately. Comparison one: *the same amount of time as Celeste*. Comparison two: *more time than Celeste*.

25 **Celeste's request for some tax-deductible, pink jellybeans during the lecture was as justifiable as Jessica's demand for a ten-minute standing ovation every time she said the words 'avoidance strategy', if not more justifiable.** In the original sentence the first comparison is incomplete because it contains only one *as*. If you untangle it from the second comparison, you hear what's missing: *Celeste's request for tax-deductible, pink jellybeans during the lecture was as justifiable than a ten-minute standing ovation every time she said the words 'avoidance strategy'.* The corrected version contains two complete comparisons.

The Pembroke: You Won't Go Broke, but You Won't Eat Well Either

A recent meal at The Pembroke was **the most distressing** **26**
experience I've had since becoming a restaurant critic. First of
all, the tables are as close together, if not closer together, than
bus passengers during rush hour **as close together as bus** **27**
passengers during rush hour, if not closer. I truly did not want to
hear my neighbours' conversation about their grandchildren, who
are, they claim, **so clever that no IQ test can measure them**. Nor **28**
did I want to chew each bite of steak for ten minutes because the
steak was tougher than **any other meat** I've eaten in my life. The **29**
wine list of The Pembroke is **the least interesting of all the** **30**
restaurants in the universe that serve wine. I am, I admit, a wine
snob, but even people who drink wine only once a year will have a
hard time finding something that is as watery, if not more watery,
than the house red **as watery as the house red, if not more** **31**
watery. I was surprised to realise that I was less impressed than **the**
32 **other diners** munching happily in the restaurant. Surely The
Pembroke can do better! The potato was much **more inedible than** **33**
an uncooked steak and **more expensive than filet mignon**. I **34**
recommend that you find a place with better food. The Pembroke
must revise its menu and its layout immediately, or the restaurant will
be **so unpopular that it will go out of business**. **35**

26 The expression *the most distressing* must be placed in context. Your answer probably differs from ours, but as long as it indicates the context, you're okay.

27 If you're doubling a comparison, each separate comparison must be complete.

28 In informal English saying that your grandchildren are *so clever*, when you mean *very clever*, is fine. In formal, standard English, however, a *so* statement must be accompanied by a *that* statement in order to complete the comparison.

29 Steak is a meat, and so the word *other* must be inserted.

30 Your completion may be different from ours, but the context of *least interesting* must appear.

31 Each element of a double comparison must be complete.

32 The critic is clearly a diner, and he or she can't be *less impressed* than him- or herself. Insert *other* and the logic is saved.

33 You can correct this comparison in about a zillion ways. We've provided one possibility, but anything you come up with is fine so long as the comparison is complete.

34 This comparison has to be completed. We supply one option, but don't worry if yours is different. Just be sure that the comparison is complete.

35 The *so* statement can't make a comparison by itself; you have to add a *that* statement to complete the comparison.

Part V
Writing with Style

'Hi – I'm Gerry & I teach English
grammar – Gerry is short for
Gerund by the way.'

In this part . . .

Completing the exercises in this part is the equivalent of designing clothes for a Parisian fashion house. If you can make it through this material, you'll have arrived on the most glamorous of all English language catwalks. The topics in this part include more than grammar; and when you conquer them, your writing will be as stylish as a supermodel is tall and thin.

Chapter 18 tackles parallelism, the grammar term for order and balance in a sentence. (In fashion terms, how not to wear hot pants and wellies, unless you're Kate Moss at Glastonbury.) Chapter 19 gives you tips on adding variety to sentences, so you don't end up wearing the same outfit . . . er, structuring every sentence the same way all the time. Chapter 20 concerns those little errors that can sabotage your writing. So, when you're ready, let the search for linguistic sartorial elegance begin!

Chapter 18

Practising Parallel Structure

....

In This Chapter
▶ Creating balanced sentences
▶ Maintaining consistent tense, person and voice
▶ Dealing with paired conjunctions

....

Maths teachers have all the luck. Not only can they play with compasses and protractors, but they also get to draw little circles and squares and parallel lines. English has parallels too, but in grammar parallels are created with words, not with pencils and rulers. And that's much less fun!

Grammatical parallelism may not be party material, but it's essential to good writing. *Parallelism* refers to order and balance, the quality a sentence has when it flows smoothly. Parallel sentences don't start out in one direction (towards your grandma's house) only to veer suddenly off the road (perhaps to a great little fish and chip shop you know 500 kilometres away). This chapter provides a road map and some practice drives to keep your sentences on track.

Understanding When Geometry Invades English: Parallelism Basics

When a sentence is parallel, everything performing the same function in the sentence has the same grammatical identity. If you have two subjects, for example, and one is an infinitive (such as *to ski*), the other subject needs to be an infinitive as well (such as *to fracture*). You can't mix and match; *to ski* and *fracturing* shouldn't show up as paired (or part of tripled or quadrupled or whatever) subjects. Have a look at these sentences:

▶ **Nonparallel:** Suzy didn't enjoy paying full price for a lift ticket and that the cashier treated her rudely.

▶ **Parallel:** Suzy didn't enjoy paying full price for a lift ticket and being treated rudely by the cashier.

In checking for parallelism, don't worry about terminology. Just read the sentence aloud and listen: parallel sentences sound balanced, whereas nonparallel sentences often sound lopsided.

Keep your balance while you look at the following sentences. Decide whether or not they're parallel. If they are, write 'correct' in the blank after each sentence. If they're nonparallel, correct the sentence in the blanks provided.

0. Sliding down Thunder Mountain, artfully spraying snow across his rival's face, and to get the best seat in the ski lodge were Robert's goals for the afternoon.

A. **Sliding down Thunder Mountain, artfully spraying snow across his rival's face, and getting the best seat in the ski lodge were Robert's goals for the afternoon.** The sentence has three subjects. The first two subjects are verb forms ending in *-ing* (gerunds, in official grammar terminology), but the third is an infinitive (the *to* form of a verb): you have a mismatch. The suggested answer makes all three subjects into gerunds. Here's another possibility: **To slide down Thunder Mountain, to spray snow artfully across his rival's face, and to get the best seat in the ski lodge were Robert's goals for the afternoon.** Now all are infinitives, and the sentence is parallel.

1. The ski pants that Robert favours are green, skin-tight and they stretch.

_____

_____

2. When he squeezes into those pants and zipping them up with great difficulty, Robert feels cool.

_____

_____

3. In this ski outfit, Robert can breathe only with great difficulty and effortfully.

_____

_____

4. The sacrifice for the sake of fashion is worth the trouble and how he feels uncomfortable, Robert says.

_____

_____

5. Robert insists that sliding down the mountain and coasting to a full stop are easier in clothing that resembles a second skin.

_____

_____

6. Robert won't share a ski lift with anyone wearing even slightly tatty ski outfits. He's been known to object to secondhand clothing and how some equipment has been used before.

_____

_____

7. 'With a brand new parka or wearing a warm face mask, I'm ready for anything,' he says.

_____

_____

8. He reckons face masks are useful on the slopes and essentially for post-season bank robberies.

_____

_____

9. Robert's mum thinks ski pants should be recycled if they are ripless and no stains.

_____

_____

10. However, robbing banks and to mug people on the street is more difficult in ski pants.

_____

_____

11. Robbers need speed and to be anonymous, but they also need pockets.

_____

_____

12. Stashing stolen money and where to put an unwanted ski mask are important issues.

_____

_____

13. Robert, who is actually quite honest and not having the inclination to rob anyone, nevertheless thinks about crime and fashion.

_____

_____

14. He once wrote and had edited a newsletter called *Crimes of Fashion*.

_____

_____

15. Skiing and to pursue a career as a police community support officer are Robert's dreams.

_____

_____

Avoiding Unnecessary Shifts in Tense, Person and Voice

Driving instructors spend years of their lives patiently explaining that changing gears at the wrong time is bad for (a) the engine and (b) their nerves. But no matter how you try during your first lessons, it can be difficult to tell whether that grinding comes from the gears or your instructor's teeth.

Sentences need to stay in gear as well, unless the meaning requires a shift. Every sentence has tense (the time of the action or state of being), person (who's talking or being talked about) and voice (active or passive). A sentence has a parallelism problem when one of these qualities shifts unnecessarily from, say, present to past tense, or from first person (the _I_ form) to third (the _he, she, it_ or _they_ form). Also, a sentence mustn't drift from singular to plural without good reason. For help with verbs, check out Chapters 1 and 2. Pronoun tips are in Chapters 3 and 11.

Some shifts are crucial to the meaning of the sentence. If _I kiss you_ and then _she leaves me_, the shift from one person to another is part of the meaning being communicated. That sort of sentence is fine. What's not parallel is a statement such as _I kiss her because you always end up being way too emotional in awkward situations_, where the _you_ is a stand-in for _I_ or _everyone_.

Hop in for a test drive and check out the following sentences. If everything's okay, write 'correct' in the blank after each sentence. Rewrite the nonparallel sentences so that they're correct.

Q. The professor introduced the speaker, and then the amoeba slides were shown by me.

A. **The professor introduced the speaker, and then I showed the amoeba slides.** The original sentence unwisely shifts from active voice (_The professor introduced_) to passive (_slides . . . were shown_). Verdict: crunched gears, caused by a lack of parallelism.

16. If anyone has studied biology, you know that a person must remember the names of hundreds, if not thousands, of organisms.

_____

_____

17. Who gave those names, and why?

_____

_____

18. The Amoeba family provides a good example of the process, and so its name will be explained.

_____

_____

19. You may not know that the first example of this single-celled organism had been called Amy.

_____

_____

20. When you split them in half, the new organisms name themselves.

_____

_____

21. The right half of Amy was still called Amy by herself, but the left half now called herself Bea.

_____

_____

22. The next time Amy and Bea split, you have four new organisms.

_____

_____

23. People can't imagine a conference among four single-celled organisms unless you witness it.

_____

_____

24. Amy Right Half favoured a name that people will notice.

_____

_____

25. Amy Left Half thought about the choice for so long that her swimming was neglected.

_____

_____

26. Bea Right Half, a proto-feminist, opted for 'Amy-Bea', because she wants to honour both her parents.

_____

_____

27. Everyone always pronounced 'Amy-Bea' very fast, and soon 'Amoeba' was their preferred spelling.

_____

_____

28. Single-celled organisms should have simple names that can be remembered by biology students.

_____

_____

29. Bea Left Half, by the way, will change her name to Bea-Amy when she reached the age of 17 days.

_____

_____

30. You know what a teenager is like; they always have to assert their identities.

_____

_____

Matchmaking – The Basics: Either/Or, Not Only/But Also and Similar Pairs

Like lots of dating couples, some words that join ideas (conjunctions, in grammar-speak) arrive in pairs. Specifically, _either/or, neither/nor, not only/but also_ and _both/ and_ work as teams. Also, like many once happy couples, these conjunction pairs tend to drift apart. Your job as a writer is to keep them together by ensuring that they link parallel elements. All you have to do is check that the elements being linked by these words have the same grammatical identity (two nouns, two noun-verb combinations, two adjectives or two whatevers). Have a look at the following examples, in which the linked elements are underlined and the conjunctions are italicised:

- **Nonparallel:** Michelle was _not only_ <u>anxious</u> to achieve fame _but also_ <u>she wanted</u> to make a lot of money.

- **Parallel:** Michelle was _not only_ <u>anxious</u> to achieve fame _but also_ <u>keen</u> to make a lot of money.

In the nonparallel sentence, the first underlined element is a description (an adjective), but the second contains a subject-verb combination that can stand alone as a complete sentence. Clearly these two aren't going to make it through their first date. They're not a well-matched coupled. Nor can you correct the problem by deleting _she_ from the nonparallel sentence, because then you're pairing a description with a verb. Divorce court looms!

The linked elements in the parallel example are both adjectives (*anxious* and *keen*).

A good way to check parallelism in this sort of sentence is to underline the elements, as we do in the preceding example sentences. Then you can focus on whether or not they match.

Parallel or nonparallel? Take a look at the following sentences. If they're parallel, write 'correct' in the blanks. If they aren't, correct them.

0. The bird both swooping over her head and the thing that she found in the back garden startled Lola.

A. **Both the bird that swooped over her head and the thing that she found in the back garden startled Lola.** In the original sentence, *swooping over her head* and *thing in the back garden* don't match. The first element has an *-ing* verb (*swooping*) and the second doesn't. The corrected version matches *bird that swooped* to *thing that she found*.

31. When she travels to the biker convention next week, Lola intends to show off both her new Harley and to display her new tattoo.

_____

_____

32. Either Lulu will accompany Lola or stay home to work on a screenplay about bikers.

_____

_____

33. Neither Lulu plans ahead nor Lola.

_____

_____

34. Lola not only writes screenplays about bikers but also about alien invasions.

_____

_____

35. Lulu both is jealous of Lola's writing talent and the award for 'best cycle' on Lola's mantelpiece.

_____

_____

36. Lola scorns not only awards but also refuses to enter most contests.

_____

_____

37. Neither the cycling award nor the trophy for largest tattoo has any significance for Lola.

_____

_____

38. Lulu, on the other hand, both wants the cycling award and the trophy.

_____

_____

39. When she entered the Biker-Writer award last year, not only did Lulu bribe the judges, but also ran a full-page ad hyping herself up.

_____

_____

40. The judges were either unimpressed with Lulu's efforts or liked Lola better.

_____

_____

Brain Strain: Extra Practice with Parallels

Look for any parallelism problems in the letter shown in Figure 18-1, written to an elected official from an unhappy voter. You should find ten mistakes in parallelism, various shifts and conjunction pairs. When you find a mistake, correct it.

Dear Councillor Bean,

I do not like complaining or to be a nuisance, but if a person is persecuted, they should be heard. As you know, the proposed new motorway not only runs through my living room but into my stamp collecting area (which no one is allowed to go near, not even my mum) as well. When I spoke to the Highways Agency, the assistant was rude and that he took my complaint lightly. He said I should either be glad the road didn't touch the breakfast bar or the kitchen. I demand that the issue be taken seriously by you. I have written to you three times already, and you will say that you were 'working on the problem'. I am angry and in the mood to take legal action. Moving the motorway or to cancel it entirely is the only solution. I expect you to cooperate and that you will fire that rude, uppity assistant immediately.

Yours sincerely,

Joshua Hickman

Figure 18-1:
A disgruntled citizen writes an unparalleled letter.

Answers to Parallelism Problems

1. **The ski pants that Robert favours are green, skin-tight and stretchy.** The original sentence links two adjectives (*green* and *skin-tight*) with a clause containing a subject and verb (*they stretch*). The corrected version relies on three adjectives (*green*, *skin-tight* and *stretchy*) to describe Robert's favourite pants.

2. **When he squeezes into those pants and zips them up with great difficulty, Robert feels cool.** The original sentence isn't parallel because the *and* joins two verbs (*squeezes* and *zipping*) that don't match. In the corrected version, *and* links *squeezes* and *zips*. Another possible correction is, **Squeezing into those pants and zipping up with great difficulty, Robert feels cool.** Now s*queezing* parallels *zipping*.

3. **In this ski outfit, Robert can breathe only with great difficulty and effort.** The original sentence has *difficulty* (a noun) and *effortfully* (an adverb). But they don't mix together well. The correction pairs two nouns (*difficulty* and *effort*).

4. **The sacrifice for the sake of fashion is worth the trouble and discomfort, Robert says.** The clanger (the original sentence) joins a noun, *trouble*, and a whole clause (that's the grammar term for a subject/verb combination), *how he feels uncomfortable*. But those two items aren't parallel. The correction links two nouns, *trouble* and *discomfort*.

5. **correct.** The sentence yokes two -*ing* forms (*sliding* and *coasting*).

6. **Robert won't share a ski lift with anyone wearing even slightly tatty ski outfits. He's been known to object to secondhand clothing and used equipment.** You're okay with two nouns (*clothing* and *equipment*). You're not okay with a noun (*clothing*) and a clause (*how some equipment has been used before*), which is what is in the original sentence.

7. **'With a brand new parka or a warm face mask, I'm ready for anything,' he says.** The *or* in the original sentence links *with a brand new parka* and *wearing a warm face mask*. The second term includes a verb form (*wearing*), and the first doesn't, and so you know that the parallelism isn't working correctly. In the correction, *parka* and *face mask* are linked, and because they're both nouns, the parallelism works.

8. **He reckons face masks are useful on the slopes and essential for post-season bank robberies.** The original sentence isn't parallel because is *useful* and *essentially* don't match. The corrected sentence pairs *useful* and *essential*, two adjectives, and so it's fine.

9. **Robert's mum thinks ski pants should be recycled if they are ripless and clean.** *Ripless* is an adjective, but *no stains* is a noun phrase. The corrected version has two adjectives (*ripless* and *clean*).

10. **However, bank robberies and street muggings are more difficult in ski pants.** In the correction two nouns are matched (*robberies* and *muggings*). You can also go for two -*ing* forms (*robbing banks* and *mugging people*). Just be sure that the two subjects have the same grammatical form.

11. **Robbers need speed and anonymity, but they also need pockets.** The original sentence falls off the parallel tracks because *speed* is a noun and *to be anonymous* is an infinitive. The correction joins two nouns, *speed* and *anonymity*.

12. **How to stash stolen money and where to put an unwanted ski mask are important issues.** In the correction, the subjects are both clauses; that is, they're both expressions containing subjects and verbs. (Think of a clause as a mini-sentence that can sometimes, but not always, stand alone.) Two clauses = a correct pairing. The original sentence derails because the first subject (*stashing stolen money*) is a gerund, and the second is based on an infinitive (*to put*).

13 **Robert, who is actually quite honest and not inclined to rob anyone, nevertheless thinks about crime and fashion.** The original sentence links an ordinary description (*honest*) with an -*ing* verb form (*not having the inclination to rob anyone*), which doesn't work. The correct answer matches two descriptions, *honest* and *inclined*.

14 **He once wrote and edited a newsletter called *Crimes of Fashion*.** The answer matches two past tense verbs, *wrote* and *edited*. The original matched a past (*wrote*) and a past perfect (*had edited*) without any valid reason for a different tense, and so it wasn't parallel.

15 **To ski and to pursue a career as a community police officer are Robert's dreams.** Pair two infinitives (*to ski* and *to pursue*) and you're fine. Or *skiing* and *pursuing* are fine, too.

16 **If you've studied biology, you know that a person must remember the names of hundreds, if not thousands, of organisms.** The original sentence shifts from *anyone* (third person) to *you* (second person). The correction stays in second person. Another possible correct is to pair *anyone* with *he or she*.

17 **correct.** Two questions. No shifts, no problem.

18 **The Amoeba family provides a good example of the process, and so I will explain its name.** The original sentence shifts unnecessarily from active (*provides*) to passive (*will be explained*). The corrected sentence stays in the active voice. True, it contains a shift from third person (talking about the Amoeba family) to first, but that shift is justified by meaning.

19 **You may not know that the first example of this single-celled organism was called Amy.** The original sentence shifts inappropriately from present tense (*may not know*) to past perfect (*had been called*). You don't need to use the past perfect, because you're not talking about something that happened further in the past than something else. The past simple is fine here.

20 **When they split in half, the new organisms name themselves.** The original sentence isn't parallel because it moves from the second person *you* to the third person *organisms*. The correction stays in third person (talking about someone), with *they* and *organisms*.

21 **The right half of Amy still called herself Amy, but the left half now called herself Bea.** In the original, the extra *was* and *by* in the first half of the sentence unbalances the sentence by making that part passive. The correction eliminates the problem by making both parts of the sentence active.

22 **The next time Amy and Bea split, they formed four new organisms.** Parallel statements need to stay in one person, in this case third person, talking about *Amy*, *Bea* and *they*.

23 **People can't imagine a conference among four single-celled organisms unless they witness it.** The issue here is pronouns. It doesn't work to begin with *people* (third person) and then shift to *you* (second person).

24 **Amy Right Half favoured a name that people would notice.** The first verb in the original (*favoured*) is past, but the second (*will notice*) shifts illogically to the future. That's not right. In the correction, the past tense *favoured* is matched with the past tense (*would notice*).

25 **Amy Left Half thought about the choice for so long that she neglected her swimming.** Why change from active (*thought*) to passive (*was neglected*) when two actives work better?

26 **Bea Right Half, a proto-feminist, opted for 'Amy-Bea', because she wanted to honour both her parents.** The original sentence has a meaningless tense shift, from past (*opted*) to present (*wants*). The correction stays in past tense (*opted, wanted*).

27 **Everyone always pronounced 'Amy-Bea' very fast, and soon 'Amoeba' was the preferred spelling.** The original sentence shifts from singular (*everyone*) to plural (*their*). The answer avoids the problem by dropping the second pronoun entirely.

28 **Single-celled organisms should have simple names that biology students can remember.** The shift from active in the original (*should have*) to passive (*can be remembered*) isn't a good idea. The verbs in the correction (*should have, can remember*) are both active. The result is much better.

29 **Bea Left Half, by the way, will change her name to Bea-Amy when she reaches the age of 17 days.** The original contains an illogical tense shift. The first verb is future (*will change*) and the second is past (*reached*), making the sentence unbalanced. In the correction, both actions are in the future. One verb uses a *will* form (*will change*). The other uses a present simple form with future meaning (*when she reaches*).

30 **You know what teenagers are like; they always have to assert their identities.** The corrected sentence stays in plural (*teenagers, they*), but the original improperly shifts from singular (*a teenager*) to plural (*they*).

31 **When she travels to the biker convention next week, Lola intends both to show off her new Harley and to display her new tattoo.** The paired conjunction here is *both/and*. The correction pairs two infinitives (*to show off* and *to display*), in contrast to the original sentence, which joins a noun (*her new Harley*) and an infinitive (*to display her new tattoo*).

32 **Lulu will either accompany Lola or stay home to work on a screenplay about bikers.** The elements joined by *either/or* in the original sentence don't match. One is a subject-verb combo (*Lulu will accompany*) and one just a verb (*stay*). The new version links two verbs (*accompany* and *stay*).

33 **Neither Lulu nor Lola plans ahead.** The corrected sentence links two nouns (*Lulu* and *Lola*) with the *neither/nor* conjunction pair. The original sentence fails the parallelism test because it links a subject-verb (*Lulu plans*) with a noun (*Lola*).

34 **Lola writes screenplays not only about bikers but also about alien invasions.** The original isn't parallel because the first element joined by *not only/but also* includes a verb (*writes*) but the second doesn't. The new version joins two prepositional phrases (*about bikers* and *about alien invasions*).

35 **Lulu is jealous of both Lola's writing talent and the award for 'best cycle' on Lola's mantelpiece.** Here you're working with *both/and*. In the original sentence *both* comes before *is*, a verb, but no verb follows the *and*. In the correction, each half of the conjunction pair comes before a noun (*talent* and *award*).

36 **Lola not only scorns awards but also refuses to enter most contests.** The conjunction pair, *not only/but also*, links two verbs here (*scorns* and *refuses*). The original sentence joins a noun, *awards*, to a verb, *scorns*. Oops!

37 **correct.** The *neither/nor* combination comes before two nouns in the sentence (*award* and *trophy*). Verdict: the sentence is parallel.

38 **Lulu, on the other hand, wants both the cycling award and the trophy.** In the original sentence, *both* comes before a verb (*wants*), but *and* comes before a noun (*trophy*). The new version performs better, linking two nouns (*award* and *trophy*).

39 **When she entered the Biker-Writer award last year, not only did Lulu bribe the judges, but she also ran a full-page ad hyping herself up.** The two conjunctions (*not only/but also*) link subject-verb combinations in the corrected version (*did Lulu bribe* and *she ran*), but in the original these conjunctions link a subject-verb and a verb (*did Lulu bribe* and *ran*).

40 **Either the judges were unimpressed with Lulu's efforts or they liked Lola better.** The *either/or* pair in the corrected sentence connects two complete sentences (*the judges were unimpressed* and *they liked Lola better*). The original is mismatched because a description (*unimpressed*) follows *either*, but a verb (*liked*) follows *or*.

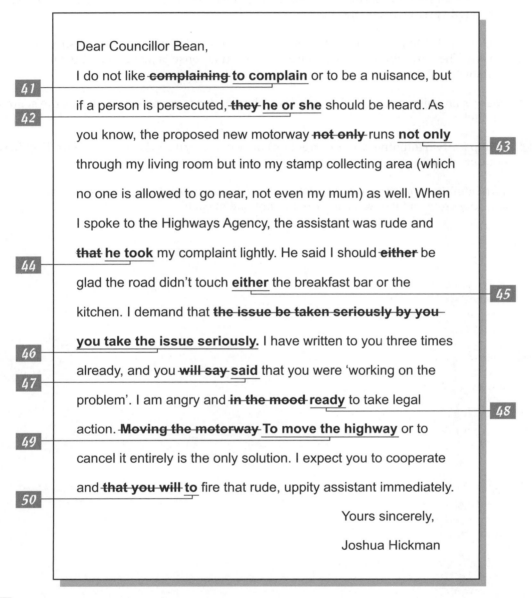

Dear Councillor Bean,

41 I do not like ~~complaining~~ **to complain** or to be a nuisance, but

42 if a person is persecuted, ~~they~~ **he or she** should be heard. As

you know, the proposed new motorway ~~not only~~ runs **not only** **43**

through my living room but into my stamp collecting area (which

no one is allowed to go near, not even my mum) as well. When

I spoke to the Highways Agency, the assistant was rude and

44 ~~that~~ **he took** my complaint lightly. He said I should ~~either~~ be

glad the road didn't touch **either** the breakfast bar or the **45**

kitchen. I demand that ~~the issue be taken seriously by you~~

46 **you take the issue seriously.** I have written to you three times

47 already, and you ~~will say~~ **said** that you were 'working on the

problem'. I am angry and ~~in the mood~~ **ready** to take legal **48**

49 action. ~~Moving the motorway~~ **To move the highway** or to

cancel it entirely is the only solution. I expect you to cooperate

50 and ~~that you will~~ **to** fire that rude, uppity assistant immediately.

Yours sincerely,

Joshua Hickman

41 You can change *complaining* to *to complain*, as we do, or you can change *to be* to *being*. Both options make a parallel sentence.

42 *A person* is singular, but *they* is plural. We change *they* to the singular *he or she*, but if you want to keep *they*, you can scrap *a person* and insert *people* instead.

43 Each part of the *not only/but also* pair needs to go before a prepositional phrase.

44 The *and* may link *was* and *took*, two verbs, but not a verb (*was*) and a subject-verb combination (that he *took*). Another way to correct this sentence is to select an adjective to replace *he took my complaint lightly* – *dismissive*, *flippant*, *disrespectful* or a similar word. Then the verb *was* goes before two adjectives, *rude* and *dismissive*, perhaps.

45 After the correction shown in the figure, each half of the conjunction pair *either/or* comes before a noun. In the original, the *either* comes before a verb (*be*) and the *or* before a noun (*kitchen*).

46 The original sentence switches from active (*I demand*) to passive (*be taken . . . by you*). The corrected version avoids the shift.

47 The original shifts from present perfect tense (*have written*) to future (*will say*) for no good reason. The correction is in past tense because that tense is justified by the meaning of the sentence.

48 *Angry* is an adjective, but *in the mood* is a phrase. *Ready*, an adjective, makes the sentence parallel.

49 Plump for two infinitives (our correction) or two *-ing* forms (*Moving* and *cancelling*) here, but not one of each.

50 Two infinitives (*to cooperate*, *to fire*) are legal, as are two subject-verb combinations (*that you will cooperate* and *that you will fire*), but not one of each.

Chapter 19

Spicing Up and Trimming Down Your Sentences

*T*ake a look at the following paragraph:

> As she writes this, the rain beats down on her window. How glad she is not to be outside! Smiling, she types away, dry and cosy.

Now compare it to this one:

> She is writing. The rain beats down on her window. She is glad that she is not outside. She is smiling. She types away. She is dry and cosy.

We hope you agree that the first version is better, because variety is not only the spice of life but also the spice of writing. In this chapter you practise adding variety to your sentences by altering the underlying structure and combining ideas. In addition, you discover how to cut repetitive or awkward expressions. Have you got your scissors handy? Let's start snipping.

Beginning with a Bang: Adding Introductory Elements

The spine of most English sentences is a subject-verb combination: *Alison walks, Fido sits* and so on. Most sentences also have some sort of completion, what grammarians call a complement or an object: *Alison walks around the kitchen* or *Fido sits on Alison's foot*.

Even when you throw in some descriptions, this basic skeleton can be boring if it's the only structure you ever use. The easiest and most effective way to change the basic pattern is to add an introductory element, which is italicised in the following examples:

> *Sticking her finger in the jar*, Alison stirred the peanut butter dreamily. (The introductory verb form tells something Alison did.)

Despite the new polish on her nails, Alison was unwilling to eat with a fork. (The introductory phrase gives information about Alison's readiness to get down and dirty with the peanut butter.)

When she had finished the whole jar, Alison wondered what finger food she could eat next. (The introductory statement has a subject and a verb, *she had finished*, and in grammar terms is a clause. Again, you get more information about Alison.)

As always in grammar, you don't need to clutter your mind with definitions. Just try some of the patterns, but be sure to avoid a common error: the subject of the main part of the sentence must be the one doing the action or the one in the state of being that the introductory verb form describes. Check out Chapter 15 for more information on this sort of error.

Put boring writing behind you by combining the two statements in each of the following questions, making one of the statements an introductory element. Note that several answers are possible for each exercise. Your answer may differ from the one we provide in the answers section and still be correct. Check to see that you express the same ideas as the original statements and that the action or state of being expressed by the introductory verb form relates to the subject of the main portion of the sentence.

Q. The letter said that the bank manager wanted to see Fiona immediately. Fiona started wondering how serious her financial situation was.

A. **Realising that the bank manager wanted to see her immediately, Fiona started wondering how serious her financial situation was.** This possibility is just one of many. You can also say: **Now that Fiona knew that the bank manager wanted to see her immediately, she started wondering how serious her financial situation was.**

1. Fiona was considering retirement. Fiona's bank manager thought that Fiona should work at least 100 more years.

_____

_____

2. Fiona wanted to drink tequila sunrises on a tropical island. Fiona also wanted to keep her house.

_____

_____

3. Fiona's entire plan was impractical. An especially unrealistic part allowed Fiona to relax in a hammock all day, drinking cocktails.

_____

_____

4.   The bank manager spoke to Fiona in a loud voice. He pointed out that Fiona had 37 pence in her savings account. He said she had a mortgage that was 16 times her annual income.

_____

_____

5.   The bank manager angered easily. Fiona brought out the worst in him.

_____

_____

6.   Fiona considered robbing the bank. Fiona was an honest woman.

_____

_____

7.   Fiona was an honest woman. Fiona told the bank manager every detail of her bank robbing fantasy.

_____

_____

8.   The bank manager took lots of notes to try to keep himself awake. He was bored out of his mind.

_____

_____

9.   The bank manager promised not to report Fiona to the police for her dishonest daydreams. He thought he was showing his gentler side.

_____

_____

10.   The bank manager decided to rob the bank. He wanted to drink cocktails on a tropical island.

_____

_____

Smoothing Out Choppy Sentences

A subordinate doesn't refer to the poor office assistant who has to make coffee for everyone at work. Instead, a *subordinate* is the part of the sentence that, though still containing a subject and a verb, occupies a position of lesser importance in relation to the rest of the sentence. In the world of grammar, the full name is a *subordinate clause*. No need to remember the name, but do remember that subordinate clauses can fall at the beginning, middle or end of the sentence.

Here are some examples, with the subordinate in italics:

> The box, *which Pandora was told never to open*, practically screamed, 'Look inside!'

> *After she had prised off the lid*, Pandora ran screaming down the hall.

> Pandora is hoping to repair *whatever was damaged if she ever manages to replace the lid*. (This sentence has two subordinates, *whatever was damaged* and *if she ever manages to replace the lid*.)

As you can see, subordination is useful for placing one idea inside another. If you have a lot of short sentences strung together, subordination can make your writing less choppy.

Take a shot at inserting ideas inside other ones. Combine the ideas in these exercises into one sentence per question, using subordinate clauses.

Q. Pandora's boss held a press conference. The boss issued a statement about 'the incident'.

A. **Pandora's boss held a press conference at which he issued a statement about 'the incident'.** More than one answer is possible. Here's another: **Pandora's boss, who held a press conference, issued a statement about 'the incident'.**

11. Josie Shmo is a prize-winning reporter. She asked the boss a number of questions.

_____

_____

12. The boss asked Josie to sit down and be quiet. Josie refused. She was still looking for information about 'the incident'.

_____

_____

13. MI5 was interested in the case. The agency sent several agents. The agents were supposed to investigate.

_____

_____

14. Pandora didn't want to talk to the agents. Her boss had told her that her job was in jeopardy.

_____

_____

15. Pandora bought a train ticket. She slipped out of the office with the box.

_____

_____

16. MI5 may track her down. The agency will deal with her harshly.

_____

_____

17. Pandora is away. The boss is trying to manage the news media.

_____

_____

18. Pandora has offered her story to an independent film company. The film company seems interested.

_____

_____

19. The box has been placed in the most secure place the film company could think of. The place is located on a small island off the eastern tip of Anglesey.

_____

_____

20. Some people know what is in the box. Those people are in danger.

Being Awkward but Interesting: Reversed Sentence Patterns

What wakes up an audience faster than a triple latte? The words *in conclusion*. Knowing that a speech is almost over makes the listener just a little bit more attentive. Similarly, in writing, the end of a chapter or a paragraph – and even the end of an individual sentence – may be a high-interest spot. Yet most writers fail to take advantage of this phenomenon. Instead, they lull the reader with the usual subject-verb-object/complement pattern. Run your eyeballs over these two examples:

> The hungry bear ran through the trees, across a clearing and towards our Robin Reliant.

> Through the trees, across a clearing and towards our Robin Reliant ran the hungry bear.

Nothing is wrong with the first sample sentence, but isn't the second a nice change of pace? In the second, *the hungry bear* is a punch line. The sentence leads the reader through the bear's route before revealing *the bear* as the subject. Granted, you don't want to reverse all your sentences or you simply create another pattern with the potential to bore your reader. But stick an occasional reversed sentence in your writing, and your reader is going to be grateful.

Don't reverse sentences by lapsing into passive voice. Active voice is when the subject does the action (*Dawn pushed Peter*); passive is when the subject receives the action (*Peter was pushed by Dawn*). Passive voice isn't wrong, and can come in handy very occasionally when you don't want to say who did what (*The window was broken*). But using the passive can be wordy and awkward. If you can stay active, do so.

These sentences are in the usual order. So get into reverse gear and reword. Aim for the same meaning expressed in a different order. To keep you awake, we put in a couple of passive-voice sentences. Change them to active voice (any order) for a better, stronger expression.

Q. The paperboy shoved a shredded mass of Sunday newspaper through our very small letter box.

A. **Through our very small letter box, the paperboy shoved a shredded mass of Sunday newspaper.**

21. Fido, our lovable pooch, came sprinting from the kitchen, sliding through the sitting room and making a beeline for the front door.

_____

_____

22. The closed front door was in Fido's way.

_____

_____

23. The newspaper and supplements were not chewed by Fido.

_____

_____

24. Fido did place a few tooth marks and about a hundred scratches on the front door.

_____

_____

25. Puppy obedience school was unsuccessful for Fido.

_____

_____

26. The paperboy stood on the front porch listening to Fido's frantic efforts.

_____

_____

27. He was no fan of dogs.

_____

_____

28. His left leg was marked by seven dog-bite scars.

_____

_____

29. Fido was not to blame for the paperboy's tooth marks.

_____

_____

30. The postie's scars, on the other hand, were inflicted by Fido.

_____

_____

Shedding and Eliminating Redundancy

Don't you hate listening to the same thing twice? We hate listening to the same thing twice. You probably hate listening . . . okay, you get the point by now! Repetition is boring. Try to avoid it in your writing, regardless of the form it takes – and it takes many forms, including doubled adjectives (_calm and serene_), extra phrases (_six feet tall in height_) or just plain saying the same thing two different ways (_in my opinion, I think_).

Rewrite the following sentences, eliminating the extra words (if any) to avoid redundancy.

Q. Feeling wound up and extremely tense, Susannah approaches the starting line where the race will begin.

A. **Extremely tense, Susannah approaches the starting line.** You can, of course, cut _extremely tense_ and stay with _feeling wound up_. Just don't use both _tense_ and _wound up_ because they say pretty much the same thing. The other cut (_where the race will begin_) is justified because that's what _a starting line_ is.

31. Susannah's new and innovative racing strategy is to peel away quickly from the crowd and separate herself.

_____

_____

32. Susannah thinks personally, from her own point of view, she's got a great chance of winning and finishing in first place.

_____

_____

33. The spikes that she's installed and put in on her tyre rims should easily and without much effort cut her opponents' tyres.

_____

_____

34. 'It's their tough luck and hard cheese,' she says to herself, 'if they're not prepared for a few sharp digs in this race.'

_____

_____

35. There are two sides to every story, of course; Susannah and the other competitors have different ideas about what is fair and unfair in a motorbike race.

_____

_____

36. A little sharp object can alter the outcome of the race in an important and significant way.

_____

_____

37. Susannah says that at this moment in time, now, she is ready to win legally or not at all.

_____

_____

Brain Strain: Extra Practice Honing Your Sentences

Figure 19-1 contains part of a short story that needs some major help. Revise it as you see fit, paying attention to varied sentence patterns, unnecessary words and choppiness.

Chelsea fainted. Chelsea was lying on the floor in a heap. Her legs were bent under her. She breathed in quick, shallow breaths at a rapid rate. Liam came running as fast as he could. He neared Chelsea and gasped. 'Sweetheart,' he said. His heart was beating. His cardiologist would be worried about the fast rate. Liam did not care. Liam cared only about Chelsea. She was the love of his life. She was unconscious. He said, 'Babes, I didn't mean that we actually have to pawn your engagement ring.' He knelt next to her.

Figure 19-1:
Short story excerpt with horrid sentence structures.

Answers to Sentence Improvement Problems

1 **Despite the fact that Fiona was considering retirement, her bank manager thought that Fiona should work at least 100 more years.** This answer begins with a prepositional phrase. You may also start with *Although Fiona was. . .* or *Contrary to Fiona's desire to retire. . . .*

2 **In addition to her desire to drink tequila sunrises on a tropical island, Fiona also wanted to keep her house.** You can start here with a prepositional phrase, but a clause (*Even though Fiona wanted to drink tequila sunrises on a tropical island*) would also be a good beginning, pairing nicely with the rest of the sentence (*she also wanted to keep her house*).

3 **Impractical in every way, the plan was especially unrealistic in allowing Fiona to relax in a hammock all day, drinking cocktails.** The introduction here is just another way to describe *the plan*, the subject of the main part of the sentence.

4 **Speaking to Fiona in a loud voice, the bank manager pointed out that she had 37 pence in her savings account and a mortgage that was 16 times her annual income.** Here the introductory verb form lets you combine the original sentences nicely into one, instead of keeping them as three separate statements.

5 **Angering easily, the bank manager admitted that Fiona brought out the worst in him.** We added *admitted* so that *the bank manager* is the subject of the sentence. You would create a dangler (see Chapter 15 for more on the dangers of danglers) by leaving *Fiona* as the subject and beginning with *angering* or a similar expression. In such a sentence, *Fiona* would be the one *angering easily* – not the meaning you want to convey. Another possible correction: **Bringing out the worst in the bank manager, Fiona angered him easily.**

6 **Even though she is an honest woman, Fiona considered robbing the bank.** The first part of the sentence is a clause because it has a subject and a verb, but it depends upon the statement in the second part of the sentence to complete the thought.

7 **Because she was an honest woman, Fiona told the bank manager every detail of her bank robbing fantasy.** You may think that you're not allowed to begin a sentence with *because* but you can, as long as you have a complete thought in the sentence.

8 **Bored out of his mind, the bank manager took lots of notes to try and keep himself awake.** The introduction *Bored out of his mind* is a way to describe *the bank manager*, the subject of the main part of the sentence.

9 **By promising not to report Fiona to the police for her dishonest daydreams, the bank manager thought he was showing his gentler side.** The introductory clause *By promising. . .* describes the *bank manager*.

10 **With cocktails on a tropical island in his future, the bank manager decided to rob the bank.** In this correction, a nice set of prepositional phrases packs an opening punch.

11 **Josie Shmo, who is a prize-winning reporter, asked the boss a number of questions.** You can also drop the *who is*, leaving *a prize-winning reporter* to do the job. (The shortened form is called an appositive, but you don't need to know that. Also, best not to ask what was in the box.)

12 **The boss asked Josie to sit down and be quiet, but Josie, who was still looking for information about the 'incident', refused.** Here *who* connects the extra information about *Josie* firmly to the rest of the sentence.

13 **MI5, which was interested in the case, sent several agents who were supposed to investigate.** The pronoun *which* stands in for *the MI5* and introduces extra information about that secretive agency.

14 **Pandora didn't want to talk to the agents because her boss had told her that her job was in jeopardy.** This combined sentence has a cause-and-effect structure introduced by the word *because*.

15 **When she slipped out of the office, Pandora bought a train ticket.** The word *when* ties the information about slipping out to the reason Pandora slipped out.

16 **If MI5 tracks her down, the agency will deal with her harshly.** Ignoring MI5 isn't usually a clever thing to do. Writing choppy sentences isn't clever either! *If* expresses a possibility, as does the verb *may* in the original. However, *if* has the advantage of letting you combine ideas together in one sentence.

17 **While Pandora is away, the boss is trying to manage the news media.** A time expression works nicely here, tying Pandora's absence to the boss's press conference.

18 **Pandora has offered her story to an independent film company that seems interested.** When you use *that* to introduce an idea, a comma is seldom necessary.

19 **The box has been placed in the most secure place the film company could think of, which is on a small island off the eastern tip of Anglesey.** When you use *which* to introduce an idea, a comma usually separates the *which* statement from the rest of the sentence. (Check out Chapter 5 for more information on comma use.)

20 **Whoever knows what is in the box is in danger.** When you're tucking ideas into your sentences, don't forget *whatever* and *whoever* – very useful little words!

21 **Sprinting from the kitchen, sliding through the sitting room and making a beeline for the front door came Fido, our lovable pooch.** By placing the subject, *Fido*, near the end, you make the sentence more dramatic.

22 **In Fido's way was the closed front door.** Not a big change, but placing the *closed front room door* at the end is a way to emphasise the tragedy of the barrier that the eager dog can't surmount.

23 **Fido didn't chew the newspaper and supplements.** The original sentence is passive, not usually a good choice. The correction is a straightforward, active voice, subject-verb-object order. You can also change the standard order and place the object before the subject and verb.

24 **On the door a few tooth marks and about a hundred scratches placed Fido.** The new order is dramatic, emphasising *Fido*. It may sound awkward to your ear, however. That's the tradeoff with reverse order sentences. You gain interest but startle (and perhaps irritate) your reader. Use this sort of sentence very sparingly!

25 **Unsuccessful for Fido was puppy obedience school.** Leading with the description *unsuccessful* is a surprising, and therefore interesting, choice.

26 **On the front porch listening to Fido's frantic efforts stood the paperboy.** Leading with phrases (*on the front porch* and *listening to Fido's frantic efforts*) is unusual but effective.

27 **No fan of dogs was he.** This reverse-order sentence has a comic effect, highlighting *no fan of dogs* by placing it in an unexpected position.

28 **Seven dog-bite scars marked his left leg.** Like question 23, the original sentence uses the passive voice. The correction uses the active voice. You can also change the standard order and put the object before the subject and verb: *His leg seven dog-bite scars marked.*

29 **Not to blame for the paperboy's tooth marks was Fido.** Leading with a negative (*not*) isn't something you want to do every day, or you end up sounding like Yoda, but occasionally, you can get a lot of attention with this pattern.

30 **On the other hand, Fido did inflict the postie's scars.** The passive voice of the original is a real no-no. You do know, because the sentence tells you, who chomped on the postie. Passive voice is therefore unnecessary and awkward.

31 **Susannah's new racing strategy is to peel away quickly from the crowd.** You can cut *new* and leave *innovative* if you prefer, but don't use both. Also, you can drop *to peel away quickly from the crowd* and leave *separate herself*. If that's your option, you may want to move *quickly* to the end of the sentence, just to retain the idea of speed.

32 **Susannah thinks she's got a great chance of winning.** Why say *personally* or *from her own point of view* when you start the sentence with *Susannah thinks*? *Winning* and *finishing in first place* are the same; choose either one.

33 **The spikes that she's installed on her tyre rims should easily cut her opponents' tyres.** More doubles: *installed* and *put in* match, as do *easily* and *without much effort*. Choose one of each, but not both.

34 **'It's their tough luck,' she says to herself, 'if they're not prepared for a few sharp digs in this race.'** With *tough luck* and *hard cheese* meaning the same, choose one and drop the other.

35 **Susannah and the other competitors have different ideas about what is fair in a motorbike race.** The whole first part of the sentence is unnecessary. Of course differing points of view exist, and as the sentence goes on to specify details, the general statement is a waste of words. Also, if the bikers can't agree on what's fair, by definition they also don't agree on what's unfair, and so that part of the statement may also be cut.

36 **A little sharp object can alter the outcome of the race in an important way.** If you prefer, drop *important* and keep *significant*. Just don't use the two together.

37 **Susannah says that now, she is ready to win legally or not at all.** When you say *at this moment* you don't need to add *in time* or *now*. (If you want to keep *at this moment*, go for it but drop *in time* and *now*.)

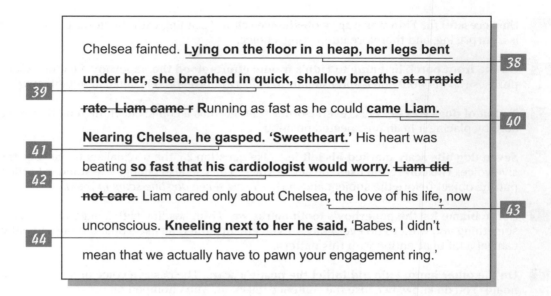

38   You can combine the following three sentences quite easily: *Chelsea was lying on the floor in a heap, Her legs were bent under her* and *She breathed in quick, shallow breaths*. The ideas in the first two sentences are turned into introductory elements, with the last of the three sentences as the main idea. If you add an introductory element with a verb form, ensure that the subject of the main section of the sentence is the person or thing doing the action or in the state of being mentioned in the introduction. Another possible combination: *After Chelsea fainted, she was lying on the floor in a heap. With her legs under her, she breathed in quick, shallow breaths.*

39   The revision cuts repetition; *rapid* and *quick* are the same.

40   We reversed the sentence *Liam came running as fast as he could* to create an interesting variation on the standard sentence pattern.

41   The revision combines two sentences: *He neared Chelsea and gasped. 'Sweetheart,' he said.* The new version, with an introductory element (*Nearing Chelsea*), is more concise. Another possibility is *He neared Chelsea and gasped, 'Sweetheart.'*

42   A subordinate (*that his cardiologist would worry*) tucks an idea from one sentence into another.

43   The original story ends with several short, choppy sentences. The revision combines all but the last sentence.

44   The last two sentences of the original combine with an introductory verb form, *kneeling*. If you begin with *kneeling*, be sure that *he* or *Liam* is the subject of the main part of the sentence. You can also revise this section in this way: *'Babes, I didn't mean we actually have to pawn your engagement ring,' he said as he knelt next to her.*

Chapter 20

Steering Clear of Tricky Word Traps

*T*he saying goes that little things mean a lot, and in this chapter we put your writing under the microscope. Those tiny mistakes – for example, a nonstandard expression, a faulty irregular verb or the wrong word from a pair of similar words – come into focus here. Peer through the lens with us and you can keep clear of some of these troublesome errors.

Separating Almost-Twins: Commonly Confused Words

Do you know any twins who resemble each other but have completely different personalities? One is a professional hang glider, perhaps, and the other a librarian. If so, you understand that each half of a similar-looking pair may function in a vastly different way, and woe betide the writer who sends one word to do the other's job.

This section highlights some often confused words that trip up people. For example:

✔ **Affect** usually expresses action: Kevin's tantrum did not *affect* his mother's decision to leave the sweetie aisle immediately.

✔ **Effect** is most often used as a noun and means 'result': one *effect* of Kevin's tantrum was a trip to the naughty step when he and his mummy got home from the supermarket.

Affect and *effect* can be used in other ways, though much less frequently. *Affect* as a noun means 'the way someone displays emotions'. *Effect* as a verb means 'bring about a change in the face of opposition'. In this chapter, though, we concentrate on the more common usage of each word.

Now that you've got to grips with those almost-twins, check out the next set of commonly confused words.

Both *farther* and *further* can refer to distance, and both are acceptable in the following sentences:

✔ **Farther:** Kevin runs *farther* than anyone else when jelly babies are at stake.

✔ **Further:** Kevin runs *further* than anyone else when jelly babies are at stake.

Most people use *further* when talking about distance. But bear in mind that some people (including the *For Dummies* editors) insist that *farther* is the only correct option in this context. If you want to talk about intensity, degree, time and so on, only *further* works. In addition, *further* is used as an expression meaning 'what's more' or 'that's not all':

> **Wrong:** Farthermore, he'll run anywhere for something sweet.
>
> **Why that sentence is wrong:** *Farthermore* doesn't exist as a word in English.
>
> **Correct:** Furthermore, he'll run anywhere for something sweet.

So, an easy way around the *further* or *farther* dilemma is to use *further* all the time and just forget about *farther*. Of course, if your boss insists on *farther* for distance, you know what to do.

Other pairs (or triplets) are quite different in appearance, but for some reason people mix them up:

> ✔ **As** expresses similarity, and it's the word you want in front of a subject-verb combination: Kevin screams as Louise does, but he gets many more sweets for his tears. (Here, the subject-verb combination is *Louise does*.) *As* can also be used before an expression beginning with a preposition: In 2005, *as in 2004*, Kevin was the supermarket screeching champion.
>
> ✔ **Like** expresses similarity too but is used before a noun or a pronoun, not before a subject/verb combination: Louise bawls *like* Kevin.
>
> ✔ **Such as** introduces examples: Kevin's grandma has a supply of sweets *such as* sherbet dib dabs, dolly mixtures and licorice comfits.

The next commonly confused words often go together, but they aren't interchangeable:

> ✔ **Imply** is 'hint' or 'make a suggestion': Kevin never actually asked for a wine gum, but he strongly *implied* – by talking about how much he enjoyed eating soft, chewy, sweet things – that one would be welcome.
>
> ✔ **Infer** is 'draw a conclusion or figure something out from a suggestion': Hearing Kevin's 'Ode to a Wine Gum', Grandma *inferred* that the packet of sweets she'd left in her coat pocket would probably be gone after Kevin's visit.

Can you tell the following twins and triplets apart? Circle the best word or phrase in each set of brackets.

Q. Fuelled by the caffeine in two double lattes, Jake drove (farther/further) than anyone else.

A. **further** or **farther**. When you're dealing with distance, either of these words is fine.

1. The judge insisted on (farther/further) proof that the police officer's speed gun was broken.

2. Jake gave the judge tons of proof, (like/as/such as) a photo of his car, a statement from all his pals about how slowly he always drives and a 'best attendance certificate' he earned in primary school.

3. He waved his wallet about vigorously, hoping to (imply/infer) that it was empty and that paying a fine was out of the question.

4. (Like/As) judges often do, Judge Carter stubbornly refused to hear his side of the story.

5. '(Farthermore/Furthermore) I don't want to hear another peep out of you,' she snarled.

6. (Like/As) a statue, Jake shut up and sat as still as a stone.

7. The judge, unfortunately, (implied/inferred) from his behaviour that he was silently protesting her ruling.

8. The (affect/effect) of this decision was disastrous.

9. Nothing Jake said, when he finally started talking again, (affected/effected) the judge's ruling.

10. Jake explained that financial setbacks (like/as/such as) speeding tickets would completely wreck his budget.

11. 'I can't convince romantic partners to spend (farther/further) time with me, without reservations at expensive restaurants,' he pleaded.

12. The judge, a realist and a romantic, sentenced Kevin to 100 hours' community service at a local cafe. The (affect/effect) of this sentence, she suggested, may be twofold. Kevin could reflect on the error of his speeding ways and he may meet someone content with beans on toast – someone who loves him for who he is, not for the swiftness of his car or the girth of his wallet.

Comparing Quantities without Numbers

The reason why different words are used to describe singulars and plurals when you're counting or measuring is lost in the fog of the history of English:

- **More than**, **many** and **fewer** work for plurals: for example, *more than* 19 witnesses, *many* problems and *fewer* than 50 coffee cups. These words work well with things you can count (also known as *countable nouns*).

- **Much** and **less** take you into singular territory: for example, *less* interest in the sport and *much* unrest. These words are best with things you can measure but not count (also known as *uncountable nouns*).

The word *over* is sometimes confused with *more* or *more than* when figures are involved. In general, after numbers, *more than* is preferred: *more than 200* applicants went for the job. But watch out for one exception. After ages (even though *18 years* is a number), *over* works better: they won't serve you unless you're *over 18*.

The following list clarifies the correct use of some more often confused words:

- **Amount** is appropriate when the item you're discussing is uncountable (and therefore singular): the *amount* of enthusiasm.

- **Number** is correct when the item is countable (and therefore plural): the *number* of bowties.

- **Between** is the word you want when you're talking about two people or things: I'm having trouble choosing *between* the pistachio and the chocolate chip.

- **Among** is for groups of three or more: *among* the 12 candidates for mayor, Hilary stands out.

Uncover your toes (in case you need to count higher than ten) and have a go at the following questions. Circle the correct word in each set of brackets.

Q. The boss sent (more than/over) 300 memos last week badgering us to work efficiently.

A. **more than.** *Memos* is a countable plural noun and you have a number (*300*), which calls for *more than*.

13. We employees, all 4,546 of us, discussed the memos (between/among) ourselves, and despite (many/much) difference of opinion, we eventually agreed on one thing.

14. We decided that email uses (fewer/less) paper and is easier to ignore.

15. The boss's (many/much) memos this week have been highlighting the (number/amount) of paper we waste.

16. Yesterday morning the office manager collected (more than/over) 5,000 sheets of paper from our desks, all emails from the boss that we had printed out.

17. Surely it takes (fewer/less) energy to shelve the issue altogether.

18. Later in the afternoon the boss caught shredding fever and by home time there were (less/fewer) than five notes left on his desk.

19. The (number/amount) of confidential material he shredded is impossible to determine.

20. But now that we've all read every one of his highly classified personal files, what we can determine without doubt is that he really doesn't know the difference (between/among) a photocopier and a shredder.

Bursting Your Bubble: Sorry, but Some Common Expressions Are Wrong

Take a look at the following paragraph:

> English *should of* been easier, *I can't help but* think. *Being that* English is difficult to learn, I'm going to *try and* spend more time studying it. *Irregardless*, I'll still have time to practise origami, a hobby that I *can't hardly* resist because it does *not* have *no* stress attached to it.

By now you've probably figured out that the italicised words and phrases are all problematic. In standard English, they don't exist. If you're using any made-up expressions, now's the time to remove them from your speech and writing and substitute the correct words, which you can see in Table 20-1.

Table 20-1	Correcting Made-Up Words
Wrong	*Right*
Should of	Should have, should've
Would of	Would have, would've
Could of	Could have, could've
Cannot help but	Cannot help [insert the *-ing* form of the verb]: *Cannot help wondering,* for example
Being that	Because or since
Try and	Try to
Irregardless	Regardless
Can't hardly	Can hardly or can barely

Here's your challenge: Rewrite the following sentences, substituting correct standard English for any nonstandard terms. We throw a few correct sentences into the mix, and so when you find one, simply write 'correct' in the blank.

Q. Jim believes he couldn't of got a more annoying nursery school teacher than Mrs Campbell.

A. **Jim believes he couldn't have got a more annoying nursery school teacher than Mrs Campbell.** The expressions *couldn't of* sounds like c*ould've,* but *could've* is the contraction of *could have,* not *could of.*

21. Irregardless of the teacher's views on technology in the classroom, Mark sends a text to his brother.

_____

_____

22. Jim doesn't answer immediately, being that he's in the middle of the sandbox.

_____

_____

23. 'I'll try and answer Mark after a snack,' he thinks.

_____

_____

24. The teacher doesn't want no distractions from the carrot and apple snacks she has prepared, and so she confiscates Jim's mobile phone, which he uses to send texts and keep track of who he's playing with each afternoon after school.

_____

_____

25. Jim should of hidden his phone until nap time.

_____

_____

26. Mark can't hardly believe some of the stories Jim tells about nursery school.

_____

_____

27. Mark remembers his own days in finger-paint land, which he should of treasured.

_____

_____

28. Because the primary school and the nursery school are in the same building, Mark could of walked out of his classroom and spoken directly to Jim.

_____

_____

29. Jim can't help wondering about his phone, which now resides on the teacher's desk.

_____

_____

30. Being that the day is almost over, Jim asks the teacher to return his phone.

_____

_____

31. 'Being in nursery school is really annoying sometimes,' Jim thinks.

_____

_____

32. 'I can't hardly wait until I'm in big school,' he says.

_____

_____

Tackling Verbs That Give You a Headache

Sit (not *set*) yourself down for some practice with four headache-inducing verbs. Afterwards you can *lie* (not *lay*) down for a rest.

- ✔ To **lie** is 'to rest or recline the body'. (Yes, it also means that you aren't telling the truth, but that definition isn't a problem.) The past tense of *lie* is *lay*. The past participle (the form of the verb *lie* that goes with *has*, *have* or *had*) is *lain*.

- ✔ To **lay** is 'to place something' or 'to put'. The past tense of *lay* is *laid*. The past participle is *laid*.

- ✔ To **sit** is 'to bend your knees and put your bottom on some sort of surface'. The past tense and the past participle are both *sat*.

- ✔ To **set** is 'to place, to put something somewhere'. The past tense and the past participle forms are also *set*.

To tell the difference between these two pairs of verbs, think of *lie* and *sit* as actions that a person does to himself or herself: I *lie* down, I *sit* in the chair. *Lay* and *set*, on the other hand, are actions that a person does to something else: I *lay* the baby carefully in her cot, I *set* the vase down on the piano.

Don't set down your pen until you try the following questions. Circle the correct form of the verb in the brackets.

Q. In my favourite soap opera, *Ear, Nose and Throat*, the main character (lies/lays) in bed, comatose.

A. **lies.** The character, in suitably pale makeup, reclines in bed, and so *lies* is correct.

33. In the world of soaps, the rule is that the doctor must (sit/set) by the bed every day with a look of concern and love on his or her face.

34. In yesterday's episode, the doctor (sit/sat/set) a bouquet of flowers on the bedside locker.

35. When the nurse told the doctor to go home and (lie/lay) down, the doctor replied that he would 'just (sit/set) down for a while'.

36. Last week the doctor (lay/laid) a wreath on the tomb of the unknown soldier.

37. I think the wreath that (lies/lays) there is a sign that the soldier is really the doctor's long lost lover.

38. I reckon that the long lost lover will suddenly show up and (sit/set) down next to the doctor in the cafeteria and give him the shock of his life.

39. They will both be ready to live happily ever after, but first the lover will have to (sit/set) aside everything else and do some explaining.

40. While the doctor (sits/sets) there crying glycerin tears, the lover will explain what happened to the evil twin and other soap mysteries.

Combining Rightfully Independent Words

Some words (such as *a lot*) are often wrongly written as a single word (*alot*). Because language and grammar change over time, some words that used to be considered wrong (such as *alright*) are now acceptable in informal writing (along with the previously considered only correct option, *all right*). If your boss is the old-fashioned kind, however, keep him or her happy on this one and stick to *all right*.

Some pairs of words have both a single- and a double-word form. Here's what each form means:

- *Already* (by this time) and *all ready* (completely prepared)
- *Everyday* (ordinary) and *every day* (daily)
- *Everyone* (all the people) and *every one* (each one)
- *Sometime* (at an unspecified moment) and *some time* (a period of time)

Can you find the correct form in the following pairs? Circle your choices.

Q. Because Jennifer sneezes (alot/a lot), Abigail has (already/all ready) packed a dozen handkerchiefs.

A. **a lot, already.** The single-word form *alot* is never correct. In the second set of brackets, the meaning you want is 'by this time', and so *already* is correct.

41. Abigail hopes Jennifer's sneezing will end (sometime/some time) soon.

42. Jennifer has devoted (sometime/some time) to the study of the nose and its explosions.

43. She has discovered that most people sneeze at least once (everyday/every day).

44. Jennifer herself sneezes at least ten times a day, and so she buys (alot/a lot) of tissues.

45. When Abigail arrived to take Jennifer to the airport, Jennifer was (already/all ready).

46. Jennifer had her (everyday/every day) handkerchief, a blue cotton square, all ready in her carry-on bag.

47. Abigail had packed a fresh outfit for (everyday/every day) of the trip.

48. 'We're (already/all ready) late. Come on, let's go!' shouted Abigail impatiently.

49. 'It always takes us (sometime/some time) to get to the airport and through security,' she snapped.

50. 'There's no need to rub it in,' snorted Jennifer. 'Is it my fault they always want to x-ray (everyone/every one) of my hankies – used or unused?'

Brain Strain: Extra Practice with Tricky Words

Figure 20-1 shows a poorly-written obituary. Whenever you encounter a misused word, correct the clunker. You should find ten mistakes.

Ancient Egypt Specialist Dies at 81

Lloyd Demos died yesterday as he was pursuing farther study in ancient Egyptian culture. Demos, who effected the lives of many residents of our town, had alot of varied interests. By the time he died he had all ready learned 12 languages, including ancient Egyptian, and spent some time everyday studying Egyptian grammar so that his writing would be alright. Demos had just set down to supper when the Grim Reaper appeared at his door. Irregardless, Demos insisted on finishing his mashed potatoes, though he was heard to say, 'I would like to lay down for a while.' Even though Demos was more than 80 he will be fondly remembered by young and old alike.

Figure 20-1: Obituary filed with errors.

Answers to Tricky Word Problems

1 **further.** In this sentence you want a word that indicates 'more' or 'a greater degree' not the idea of distance, and so *further* fits the bill.

2 **such as.** These words introduce a list of examples (the car photo, the statement from friends and the attendance award), meaning that *such as* is the best choice.

If you introduce examples with *like*, you exclude those examples. In this answer, using *like* means that Jake *didn't* provide a photo of his car, a statement from his friends or an attendance certificate. Instead, he provided items that were *similar* to those on this list.

3 **imply.** Jake is hinting that his finances are in bad shape, and *to imply* is 'to hint'.

4 **As.** In front of a subject/verb combination, *as* is the only appropriate choice.

5 **Furthermore.** Sometimes you can use *farther* and *further* interchangeably but in this instance (*furthermore*), you can't. *Further* is the only word that works here.

6 **Like.** Jake resembles a statue, and *like* expresses similarity. Because no verb follows, *like* is better than *as*.

7 **inferred.** The judge figured out that Jake was annoyed with the speeding ticket, and so *inferred* is the correct verb here.

8 **effect.** The sentence calls for a noun meaning *result*. Bingo: *effect* wins.

9 **affected.** Here you're looking for a verb that's the same as *influence*: *affect* is that verb.

10 **such as.** The tickets are presented as an example of budget-wreckers, and *such as* introduces examples.

11 **further.** When you're talking about time, *farther* isn't an option, because *farther* only refers to distance (whereas, *further* can be used to talk about time or distance).

12 **effect.** The judge is talking about the result of Jake's sentence, and so you want *effect*.

13 **among, much.** Because more than two employees are talking, you want *among. Between* works for couples, not mobs. In the second brackets, *much* is the correct choice because *difference* is uncountable and singular.

14 **less.** The word *paper* is uncountable and singular, and so *less* is appropriate.

15 **many, amount.** *Many* works for countable nouns (such as *memos*). In the second answer, the uncountable *paper* is the issue, and *amount* is for uncountable nouns (*number* works with countable nouns).

16 **more than.** When you're talking about *sheets*, you're in countable land and you're counting a number. Use *more than*.

17 **less.** Although *fewer employees* are necessary to shelve the issue, the task takes *less energy*, because *energy* is a singular, uncountable noun.

18 **fewer.** The word *notes* is a countable noun, and so *fewer* is needed.

19 **amount.** *Material* is an uncountable noun, and so *amount* is the right choice here.

20 **between.** When comparing two office machines, *between* is correct.

21 **Regardless of the teacher's views on technology in the classroom, Mark sends a text to his brother.** *Irregardless* doesn't exist in English. Use *regardless* instead.

22 **Jim doesn't answer immediately because he is in the middle of the sandbox.** Another non-existent expression is *being that*. Use *because* or *as*.

23 **'I'll try to answer Mark after a snack,' he thinks.** The expression *try and* says that the speaker is going to do two things: *try* and *answer*. But the real meaning of the sentence is 'try to answer'.

24 **The teacher doesn't want any distractions from the carrot and apple snacks she has prepared, and so she confiscates Jim's mobile phone, which he uses to send texts and keep track of who he's playing with each afternoon after school.** Double negatives are a no-no. Change *doesn't want no* to *doesn't want any*.

25 **Jim should have hidden his phone until nap time.** The expression *should of* sounds like *should've*, but *should've* is the contraction of *should have*, not *should of*.

26 **Mark can hardly believe some of the stories Jim tells about nursery school.** *Can't hardly* is a double negative, which reverses the intended meaning of the sentence. Go with *can hardly*, which means that Mark thinks Jim is exaggerating.

27 **Mark remembers his own days in finger-paint land, which he should've treasured.** The contraction *should've* is the short form of *should have*.

28 **Because the primary school and the nursery school are in the same building, Mark could have walked out of the classroom and spoken directly to Jim.** Either *could have* or *could've* is fine, but stay away from *could of*.

29 **correct.** The expression *can't help* is fine when it precedes the *-ing* form of the verb. Just don't place it with *but*, because then you have a double negative.

30 **Because the day is almost over, Jim asks the teacher to return his phone.** Delete *being that* wherever you find it; send in *because* instead.

31 **correct.** In this sentence *being* is fine because it's a verb, not a faulty substitute for *because*.

32 **'I can hardly wait until I'm in big school,' he says.** *Can't hardly*, a double negative, flips your meaning. *Can hardly* says that waiting is a difficult task for young Jim.

33 **sit.** The doctor isn't placing something else on the bed but is resting beside the bed. Go for *sit*.

34 **set.** To place something somewhere calls for the verb *set*.

35 **lie, sit.** Both of these spots call for personal body movements, not the placement of something else. *Lie* and *sit* deal with flopping in bed or relaxing on a couch or in a chair.

36 **laid.** Because the doctor placed the wreath, the verb of choice is to *lay*, and the past tense of *lay* is *laid*.

37 **lies.** This one is a bit tricky. The doctor *lays* the wreath, but the wreath itself just *lies* (rests) there.

38 **sit.** The lover will pull out a chair and sit in it, not place an object somewhere.

39 **set.** The lover will put everything else to one side. You want the verb *set* here.

40 **sits.** The doctor isn't placing something, just staying in a chair, crying. The verb *to sit* is the right one.

41 **sometime.** The sentence refers to an unspecified time in the future, and so you need *sometime* here.

42 **some time.** Jennifer has spent a period of time (or *some time*) researching her nasal issues.

43 **every day.** Here you're going for 'daily', and so the two-word form does the job.

44 **a lot.** Not one word, but two. (Things may change in the future but, for now, *alot* still isn't considered correct in standard English.)

45 **all ready.** She had her suitcase, her carry-on bag, her hanky case and every other case prepared. Therefore, *all ready* is correct here.

46 **everyday.** Her ordinary handkerchief (that is, her *everyday* handkerchief) isn't as fancy as the silk number she carries when she's dressed up.

47 **every day.** The meaning implied here is 'every single day'.

48 **already.** Abigail means 'by this time'.

49 **some time.** Because Jennifer never remembers the quickest way to the airport, the journey does indeed take a period of time (*some time*).

50 **every one.** Here you mean 'each one', and so you need two words, not one.

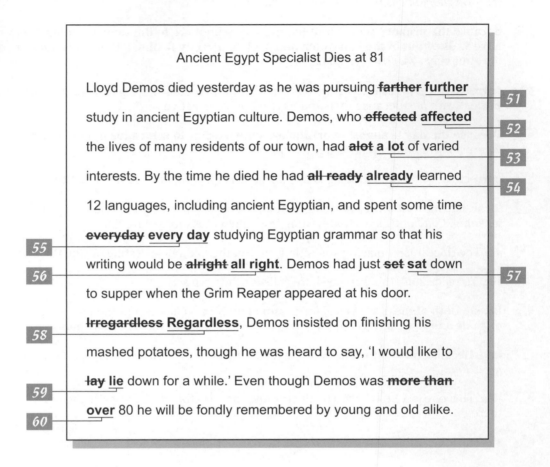

Ancient Egypt Specialist Dies at 81

Lloyd Demos died yesterday as he was pursuing ~~farther~~ **further** 51 study in ancient Egyptian culture. Demos, who ~~effected~~ **affected** 52 the lives of many residents of our town, had ~~alot~~ **a lot** of varied 53 interests. By the time he died he had ~~all ready~~ **already** learned 54 12 languages, including ancient Egyptian, and spent some time 55 ~~everyday~~ **every day** studying Egyptian grammar so that his 56 writing would be ~~alright~~ **all right**. Demos had just ~~set~~ **sat** down 57 to supper when the Grim Reaper appeared at his door. 58 ~~Irregardless~~ **Regardless**, Demos insisted on finishing his mashed potatoes, though he was heard to say, 'I would like to 59 ~~lay~~ **lie** down for a while.' Even though Demos was ~~more than~~ 60 **over** 80 he will be fondly remembered by young and old alike.

51 *Farther* refers to distance; *further* is for time, intensity or duration.

52 *Effected* can be a verb, but as such it means 'to be the sole agent of change'. In this sentence 'influenced' is the more likely meaning, and so you want *affected*.

53 *A lot* is always written as two words.

54 *All ready* as two words means 'completely prepared', but in this sentence you want 'by this time', which is the definition of *already*.

55 *Everyday* as one word means 'ordinary'. As two words, it means 'daily', which is the meaning you want here.

56 *Alright* is often used informally nowadays, but *all right* is more appropriate in formal writing.

57 *Sat* is the past tense of *sit*, which is the verb you want for describing Lloyd's plopping himself in a chair. *Set* is to place something somewhere.

58 *Irregardless* doesn't exist, but *regardless* expresses the same idea.

59 *Lie* is to rest or recline; *lay* is to put something down somewhere.

60 *Over* is the better choice than *more than* with ages (such as *80*).

Part VI
The Part of Tens

'Is that all the help I get? Keep
using the Computer Grammar Checker?
A fine muse you are!'

In this part . . .

The renowned Dummies Part of Tens gives you a list of overcorrections – mistakes people make, usually when nerves kick in, when they're trying to speak or write more formally than usual. Often in these tricky situations some of the fundamental rules of grammar can get overlooked.

This part also shows you the worst, avoid-at-all-cost, common errors that can sink your writing faster than a big hole in the side of the tiny plastic boat in your bathtub. No exercises here – just the best tips for improving your English. Sail on.

Chapter 21

Ten Overcorrections

Have you ever found yourself in front of an interview panel, a new boss or the love of your life's parents, desperately trying to impress? Suddenly you find the grammar/ style part of your brain going into overdrive. *Who* becomes *whom* for no reason at all. Verb tenses tangle up, and *had* is suddenly as common as shoulder pads at a 1980s party. This tendency is called *overcorrection* and, in many ways, overcorrection is almost as bad as the error you're trying to avoid. If you want to identify what not to wear in terms of grammar and style, read on.

Substituting 'Whom' for 'Who'

True, some people never utter the word *whom*, even when it's necessary in a sentence. But throwing *whom* into every situation also isn't a good idea. In fact, sentences requiring *whom* are quite rare and you need the word only when the sentence calls for an object of some sort. (Check out Chapter 10 for more information on *who* and *whom*.)

Objects receive the action of the verb, as in *Whom did you call?* In this sentence, *whom* receives the action of the verb *did call*. (*You*, in case you're wondering, is the subject.) The problem with *whom* is that when it does show up, it's often in a sentence containing other thoughts, and so you have to sort out the various threads. One common error is *Whom shall I say is calling?* Sounds nice, doesn't it, but it's wrong. Untangling shows you the answer to that question would be: *I shall say whom is calling. Whom is calling?* Nope. *Who is calling* is correct, which means the question needs to be *Who shall I say is calling?*

Inserting Unnecessary 'Hads'

As a helping verb, *had* is very good, but don't overuse it. *Had* places an action in the past before another action in the past, as in this sentence: *Archie had already shaved when the aerosol can exploded.* On a timeline, the shaving happened before the exploding, and both happened before the present moment. The shaving part of the sentence gets the *had*. The overcorrection comes when people sprinkle *hads* all over, without rhyme or reason. For example: *Archie had already shaved when the aerosol can had exploded.*

Repeating Again and Again

You may think that using more, rather than fewer, words always makes you sound more educated, formal or knowledgeable. But take care. Sometimes you can end up simply saying the same thing twice (and making yourself sound less than clever in the process). Can you see what the problem is with these pairs of words: *PIN number*, *repeat again*, or *alternately*, *HGV vehicle*, *reverse back* and *review again*? They are all repetitious. For example, *reverse* means go back, and so *reverse back* means go back back! *PIN* means personal identification number, and so *PIN number* repeats the word *number* unnecessarily.

Sending 'I' to Do a 'Me' Job

Me sounds childlike, doesn't it? It conjures up memories of 'Me hungry!' and similar statements. But *I* isn't the personal pronoun for every sentence. *I* is a subject pronoun, meaning that it belongs in a subject spot – or after a linking verb – and nowhere else. An error that pops up frequently is using *I* as the object of a preposition: *between you and I* or *except you and I*. Oops! The correct phrases (where *me* is used correctly as an object pronoun) are *between you and me* and *except you and me*.

Speaking or Writing Passively

The government, official bodies and large faceless organisations are often guilty of this particular overcorrection. Official forms and announcements tend to throw passive verbs all over the place, perhaps because the passive voice allows the writer to omit the subject – that is, the doer of – and therefore the one responsible for – the action. How much safer a person must feel when writing that *VAT was increased last year by 2 per cent* rather than *I increased VAT by 2 per cent last year; now please vote for me in next week's election.*

One of the problems with using the passive voice in everyday writing is that it can come across as overly formal or stilted. Unless you need it (perhaps because you truly don't know who did the action or because the subject isn't the point of the sentence), opt for the active voice.

Making Sentence Structure Too Complicated

Complicated sentences don't always make your writing look more mature. Often, they just make it awkward. Stay away from sentences such as *It was this treaty that ended the war* and go for *This treaty ended the war*. Run from *That which he created yesterday is the product which will make his fortune* and race instead towards *The product he created yesterday will make his fortune.*

Letting Descriptions Dangle

Description is good, especially when you're agreeing to a blind date with someone you've never met. (In the sentence *Jake is pleasantly plump*, you discover some important information about Jake in the description *pleasantly plump*.) Descriptions containing verb forms are useful, because they give you even more information: *Jake, howling at the moon as he does every evening, is looking forward to his date*. The description *howling at the moon as he does every evening* is certainly an eye-opener, giving you a lot of information about Jake. Descriptions in the beginning of a sentence are especially effective, because they vary the usual, boring sentence pattern: *Running with his friend Wolfie, Jake often stays out all night*. The description *running with his friend Wolfie* tells you something about Jake that you probably need to know (preferably before you meet up with him for your date tonight).

But – and this is a big but – don't overuse the introductory description or you simply create a new, but immediately boring, sentence pattern. Also, be sure that the introductory description applies to the subject – the first person mentioned in the sentence. If not, you have a dangler, a truly big no-no. (We go into more detail on danglers in Chapter 15.)

Becoming Allergic to 'They' and 'Their'

For some overcorrectors, the pronouns *they* and *their* seem to be radioactive. Even when a plural is justified, the overcorrectors send in *he or she* and similar phrases. Bad idea! Plurals (*the guys, three grapefruits, both, several, a few* and so on) match with other plurals (*they* and *their*). So don't write *The six naughtiest pupils forgot his or her homework and blamed his or her dog*. Instead, keep the plurals together, as in *The six naughtiest pupils forgot their homework and blamed their dogs*.

Being Semi-Attached to Semicolons

Semicolons (the dot on top of the comma) link two complete sentences. They also separate items in a list, when at least one of the listed items contains a comma already. But that's it for using the semicolon. A semicolon isn't a fancy comma or a weak colon. It's a semicolon and proud to be one. Why are we going on about semicolons? Because a lot of people throw them around like dog treats at a kennel. Don't; throw them around. Oops. We mean *Don't throw them around*.

Not Knowing When Enough Is Enough

You can lay the blame for this overcorrection squarely at our door. We're teachers and guilty of forever asking for more, more. Did we mention already about wanting to see more detail? When a student hands in an essay about an apple, we're there with the red pens, writing *What colour is the apple? How many seeds does it have?* In the real world, however, most people aren't particularly interested in reading 15 sentences about an apple when all they really want to know is who the bad one is or which one is going to keep the doctor away. The cure for under-explaining isn't over-explaining. The best path is to provide interesting and relevant details and nothing more. And if your readers wander around wondering how many seeds were in that apple, that's their problem.

Chapter 22

Ten Errors to Avoid at All Costs

In This Chapter

▶ Mistakes that ruin your writing

▶ Relying too heavily on computers

*W*hat did you forget? Your lunch? A parachute? We ask these questions to point out that some mistakes are more serious than others. The plane's going down fast; you're standing at the open door, cold air rushing past you. Does what you've forgotten really make any difference? Well, you probably don't mind if you've left your cheese sarnie behind, but you're going to be just a little bit hacked off when you realise, just as you're about to jump, that you've forgotten to strap that essential life-saving device onto your back.

Your writing can crash and burn too, especially if you err in a few – well, ten – specific ways, which we look at in this chapter. Everyone makes mistakes, and so a small slip here and there is no biggie, but this chapter shows you how to avoid missing the runway completely and killing everyone on board, in your writing.

Writing Incomplete Sentences

Unless, of course, you want to make a style statement. Of course, the preceding sentence is incomplete. That's our attempt at irony and also a way of pointing out that sometimes breaking the rules is a good thing. You can think of writing as a forest, and an incomplete sentence as a clearing. In a forest, a clearing stands out but a forest full of clearings is no forest at all. In your writing, an occasional incomplete sentence calls attention to an important point. But a page full of incomplete sentences just draws attention to your poor writing skills, and makes your reader question whether you know how to write a complete sentence or not. That's a bad impression to give (especially when your teacher or boss is doing the reading). So, be sure that each of your sentences has a subject-verb pair, an endmark and a complete thought. (For more information on complete sentences, check out Chapter 4.)

Letting Sentences Run On and On

A run-on sentence is actually two or more sentences stuffed together without any proper glue; for example, leaving out a word such as *and* or a semicolon. The worst form of run-on is what grammarians call a comma splice, in which a comma attempts (and fails) to attach one complete sentence to another. Be especially careful with words that resemble legit joiners (*consequently, however, therefore, nevertheless* and so on). Use them for their meaning, not for their sticking abilities. (Chapter 4 explains run-ons in greater detail.)

Forgetting to Capitalise 'I'

Times change and fashions come and go. And you can see that fact clearly in the fads and phases of the letter *i*. Not that long ago if you wrote *i will c u l8er* most people would have thought you were trying to write in some sort of secret code or simply didn't know even the most basic rules of grammar and spelling. The rule, back in the day, was that the personal pronoun *I* was always capitalised and *i* was always, always, always wrong. Today, that rule still stands – in general – but our quest for faster and faster communication means that *i* is acceptable in texts and informal emails. However, in any kind of formal writing (exams, reports, CVs, job application letters) take our advice and stick to the old school *I* when writing about yourself.

Being Stingy with Quotation Marks

Whether you're writing for school, work or personal reasons, honesty requires you to credit your sources. Lifting someone else's words, dropping them into your own writing and omitting the quotation marks is just plain dishonest. At school, your teacher can fail you; in work or public life, you can get sued. The solution is simple. If the words aren't yours, credit the source, as we do here where we cite this humorous line from Milton: 'Copy from one, it's plagiarism; copy from two it's research.' (Chapter 8 contains much more on quotation marks.)

Using Pronouns Incorrectly

Pronouns – noun substitutes such as *he*, *they*, *all*, *other*, *neither* and the like – are governed by more rules than an off-peak family railcard. Even if you don't know all the finer points, never neglect the basics: pronouns can replace one and only one noun, and that noun needs to be clearly identifiable. Don't use an object pronoun (*me*, *her*, *them*) in a subject-pronoun (*I*, *she*, *they*) spot. Singular pronouns replace singular nouns, and plural pronouns replace plural nouns.

Also, don't overuse reflexive pronouns. You may think that writing *If you have any questions, please contact myself* sounds more formal, but the reflexive pronoun *myself* is incorrect here. The right pronoun is the object pronoun *me*. (Turn to Chapters 3 and 10 to take a closer look at these issues.)

Placing New Words in the Wrong Context

New words make their way into your vocabulary gradually. At first, they begin to look familiar when you come across them a few times in something you're reading. Later, you recognise them as old friends. Later still, you feel comfortable using them in your own writing. Don't skip any of these stages! Every teacher has received essays from someone who's memorised the '100 words most likely to impress your teacher' and is determined to get as much mileage out of them as possible.

The problem is that the nuances of a word's meaning are hard to grasp from a list or a couple of encounters. And premature use of vocabulary can be quite embarrassing. You may find yourself writing about *Manchester City Council's suppository of documents*. (Hint: a suppository is a way of getting medicine into the body without a needle or a spoon. Look it up, if you need to.)

Letting Slang Seep into Your Speech

Take a look at the following paragraph:

> It ain't that slang is a real downer. In fact, slang can be wicked – the real bee's knees. But if your readers aren't in the loop, they may think that you're grating their carrot sideways.

That paragraph contains a mixture of slang from several different eras. You probably recognised at least one of the slang expressions but may have missed some of the others. And that's the problem. Slang changes fast, so fast that it's almost impossible for everyone to keep up. If your readers understand that *wicked* in the sentence above is slang for *good*, that's fine. But the readers who get that reference may not realise that *bee's knees* is a term (from the 1920s) for the latest, best fashion. And if your readers are old enough to know *bee's knees*, they may not know that *in the loop* means *understanding what's going on*, that *ain't* is a corruption of *isn't*, that *a real downer* means *something that makes you feel unhappy* or that if something *grates your carrot*, it *gets on your nerves*.

The bottom line is that when you use slang, you risk confusion. In addition, slang sounds informal, and so if you want to impress a boss or a teacher, it's best to give slang a miss.

Forgetting to Proofread

Even if you finish the essay or report only ten minutes before you have to hand it in, take the time to proofread your work. Yo maye ffind tat som latters are nut where they sould be, not to mentione. punctuation,

Relying on Computer Checks for Grammar and Spelling

Those little red and green wavy lines that show up on your screen, highlighting potential mistakes, can be really helpful but they're not always accurate. First of all, plenty of eras slip through. (See what we mean? That last sentence should read *plenty of errors*.) Second, the computer often identifies a mistake when the sentence is actually correct. We were given plenty of little wavy lines while writing this book, and as you've no doubt figured out by now, we're prefect. Er . . . perfect.

Repeating Yourself

In conclusion, at the end of this chapter, we'd like to state, declare and advise that saying the same thing more than once repetitively is a real drag, an annoyance and a pain. Don't – do not – repeat, because repetition is likely to send your reader away fast and quickly, not to mention rapidly. Shall we reiterate the point or is once enough?

Appendix

Your Final Challenge

· ·

How sharp are your eyes? This appendix is the grammatical equivalent of an optician's chart. If your grammatical vision is 20/20, you should spot 30 mistakes in each of the four exercises. Of course, after you spot the errors, your mission is to correct them. The errors may involve faulty structure, word choice, punctuation, capitalisation or indeed anything we cover in *English Grammar Workbook For Dummies*.

Exercise One

Have a look at the university course overview in Figure A-1. This course description has many faults – 30, by our estimate. Your tally may differ slightly depending on how you group your answers. You can quibble later about the statistics – your mission for now is to search and destroy the mistakes.

6901 World Domination: Professor Peck, Mr Lapham, Ms Austin. One two-hour lecture period per week is required. Three periods of fieldwork per week is also required.

This course on world domination and dictatorship involve both lecture and that they put into practice what students will learn. A student will report to their faculty advisors once a month. Everyone must keep a journal of revolutions started, governments overthrown and peasants' oppressed. Readings include Karl and Groucho Marx's masterful essay, 'Laughing All The Way to The Throne', and Chairman Mayos autobiography, *Hold the Lettuce*. This is certain to interest students who's career plans are to be emperors; tsars; dictators; or reality-show winners. By the time the course ends, students have gathered all necessary information about what it takes to rule the world. We will be discussing topics like propaganda, media manipulation and telegenic coronation clothes (including crown-jewel selection). Working in the field, spy networks will be set up, this will count as a quarter of the final mark. The students's task is to outmanoeuvre everyone on the course by becoming the first to conquer a hostile country that is required for graduation. Exams also emphasises real practical skills, and theoretical ideas. Students only have to write two essays.

Figure A-1:
A scary
course
description
that needs
some work.

Admission to this course and it's sequel (Universal Domination) are by permission of the Department of Politically Science Irregardless of age or ability, applicants should be as motivated than the average first year student and should try and visit the departmental office for an interview.

Exercise Two

The publisher's letter in Figure A-2 is full of errors. Try your hand at correcting all 30.

Higgen Publishing Company

459 elm Avenue

Edinburgh

EH1 9RV

31 October 2010

Mr Chester Slonton

33 Warwickville Road

Peebles

EH45 8QP

Dear Mr Slonton,

Thank you for sending us your novel, 'The Lily Droops at Dawn'. To read over 1,000 pages about a love affair between plants is a very unique experience. In your talented hands, both of the plants becomes characters that are well-rounded and of great interest to the reader. Before Ms Higgen, whom you know is our founder, commits to publishing this masterpiece, I must ask for some real minor changes.

Most of the editors, including Ms Higgen, was confused about the names. You are absolutely right in stating that each of the lovers are in the lily family, scientifically they have similar characteristics. Calling the lovers Kerry and Terry would not of been a problem if the characters were distinguished from one another in personality or habits or appearance. Unfortunately, your main characters resembles each other in petal colour and height. True, one of the lilies is said to be smartest, but the reader doesnt know which.

A second problem are the love scenes. You mention in your covering letter that you can make them more lengthier. Ms Higgen feels, and I agree, that you write vivid; nevertheless, we think you could cut them alot without losing the reader's attention. After all, once a person has read one flower proposal, he or she has essentially read them all.

Finally, the ending needs work. When the lily droops, the book ended. Are you comfortable with a tiny change. Market research shows that books with happy endings appeal to the readers, whoever he or she may be. These volumes sell good. Instead of drooping, perhaps the lily could spread it's petals and welcome the dawn. Or become a rose.

Higgen Publishing would like this novel for their summer list. I hope that you are open to the changes I had outlined in this letter. I cannot help but mention that Higgen Publishing is probably the only publisher with experience in plant romance volumes I look forward to having talked with you about the editing process.

Yours sincerely,

Alex Higgen

Publishing Assistant

Figure A-2: A letter from a publisher (with a lot of mistakes so you know it must be fake).

Exercise Three

Ever dream of running your own newspaper? Have a look at the article in Figure A-3 and see whether you can find and edit out 30 errors, including some in the quoted material. (In real life, when you quote someone who makes a grammar error, you can usually leave the error in the quotation in order to convey the person's style or personality. But for the purposes of this exercise, please correct every mistake you find.)

Hold the Tights: a Former TV Star Plays Shakespeare

Silver, the actor that played a talking horse in the Bafta-winning series *Mr Said* is now starring in the Theatre Royal production of 'Hamlet'. The handsome blond recently agreed to discuss his approach to acting. It were never about talking, in Silvers' view. As he had munched oats and sipped delicately from a water bucket, the colt explained that he learned to talk at the age of one. Him talking was not fulfilling enough, only acting met his need for recognition.

'I started by reciting monologues for whomever would listen,' he said. Then one day I got a call from an agent offering me the part of Mr Said.' Tossing his mane dramatically, Silver continued, 'I plays that role for nine seasons. You get typecast. Nobody want to take a chance on your dramatic ability if they can find someone else for the role.' He added, 'Sitting by the phone one day, it rang, and my agent told me that I had a audition.' That audition resulted in him getting the part. Silver is the only horse that have ever played Hamlet, as far as he knows.

The actor has all ready began rehearsals. His costume includes a traditionally velvet coat but no tights. 'Between you and I,' he whispered, 'the tights snag on my hairy legs.' Director Ed Walketers asked Silver to consider shaving, and he also tried several types of material for the tights. Even Silver's wife got involved in this key costuming decision. 'No one tried harder than her to find tights I could wear,' Silver said. Nothing was suitable for this extremely unique situation.

Silver is equally as involved with the role itself. 'I relate to Hamlet's problems,' he explained. 'Us horses often find it hard to take action and being decisive.' The role is also exhausting; Silver lays down for a quickly nap everyday before going onstage as Hamlet.

Figure A-3:
A newspaper article with a plethora of errors.

Exercise Four

Don't you hate computer manuals? The one in Figure A-4 is even worse than the usual techno-babble because it contains 30 mistakes. Can you find them all and correct them?

Installing You're New Widget Wheel

To install the widget wheel, a computer should first be turned off, then follow these simple steps.

Important: If you have an A4019 or a newest model, please discard this manual. You must have sent for manual number 218B, or, in the case of a computer that previously has a widget, for manual number 330B. Being that your computer is not covered in this manual, discard it. Faulty directions have been responsible for explosions and that software crashed.

1. Unpack the widget wheel which looks like a sharks tooth.

2. Unpack the two disk poles. Grasp the disk pole that is more circular. Lining up the teeth with the teeth on the widget. *Note*: Teeth should be brushed everyday with a WidgetBrush. see enclosed order form for more information.

3. After the teeth are tight clenched, a person should insert the widget disk into slot C. However, if the widget disk has a blue strip, in which case it should be inserted into slot D. Don't mix up the slots as the computer will catch fire. Neither of these slots are open when the computer is standing upright. Sit the computer on its side before beginning this step.

4. Turn on the computer. If the screen is blank call the service specialist on 0800-555-5039. Farthermore, if the screen blinks rapid from red to green (or from blue to yellow in model 2W4T), you really need to panic. This means the widget was installed improper; the computer is all together unusable.

5. You are almost ready to enjoy your new widget!! Place a hand on the mouse that is not wearing any rings, including wedding rings. Depending upon the model number, either press firmly or softly. Some widgets can work good no matter what the pressure.

Figure A-4:
The world's biggest headache-inducer: A badly written computer manual.

Answers to Exercise One

In the following figure the errors from the original course description are in bold and crossed out, with a possible correction following each one, as well as an occasional addition of a missing word or mark. All corrections are in bold and underlined. Check the corresponding numbered explanations that follow the revised course description.

6901 World Domination: Professor Peck, Mr Lapham, Ms Austin. One two-hour lecture period per week is required. Three periods of fieldwork per week ~~is~~ **are** also required. **1**

This course on world domination and dictatorship ~~involve~~ **involves** both lecture and **2** ~~that they put into practice~~ **practical application of** what students ~~will~~ **learn**. **4** ~~A student~~ **Students** will report to their faculty advisors once a month. Everyone must keep a **5** journal of revolutions started, governments overthrown and peasants'/oppressed. Readings **6** include Karl and Groucho Marx's masterful essay, 'Laughing All ~~T~~the Way to ~~T~~the Throne' and **7** Chairman ~~Mayos~~ **Mayo's** autobiography, *Hold the Lettuce*. This **reading list** is certain to **8** **9** interest ~~students~~ **who's whose** career plans are to be an emperors'/, tsars'/, dictators'/, or **11** reality-show winners. By the time the course ends, students **will have** gathered all necessary **12** information about what it takes to rule the world. We will be discussing topics ~~like~~ **such as** **13** propaganda, media manipulation and telegenic coronation clothes (including crown-jewel selection). Working in the field, ~~spy networks will be set up~~ **students will set up spy** **14** **networks'/, this fieldwork** will count as a quarter of the final mark. The ~~students's~~ **students'** **15** **17** task **that is required for graduation** is to outmanoeuvre everyone **else** on the course by **16** **19** becoming the first to conquer a hostile country ~~that is required for graduation~~. Exams also **18** **21** ~~emphasises~~ **emphasise** ~~real~~ **really** practical skills'/ and theoretical ideas. Students **20** **22** ~~only~~ have to write **only** two essays. **23**

Admission to this course and it/'s sequel (Universal Domination) ~~are~~ **is** by permission of the **24** **25** Department of ~~Politically~~ **Political** Science. ~~Irregardless~~ **Regardless** of age or ability, **26** **28** applicants should be as motivated ~~than~~ **as** the average first year student and should try ~~and~~ **to** **29** **30** visit the departmental office for an interview.

27

1 The subject is *three periods*, a plural, and so the verb (*are*) must also be plural.

2 The subject course is singular, and so the verb (*involves*) must also be singular.

3 To keep the sentence parallel, the noun *lecture* must be coupled with another noun, not with a subject/verb combination.

4 The *practical application* happens at the same time as the learning, and so you don't want the future tense. Go for the present (*learn*).

5 The paragraph refers to *students* (plural), and so a shift in one spot to singular is inappropriate.

6 The original sentence includes the possessive *peasants'* for no valid reason. The possessive form needs to be linked to a noun, but here it comes before a verb form (*oppressed*).

7 In titles, articles (such as *the* in this title) aren't capitalised.

8 The autobiography belongs to Chairman Mayo, and so you need to show possession with an apostrophe and an *s* after *Mayo*.

9 In the original sentence the pronoun *this* is vague. Insert the clarifying expression, *reading list*.

10 The contraction *who's* means 'who is', but the sentence calls for the possessive *whose*.

11 Items in a series are separated by semicolons only when one or more of the items contain a comma. In this series, no item contains a comma, and so semicolons aren't necessary.

12 A future deadline (*by the time the course ends*) calls for the future perfect tense (*will have gathered*).

13 *Like* excludes the items listed and refers to items that are similar. In this sentence the listed items are examples and need to be preceded by *such as*.

14 The original sentence contains a dangler, *working in the field*. An introductory element containing a verb form must refer to the subject, and *spy networks* aren't *working in the field*. Reword the sentence so that the *students are working in the field*.

15 Two complete sentences can't be joined by a comma. Substitute a semicolon or create two sentences.

16 The pronoun *this* is too vague all by itself. Substitute a noun (*fieldwork*) to clarify the meaning.

17 To create a possessive form for a plural ending in the letter *s*, just add an apostrophe, not an extra *s*.

18 Each student is on the course and so must be compared to everyone *else*.

19 In the original, this misplaced description seems to say that *a country* is required for graduation, not the *task*. Descriptions need to be close to the word they describe.

20 The plural subject, *exams*, requires a plural verb, *emphasise*.

21 The description *practical* needs to be intensified by an adverb (*really*), not by an adjective (*real*).

22 If you unite two complete sentences with the word *and*, a comma goes before the *and*. If you unite two of anything else (in this sentence, two nouns – *skills* and *ideas*), no comma precedes the *and*.

23 The descriptive word *only* needs to precede the word being compared – in this case, *two* as compared to *three* or *four* or whatever the professor assigns.

24 Possessive pronouns have no apostrophes.

25 *Admission* is singular and takes a singular verb, *is*.

26 The adjective *Political* describes the noun *Science*. *Politically* is an adverb and may describe only verbs (*speaking politically*) or other descriptions (*politically inexperienced*).

27 A statement needs to end with a full stop, which is missing in the original.

28 *Irregardless* isn't standard English. Substitute *regardless*.

29 *As* and *than* don't belong in the same comparison: an *as* comparison is for equal items and a *than* comparison for unequal items.

30 *Try and* implies two actions, but the sentence refers to one that should be attempted. The correct expression is *try to*.

Answers to Exercise Two

In the following figure the errors from the original letter are in bold and crossed out, with a possible correction following each one, as well as an occasional addition of a missing word or mark. All corrections are in bold and underlined. Check the corresponding numbered explanations that follow the revised letter.

31 Proper names are capitalised.

32 The title of a full-length work (in this case, a novel) is italicised or underlined, not enclosed in quotation marks.

33 After numbers (such as, *1,000*) *more than* is preferred to *over*.

34 *Unique* is an absolute, and so no degrees of uniqueness (*very unique, a little unique* and so on) exist.

35 *Both* is plural and must be matched with the plural verb, *become*.

36 The original sentence isn't parallel because it pairs the simple description *well-rounded* with the phrase *of great interest*. The correction changes the phrase to a simple description, *interesting*.

37 You need the pronoun *who* to act as a subject for the verb *is*.

38 *Real* is an adjective and appropriate for descriptions of people, places, things or ideas. The adverb *really* intensifies the description *minor*.

39 *Most of the editors* is a plural subject and requires a plural verb, *were*.

40 *Each of the lovers* is a singular subject and requires a singular verb, *is*.

41 A comma can't join two complete sentences. Use a semicolon instead.

42 *Would of* doesn't exist in standard English. The proper expression is *would have*, here changed to the negative *would not have*.

43 The plural subject *characters* needs the plural verb *resemble*.

44 *Smartest* is for the extreme in groups of three or more. Because only two lilies are compared, *smarter* is correct.

45 The contraction *doesn't* contains an apostrophe.

Higgen Publishing Company

459 ~~elm~~ **Elm** Avenue [31]

Edinburgh

EH1 9RV

31 October 2010

Mr Chester Slonton

33 Warwickville Road

Peebles

EH45 8QP

Dear Mr Slonton,

Thank you for sending us your novel, ~~'The Lily Droops at Dawn.'~~ *The Lily Droops at Dawn.* [32] To read ~~over~~ **more than** 1,000 pages about a love affair between plants is a ~~very~~ unique [34] experience. In your talented hands, both of the plants ~~becomes~~ **become** characters that are [35] well-rounded and ~~of great interest~~ **interesting** to the reader. Before Ms Higgen, ~~whom~~ **who** you [37] know is our founder, commits to publishing this masterpiece, I must ask for some ~~real~~ **really** [38] minor changes. [33] [36]

Most of the editors, including Ms Higgen, ~~was~~ **were** confused about the names. You are [39] absolutely right in stating that each of the lovers ~~are~~ **is** in the lily family**,** scientifically they have [41] similar characteristics. Calling the lovers Kerry and Terry would not ~~of~~ **have** been a problem if [42] the characters were distinguished from one another in personality or habits or appearance. Unfortunately, your main characters ~~resembles~~ **resemble** each other in petal colour and height. [43] True, one of the lilies is said to be ~~smartest~~ **smarter**, but the reader doesn't know which. [45] [40] [44]

A second problem ~~are~~ **is** the love scenes. You mention in your covering letter that you can [46] make them ~~more~~ lengthier. Ms Higgen feels, and I agree, that you write ~~vivid~~ **vividly**; [48] nevertheless, we think you could cut them ~~alot~~ **a lot** without losing the reader's attention. After [49] all, once a person has read one flower proposal, he or she has essentially read them all. [47]

Finally, the ending needs work. When the lily droops, the book ~~ended~~ **ends**. Are you [50] comfortable with a tiny change**?** Market research shows that books with happy endings appeal to the readers, whoever ~~he or she~~ **they** may be. These volumes sell ~~good~~ **well**. Instead of [53] drooping, perhaps the lily could spread it~~'~~s petals and welcome the ~~dawn. Or~~ **dawn or** become [55] a rose. [51] [52] [54]

Higgen Publishing would like this novel for ~~their~~ **its** summer list. I hope that you are open to [56] the changes I ~~had~~ **have** outlined in this letter. I cannot help ~~but mention~~ **mentioning** that [58] Higgen Publishing is probably the only publisher with experience in plant romance volumes. I [59] look forward to ~~having talked~~ **talking** with you about the editing process. [57] [60]

Yours sincerely,

Alex Higgen

Publishing Assistant

46 The singular subject *problem* takes the singular verb *is*.

47 Double comparisons aren't correct. Use *lengthier* or *more lengthy*.

48 The verb *write* may be described by the adverb *vividly* but not by the adjective *vivid*.

49 The expression *a lot is* always written as two words.

50 The present tense verb *ends* works best with the rest of the sentence, which contains the present tense verb *droops*.

51 This sentence, a question, calls for a question mark rather than a full stop.

52 The plural pronoun *they* refers to *readers*.

53 *Good* is an adjective, but the sentence calls for the adverb *well* to describe the verb *sell*.

54 A possessive pronoun, such as *its*, never includes an apostrophe.

55 The expression *or become a rose* is a fragment and can't stand as a separate sentence.

56 A company is singular, and so the matching pronoun is *its*.

57 The helping verb *had* is used only to place one action in the past before another past action. Here, the present perfect (*have outlined*) makes the outlining more immediate, more connected to the present.

58 *Cannot help but mention* is a double negative.

59 Every sentence needs an endmark. This statement calls for a full stop.

60 *Having talked* implies a deadline, and the sentence doesn't support such a meaning.

Answers to Exercise Three

In the following figure the errors from the original article are in bold and crossed out, with a possible correction following each one, as well as an occasional addition of a missing word or mark. All corrections are in bold and underlined. Check the corresponding numbered explanations that follow the revised article.

61 The first word of a title and a subtitle must always be capitalised.

62 *Silver* identifies the actor being discussed. The original sentence has a comma at the beginning of the long, descriptive expression (*the actor that played a talking horse in the Bafta-winning series* Mr Said) but none at the end. The second comma is necessary because the information supplied is extra, not essential to the meaning of the sentence. The information needs to be set off from the rest of the sentence by a pair of commas.

63 The title of a full-length work (in this sentence, a play) needs to be in italics or underlined.

64 The singular *it* pairs with the singular verb *was*.

65 A singular possessive is formed by the addition of an apostrophe and the letter *s*.

66 The helping verb *had* places one past action before another past action, but in this sentence the actions take place at the same time. Therefore, drop the *had*.

61 Hold the Tights: ~~a~~ A Former TV Star Plays Shakespeare

Silver, the actor that played a talking horse in the Bafta-winning series *Mr Said*, is now starring **62**

in the Theatre Royal production of ~~'Hamlet'.~~ *Hamlet.* The handsome blond recently agreed to **63**

discuss his approach to acting. It ~~were~~ was never about talking, in ~~Silvers'~~ Silver's view. As **65**

64

66 he ~~had~~ munched oats and sipped delicately from a water bucket, the colt explained that he

67 learned to talk at the age of one. ~~Him~~ His talking was not fulfilling enough/; only acting met his **68**

need for recognition.

69 'I started by reciting monologues for ~~whomever~~ whoever would listen,' he said. 'Then one day I **70**

got a call from an agent offering me the part of Mr Said.' Tossing his mane dramatically, Silver

71 continued, 'I ~~plays~~ played that role for nine seasons. You get typecast. Nobody

~~want~~ wants to take a chance on your dramatic ability if ~~they~~ he or she can find someone else **73**

72

for the role.' He added, 'Sitting by the phone one day, ~~it rang~~ I heard it ring, and my agent told **74**

me that I had ~~a~~ an audition.' That audition resulted in ~~him~~ his getting the part. Silver is the only **76**

75

77 horse that **have** has ~~ever~~ played Hamlet, as far as he knows.

78 The actor has ~~all ready~~ already ~~began~~ begun rehearsals. His costume includes a **79**

80 ~~traditionally~~ traditional velvet coat but no tights. 'Between you and ~~I~~ me,' he whispered, 'the **81**

tights snag on my hairy legs.' Director Ed Walketers asked Silver to consider shaving, and ~~he~~

Silver also tried several types of material for the tights. Even Silver's wife got involved in this **82**

key costuming decision. 'No one tried harder than ~~her~~ she to find tights I could wear,' Silver **83**

said. Nothing was suitable for this ~~extremely~~ unique situation.

84

85 Silver is equally ~~as~~ involved with the role itself. 'I relate to Hamlet's problems,' he explained. '~~Us~~

We horses often find it hard to take action and ~~being~~ to be decisive.' The role is also

86 exhausting; Silver ~~lays~~ lies down for a ~~quickly~~ quick nap ~~everyday~~ every day before going **87**

88 onstage as Hamlet. **90**

89

67 The possessive pronoun *his* needs to precede an *-ing* form of a verb that's being used as a noun (in this sentence, *talking*).

68 Two complete sentences mustn't be joined by a comma. Use a semicolon instead.

69 The subject pronoun *whoever* is needed as the subject of the verb *would listen*. The preposition *for* may have confused you because normally an object follows a preposition. However, in this sentence the entire expression (*whoever would listen*) is the object of the preposition, not just the pronoun.

70 A quotation mark belongs at the beginning and the end of the quotation.

71 The past tense verb matches the meaning of the sentence.

72 The pronoun *nobody* is singular and requires a singular verb, *wants*.

73 Only singular pronouns (in this sentence, *he or she*) can refer to the singular pronoun *nobody*.

74 In the original sentence, *it* (the phone) is sitting by the phone – illogical! Reword in some way so that the speaker is sitting by the phone. Another possible correction: add a subject/verb combination to the beginning of the sentence so that it reads *When I was sitting by the phone*.

75 The article *an* goes before a vowel sound, such as the *au* in *audition*.

76 The possessive pronoun *his* needs to precede the *-ing* form of a verb that's being used as a noun (in this sentence, *getting*).

77 Because *only one horse* is the meaning of the pronoun *that*, the verb paired with *that* is singular. *Has* is singular, and *have* is plural.

78 The single word *already* means 'before this time', the meaning required by the sentence.

79 You need *begun* here. *Begun* is a past participle that you use with *has* (or *have*) to create the present perfect.

80 The adjective *traditional* describes the noun *coat*.

81 *Between* is a preposition and thus takes an object. The pronoun *me* is an object.

82 Two males appear in the sentence (*Silver* and *Ed*), and so the pronoun *he* is unclear. To make the meaning clear, substitute a noun (either *Silver* or *Ed*. The choice is yours) for *he*.

83 The missing word in the original is *did*, as in *than she did*. *Her* is inappropriate as the subject of the implied verb *did*.

84 *Unique* is an absolute and can't be compared, which means that *extremely* must be deleted.

85 The comparison *equally* can't be followed by *as*.

86 *We* is the subject pronoun needed here. *Us* is for objects.

87 To keep the sentence parallel, *to be* needs to be paired with *to take action*. Another alternative is to change *to take action* to *acting*.

88 *To lay* means 'to place something else somewhere'. *To lie* is 'to rest or to recline', the intended meaning here.

89 The noun *nap* must be described by an adjective (*quick*), not an adverb (*quickly*).

90 The single word *everyday* means 'ordinary'. In this sentence you need the two-word form, which means 'each day'.

Answers to Exercise Four

In the following figure the errors from the original manual are in bold and crossed out, with a possible correction following each one, as well as an occasional addition of a missing word or mark. All corrections are in bold and underlined. Check the corresponding numbered explanations that follow the revised manual.

91

Installing ~~You're~~ **Your** New Widget Wheel

92
93
To install the widget wheel, ~~a computer should first be turned off~~ **first turn the computer off/and** then follow these simple steps.

94
Important: If you have an A4019 or a ~~newest~~ **newer** model, please discard this manual. You

95
must ~~have sent~~ **send** for manual number 218B, or, in the case of a computer that previously

96
~~has~~ **had** a widget, for manual number 330B. ~~Being that~~ **Because** your computer is not covered

97

98
in this manual, discard ~~it~~ **the manual**. Faulty directions have been responsible for explosions

99
and ~~that software crashed~~ **software crashes**.

100
1. Unpack the widget wheel**,** which looks like a shark**'**s tooth.

101

102
2. Unpack the two disk poles. Grasp the disk pole that is more **nearly** circular. ~~Lining~~ **Line** up

103
the teeth with the teeth on the widget. *Note:* Teeth should be brushed ~~everyday~~ **every day**

104
with a WidgetBrush. ~~s~~**S**ee enclosed order form for more information.

105

106
3. After the teeth are ~~tight~~ **tightly** clenched, ~~a person should~~ insert the widget disk into slot C.

107
However, if the widget disk has a blue strip, ~~in which case it should be inserted into slot D~~

108
insert the widget into slot D. Don't mix up the slots as the computer will catch fire. Neither

109
of these slots ~~are~~ **is** open when the computer is standing upright. ~~Sit~~ **Set** the computer on its

110
side before beginning this step.

111
4. Turn on the computer. If the screen is blank**,** call the service specialist on 800-555-5039.

112
~~Farthermore~~ **Furthermore**, if the screen blinks ~~rapid~~ **rapidly** from red to green (or from blue to

113
yellow in model 2W4T), you really need to panic. ~~This~~ **Blinking** means the widget was installed

114
~~improper~~ **improperly**; the computer is ~~all together~~ **altogether** unusable.

115
116
5. You are almost ready to enjoy your new widget**!** Place a hand **that is not wearing any**

117
rings, including wedding rings, on the mouse ~~that is not wearing any rings, including~~

118
~~wedding rings~~. Depending upon the model number, ~~either~~ press **either** firmly or softly.

119
Some widgets can work ~~good~~ **well** no matter what the pressure.

120

---

91 The contraction *you're* means 'you are'. In this sentence you want the possessive pronoun *your*.

92 An introductory verb form (*to install the Widget Wheel*) must refer to the subject, but the subject in the original sentence is *a computer*. Reword the sentence so that the subject is the person who is installing – the understood *you*.

93 The adverb *then* is not capable of uniting two complete sentences on its own. Delete the comma and insert *and*.

94 The *-est* comparison singles out one extreme from a group of three or more. In this sentence you're talking about a comparison between two things only – model A4019 and the group of everything *newer*. (The group counts as one thing because the items in the group aren't discussed as individuals.)

95 The verb *send* is in the present tense and addresses what the installer must do now, not what the installer must have done previously. The present perfect tense (*have sent*) implies a connection with the past.

96 The word *previously* tips you off to the fact that you're talking about a time in the past, and so *had* works better than *has*.

97 The expression *being that* isn't standard; use *because* instead.

98 The pronoun *it* must have a clear meaning, but the original sentence provides two possible alternatives, *computer* and *manual*. The correction clarifies the meaning of *it*.

99 Two terms linked by *and* need a similar grammatical identity in order to keep the sentence parallel. The original sentence joins a noun (*explosions*) with a clause (*that software crashed*). The correction links two nouns, *explosions* and *crashes*.

100 A description beginning with *which* is usually set off by a comma from the word it describes.

101 The tooth belongs to the shark, and so you need the possessive *shark's*.

102 *Circular* is an absolute. It may be approached but not compared. The disk pole may be *circular* or *more nearly circular*.

103 The original sentence is a fragment; it contains no complete thought. The correction has a subject (the understood *you*) and a verb (*line*) and a complete thought.

104 *Everyday* means 'ordinary'. *Every day* means 'daily'.

105 A sentence always begins with a capital letter.

106 *Tightly* is an adverb, needed to describe the verb *clenched*.

107 *A person* is a new expression in this piece, which has been addressing *you* directly or by implication. For consistency, change *a person* to the understood *you*.

108 The original is a fragment, not a complete sentence. The reworded version has a complete thought.

109 The pronoun *neither* is singular and takes the singular verb *is*.

110 *Sit* is what the subject does by bending knees and plopping onto a chair. *Set* means 'place something somewhere', which is the intended meaning here.

111 An introductory expression with a verb is usually set off by a comma from the main idea of the sentence. Insert a comma after *blank*.

112 Furthermore, not farthermore, means 'what's more', and so *furthermore* is the word you need here.

113   The adverb *rapidly* is needed to describe the action *blink*.

114   The pronoun *this* is too vague. Go for the specific term, *blinking*.

115   The adverb *improperly* is needed to describe the action *installed*.

116   *All together* means 'as one'. *Altogether* means 'completely', the definition that fits this sentence.

117   Don't double up on endmarks. One per sentence does the job.

118   The description is in the wrong place in the original sentence. Place it after *hands*, the word being described.

119   The duo *either/or* needs to link words or expressions with the same grammatical identity. Move *either* so that two adverbs are linked.

120   The adverb *well* is needed to describe the verb *can work*.

Index

FOR DUMMIES®

Making Everything Easier! ™

UK editions

BUSINESS

978-0-470-74490-1

978-0-470-74381-2

978-0-470-71382-2

FINANCE

978-0-470-99280-7

978-0-470-71432-4

978-0-470-69515-9

HOBBIES

978-0-470-69960-7

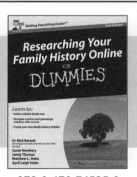

978-0-470-74535-9

978-0-470-68178-7

British Sign Language
For Dummies
978-0-470-69477-0

Business NLP For Dummies
978-0-470-69757-3

Cognitive Behavioural Therapy For
Dummies
978-0-470-01838-5

Competitive Strategy For Dummies
978-0-470-77930-9

Cricket For Dummies
978-0-470-03454-5

CVs For Dummies, 2nd Edition
978-0-470-74491-8

Divorce For Dummies, 2nd Edition
978-0-470-74128-3

eBay.co.uk Business All-in-One
For Dummies
978-0-470-72125-4

Emotional Freedom Technique For
Dummies
978-0-470-75876-2

English Grammar For Dummies
978-0-470-05752-0

Flirting For Dummies
978-0-470-74259-4

Golf For Dummies
978-0-470-01811-8

Green Living For Dummies
978-0-470-06038-4

Hypnotherapy For Dummies
978-0-470-01930-6

IBS For Dummies
978-0-470-51737-6

Lean Six Sigma For Dummies
978-0-470-75626-3

FOR DUMMIES®

A world of resources to help you grow

UK editions

SELF-HELP

978-0-470-74830-5

978-0-470-74764-3

978-0-470-74193-1

STUDENTS

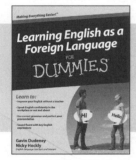

978-0-470-74747-6

978-0-470-74711-7

978-0-470-74290-7

HISTORY

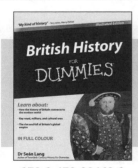

978-0-470-99468-9

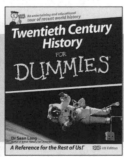

978-0-470-51015-5

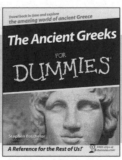

978-0-470-98787-2

Neuro-linguistic Programming Fcr Dummies
978-0-7645-7028-5

Origami Kit For Dummies
978-0-470-75857-1

Overcoming Depression For Dummies
978-0-470-69430-5

Positive Psychology For Dummies
978-0-470-72136-0

PRINCE2 For Dummies
978-0-470-51919-6

Psychometric Tests For Dummies
978-0-470-75366-8

Raising Happy Children
For Dummies
978-0-470-05978-4

Sage 50 Accounts For Dummies
978-0-470-71558-1

Starting a Business For Dummies, 2nd Edition
978-0-470-51806-9

Study Skills For Dummies
978-0-470-74047-7

Teaching English as a Foreign Language For Dummies
978-0-470-74576-2

Teaching Skills For Dummies
978-0-470-74084-2

Time Management For Dummies
978-0-470-77765-7

Understanding and Paying Less Property Tax For Dummies
978-0-470-75872-4

Work-Life Balance For Dummies
978-0-470-71380-8

Available wherever books are sold. For more information or to order direct go to www.wiley.com or call +44 (0) 1243 843291

13061 p2

FOR DUMMIES®

The easy way to get more done and have more fun

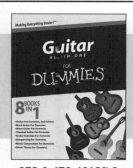

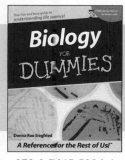

FOR DUMMIES®

Helping you expand your horizons and achieve your potential

COMPUTER BASICS

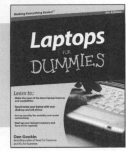
978-0-470-57829-2

978-0-470-46542-4

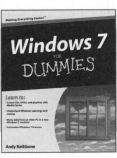
978-0-470-49743-2

DIGITAL PHOTOGRAPHY

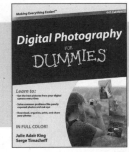
978-0-470-25074-7

978-0-470-46606-3

978-0-470-45772-6

MAC BASICS

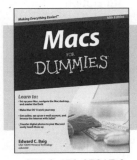
978-0-470-27817-8

978-0-470-46661-2

978-0-470-43543-4

Access 2007 For Dummies
978-0-470-04612-8

Adobe Creative Suite 4 Design
Premium All-in-One Desk Reference
For Dummies
978-0-470-33186-6

AutoCAD 2010 For Dummies
978-0-470-43345-4

C++ For Dummies, 6th Edition
978-0-470-31726-6

Computers For Seniors For Dummies ,
2nd Edition
978-0-470-53483-0

Dreamweaver CS4 For Dummies
978-0-470-34502-3

Excel 2007 All-In-One Desk Reference
For Dummies
978-0-470-03738-6

Green IT For Dummies
978-0-470-38688-0

Networking All-in-One Desk Reference
For Dummies, 3rd Edition
978-0-470-17915-4

Office 2007 All-in-One Desk Reference
For Dummies
978-0-471-78279-7

Photoshop CS4 For Dummies
978-0-470-32725-8

Photoshop Elements 7 For Dummies
978-0-470-39700-8

Search Engine Optimization
For Dummies, 3rd Edition
978-0-470-26270-2

The Internet For Dummies,
12th Edition
978-0-470-56095-2

Visual Studio 2008 All-In-One Desk
Reference For Dummies
978-0-470-19108-8

Web Analytics For Dummies
978-0-470-09824-0

Windows Vista For Dummies
978-0-471-75421-3

13061 p4